Lichens of Ireland

An illustrated introduction to over 250 species

Paul Whelan has a degree in Biology from University College Dublin and studied Computer Science and Art History at Trinity College Dublin. He published several books on Computer Aided Design in the 1990s before returning to his earlier interest in natural history and focusing on Ireland's lichen flora. In 2008 he became involved in the LichenIreland project and developed an independent website (www.lichens.ie), which susbequently won an Irish Internet Association Net Visionary Award. In 2010 he developed www.ispynature.com for primary school children. Paul lives in east Cork.

For Anna, Aine, Molly and Pip.

Ernst Haeckel (1834–1919), lichens from *Kunstformen der Natur* (1904).

[*Cladia retipora, Cladonia perfoliata, Cladonia cervicornis ssp. verticillata, Cladonia squamosa Cladonia fimbriata, Cladonia cornucopiae, Lobaria pulmonaria, Physcia aipolia, Melanohalea olivacea Flavoparmelia caperata, Anaptychia crinalis*]

Lichens of Ireland

An illustrated introduction
to over 250 species

Paul Whelan

The Collins Press

First published in 2011 by
The Collins Press
West Link Park
Doughcloyne
Wilton
Cork

Reprinted 2012

British Library Cataloguing in Publication Data
Whelan, Paul.
The lichens of Ireland : an introductory guide.
1. Lichens—Ireland. 2. Lichens—Anatomy. 3. Lichens—Ireland—Identification. 4. Lichens—Ireland—Geographical distribution.
I. Title
579.7'09415–dc22

ISBN–13: 9781848891371

This publication has received support from the Heritage Council under the 2011 Heritage Education, Community and Outreach scheme.

Design and typesetting by Paul Whelan
Typeset in Adobe Garamond Pro
Printed in Poland by Białostockie Zakłady Graficzne SA

Cover photographs
Front: watercolour of *Teloschistes chrysophthalmus* by Tobias Hodson
Back: on an ash tree near Muckross House are examples of 'old' woodland species *Lobaria pulmonaria, Lobaria virens* and *Leptogium hibernicum*

Contents

Acknowledgements

In particular I would like to thank John Douglass, lichenologist, for many enjoyable and informative field trips throughout Ireland. Thank you also to Howard Fox, lichenologist with the National Botanic Gardens, Glasnevin, Dublin, for his encouragement, and to the LichenIreland team for involving me in field work. LichenIreland is supported by National Parks and Wildlife Service; National Botanic Gardens, Glasnevin; Environment and Heritage Service and the Ulster Museum, National Museums Northern Ireland.

I would like to express my thanks to Alan Orange, the National Museum of Wales, for use of his wonderful ink drawings which help to elucidate much of the lichen terminology, and to both the British Lichen Society and LichenIreland for access to their records of Ireland's lichens at 10km resolution. Special thanks must be given to the fieldworkers who walked the length and breadth of Ireland over many years amassing more than 130,000 records of our rich lichen biodiversity. These lichenologists include Andy Acton, Brian Coppins, Sandy Coppins, Simon Davey, John Douglass, Howard Fox, Vince Giavarini, Joe Hope, Alan Orange, Ivan Pedley, David Richardson, Neil Sanderson, Jenny Seawright, Mike Simms, Robert Thompson and Stephen Ward.

Also, thank you to Gill Weyman of the Irish Wildlife Trust, Anna O'Connor and Paula Meenehan, for reading the text and making suggestions and also to Jenny Seawright for helping me locate some species to photograph for the book. And thanks to Nico Nieuwstraten, who wrote a wonderful Photoshop script file to generate the vice-county maps from the vice-county data.

Finally, I would like to express my gratitude to the Heritage Council of Ireland for financial support under the 2011 Heritage Education, Community and Outreach scheme, without whom this book would not have been published.

Paul Whelan
October 2011

Introduction

Currently, Ireland is home to almost 1,200 recorded lichens and 205 lichenicolous and non-lichenized fungi. Considering that the whole of North America has approximately 3,600 recorded species, Ireland's lichen biodiversity has a staggering richness for a country of its size and latitude. This hidden richness of our natural world was relatively neglected until recently, when the LichenIreland Project (2005–2010) began to uncover the extent of the biodiversity, particularly of our Atlantic woodlands and hyper-oceanic hazel woods.

This book is the result of my involvement in the LichenIreland project. It introduces beginners, armed with a simple hand lens, to the delightful Lilliputian world of lichens. There could be much debate as to which species should be included in a book of this nature and size. Many will feel that species 'x' should have been included. However, a selection had to be made and included are some notable species that thrive in our oceanic climate, and some dots-and-squiggles lichens that are rather difficult to identify. All will contribute in some way to challenge beginners, and prepare them for more advanced texts such as Frank Dobson's *Lichens* (6th edition) or *The Lichens of Great Britain and Ireland*, 2009 edition (British Lichen Society).

The book lacks a key. For this I make no apology as a key would take the text beyond its current scope, and possibly lose the readership for which it is intended. The book is necessarily brief and sometimes simplified, but will hopefully turn the minds of Ireland's new generation of young naturalists to the world of lichenology. A downloadable glossary (pdf) to the book is currently available at www.lichens.ie.

The lichens are listed alphabetically. This method was chosen after consideration of other possible arrangements. Presentation by body form was rejected because that classification system quickly breaks down (for example *Cladonia* lichens belong to both squamulose and fruticose forms) and classification by habitat breaks down because many species straddle more than one habitat. Similarly, classification by substrate breaks down although it was a system I gave a lot of consideration to. Alphabetic arrangement provides more immediate rewards because the beginner will quickly learn to recognise the genera and can flick to the relevant section efficiently.

All the photographs in the text were taken by the author over a three-year period of lichen hunting around Ireland. The magnified insets on many images act to either show more detail or to concentrate the eye on where to look for characteristic features (not necessarily magnified). With just a hand lens and a willingness to understand lichens, you will open up a miniature world of immense beauty. It is almost inevitable that a beginner using a hand lens for the first time will consider him or herself in the shoes of Alice in Wonderland.

Some of the earliest Irish lichen records were made *c.* 1696 by William Sherard and Caleb Threlkeld (1676–1728). In the twentieth century Matilda Knowles made significant contributions with her work on seashore zonation and her 1929 publication *History of Irish Lichens* (available on www.lichens.ie). Other twentieth century contributions were made by Lilian Porter, Robert Lloyd Praeger, Annie Lorrain Smith, John Adams and more recently Howard Fox. The LichenIreland project of 2005–2010 made a major contribution to documenting Irish lichen flora. At the time of writing a Lichen Red Data list is imminent. Nomenclature in this text is mainly according to Smith *et al.* (2009) and Hawksworth (2003).

What are lichens?

Lichens contribute to the visual 'background noise' of our environment, providing colour and texture to woodlands, parks, buildings, monuments and graveyards. They add the 'old' to old walls, gateposts and monuments, their aesthetic value only missed when they are absent.

Lichens have been used as medicines, poisons and dyes and have contributed to making many a child's doll in the form of hair or bulking out material for arms and legs. Even today they are used in the manufacture of perfume, acting as a fixative to ensure the slow release of scent. *Evernia prunastri* has been used to give some perfumes a moss-like scent. *Cladonia pyxidata* was once thought to cure whooping cough. Dyes can be extracted from lichens and used to colour wool. Extraction sometimes involved boiling or soaking them in urine. During the nineteenth century lichens became economically valuable, often demanding prices in excess of the cost of rare spices. A large cottage industry developed around lichen dyes.

Lichens act as a source of nitrogen for many plants and are frequently the first living forms to inhabit bare rock. Birds use them as nesting material and they are an essential component in food chains, being eaten by snails, slugs, insects and higher animals such as deer. Lichens act as biomonitors, some absorbing heavy metals from their environment and responding to both air and water quality.

Crustose lichens add texture and colour to headstones in a west-of-Ireland graveyard. They enhance the aesthetic quality of many buildings and monuments.

Defining a lichen

Lichens (phonetic pronunciation 'like en' or 'litch en', both acceptable) are fungi that live with a photosynthesizing partner, usually an alga or cyanobacteria. It is a clever arrangement because many fungi are saprophytes (they feed on dead organic matter such as dead plants or animals) and the algae and cyanobacteria are autotrophs, able to make their own food from sunlight, water and carbon dioxide (photosynthesis). With such a dual food source, they are unlikely to starve.

A little more detail

A standard textbook definition describes lichens as two and sometimes three organisms living together in symbiosis. This is essentially true. The three organisms in question are a fungus (related to bread mould, although a few are related to mushrooms), algae (related to seaweed or the green slime on ponds) and in some cases photosynthesizing bacteria belonging to a group called cyanobacteria. The relationship is stable and they form a distinct shape and structure (both used as identification aids) and generally live a long time. Some lichens have been estimated to be 4,500 years old. Lichen-type symbiosis has been positively identified in fossil records as old as 410 million years (Rhynie chert in Scotland). Recent studies have pushed this back to 600 million years.

In 1982 the International Association of Lichenology issued the following definition of a lichen: an 'association of a fungus and a photosynthetic symbiont resulting in a stable thallus of specific structure'.

In summary, a lichen is not a single organism, but an assemblage of two or three different species working together for survival. The fungal part is termed the *mycobiont* and the photosynthetic partner is the *photobiont*.

Damsel–tyrant duality

The dual nature of lichens was first recognized in 1869 by a German biologist, Simon Schwendener. There was great resistance to this idea at the time. He wrote: 'lichens are ... colonies ... of individuals, of which one alone plays the master, while the rest, forever imprisoned, prepare the nutrients for themselves and their master. This fungus is a fungus of the class *Ascomycetes*, a parasite which is accustomed to live upon others' work. Its slaves are green algae, which it has sought out ... and compelled into its service.' A further description around the same time, by Rev. James Crombie, a Scotsman, described the dual relationship as 'the unnatural union between a captive algal damsel and tyrant fungal master'. Regardless of which of these descriptions you favour, it was determined that the fungal partner was the dominant one. Perhaps a more concise definition of a lichen is 'a fungus that associates with a photobiont'. A fungus makes up the bulk of the lichen body, occupying 80% or more of the thallus; frequently the algal part is as low as 5%. Whether the fungus enslaves the alga or cooperation is mutual is a matter of conjecture. Both partners seem at ease with one another, although the alga has had to give up its own sex life. Only the 'tyrant' fungus is the sexually active partner.

Simon Schwendener (1829–1919) who first postulated the dual nature of lichens. This idea was rejected by many scientists of the time.

Simon Schwendener also suggested that lichens should be classified with fungi, but this was rejected by the scientific community. Since the 1950s lichens are accepted as lichenized fungi and have been accepted into the Kingdom Fungi. Despite this, the study of lichens has been considered a separate study (lichenology) from the study of fungi (mycology).

Naming lichens

Carl von Linné (Linnaeus) introduced a binomial system for naming plants and animals in the eighteenth century. Names such as *Ochrolechia parella* or *Homo sapiens* are binomial. Latin was then in use as the universal scientific language. Binomial names are derived from Latin or Greek words and written in *italics* when printed and <u>underlined</u> when handwritten. The first part of the name is the genus or group to which the organism belongs and the second part of the name is the species (*parella* or *sapiens* in the above examples) and is written in lowercase letters.

Now, while Linnaeus made major progress with naming just about every known plant and animal at the time, lichens confounded him, although he did manage to describe 109 different species. Overall, he had little time for lichens and referred to them using the Latin phrase *rustici pauperrimi* (nature's paupers).

Carl von Linné (1707–1793) described 109 lichens and referred to them as 'nature's paupers'.

As a lichen is an assemblage of two or three distinct species, each with its own binomial name, how do we name it? The name of a lichen is the name of the fungal partner. Consequentially, a name such as *Ochrolechia parella* refers to the fungus that makes up the lichen; the photobiont does not usually contribute to the lichen's name.

Mycobionts – fungi

The fungal partner in a lichen is termed the mycobiont. Fungi are a large and diverse group of organisms, comprising at least 70,000 species worldwide. Some fungal experts say the number is more likely to be 1.4 million species. Fungi are the primary 'decomposers' or saprophytes, in the biosphere. Many fungi are also parasites, feeding on living cells and tissues.

Both animals and green plants are constructed of individual block-shaped cells. Fungi, on the other hand, are composed of thread-like filaments. This filamentous structure has contributed largely to their success as a group, allowing them to grow into crevices, enabling access to carbohydrate and protein molecules of their hosts.

Nearly all fungi that form lichens in Ireland come from one group, the *Ascomycetes* or 'sac fungi', so called because they produce sexual reproductive spores in sacs or asci.

Only a handful of lichens in Ireland (less than 5%) have the mushroom-type fungi (group *Basidiomycetes*) as a mycobiont. These fungi do not produce spores in sacs, but instead on club-shaped structures, the basidia. In this book, the terms 'spores' and 'ascospores' are used interchangeably.

Photograph showing a mould growing on food (jam), illustrating the thread-like nature of fungal cells. In many crustose-type lichens the outer growth area or prothallus is similar.

A crustose lichen showing the prothallus or outer growing area. The orange-red colour is a free-living *Trentepohlia* alga.

Photobionts – algae and cyanobacteria

Photobionts use light to make molecules of glucose. This process of converting electromagnetic energy into chemical energy is termed photosynthesis. All green plants photosynthesize, as do all algae and cyanobacteria. Many lichens contain both algal and cyanbacterial photobionts in the same thallus; however, one is dominant and is termed the primary photobiont. Algal photobionts contribute sugars to the fungus; cyanobacteria also provide sugars, but additionally supply nitrogen in a form (nitrates) the fungus can use to build up its body tissue (mainly proteins).

Algae belong to the Kingdom *Protista* and those found in lichens belong to the genera *Trentepohlia* (orange in colour) and *Trebouxia* (bright green in colour). The group *Trebouxia* are unicellular and by far the most common green algae integrated into lichens, but rarely found free-living. *Trentepohlia* algae, on the other hand, grow freely outside lichens as filaments, but when part of the lichen symbiosis they become single cells. Crustose lichens tend to have *Trentepohlia* algae as their photobiont. Lichens whose only photobiont is green algae are termed chlorolichens. A group called the 'jelly lichens' have a predominance of cyanobacteria (their primary photobiont) and belong to the genera *Collema* and *Leptogium*. *Nostoc* cyanobacteria are found in jelly lichens.

This ash tree is home to dark-coloured lichens with the cyanobacteria *Nostoc*. The green lichens contain algae from the group *Trebouxioid*. Photographed in Killarney National Park.

The orange-red on this tree is a free-living version of the lichen photobiont *Trentepohlia*. It is common in many crustose lichens. Photographed in Fota Wildlife Park.

Other photobiont cyanobacteria groups include *Scytonema* and *Stigonema* (see lichens *Pilophorus strumaticus* and *Stereocaulon vesuvianum). Nostoc* is very common in free-living form in the Burren limestone karst region of Ireland. Generally it is found in small depressions in the limestone, either dried out and crisp, or as an olive green to brown wet jelly-like mass.

Morphs

There are cases of a fungus choosing from one of two photobionts, producing morphs. For example, *Sticta canariensis* may take cyanobacteria or green algae as its primary photobiont. If it chooses the cyanobacteria as its primary partner, the result is a cyanobacterial morph named *Sticta dufourii*, whereas if the green algae is its primary photobiont then the green morph is *Sticta canariensis*.

Left: The photobiont *Nostoc* (cyanobactieria) can be found free-living in solution pans or kamenitzas in the Burren, Co. Clare. When the solution pans dry, *Nostoc* becomes black, crisp and brittle. Once it rains *Nostoc* immediately absorbs the water and swells becoming jelly-like . **Right**: A film of *Nostoc* lifted out of a kamenitza. *Nostoc* is found in *Collema*, *Peltigera* and *Leptogium* lichens.

Thallus anatomy

Anatomy of an idealized lichen is shown in the illustration below. The imaginary section is through the lichen body or thallus.

Upper cortex: The upper surface is a layer of tightly bound fungal threads or hyphae. It functions to protect the photobiont from direct sunlight and its permeability strikes a balance between allowing water to soak in, yet not dry out. Lichens do not have specialized structures to prevent water loss as do flowering plants (stomata).

Photobiont layer: Directly below the upper cortex is a layer of fungal hyphal threads, where the photobiont gathers to capture sunlight and photosynthesize. If the surface of a typical crustose lichen is scraped, the algal layer is visible. If the scrape exposes a green colour, the photobiont is a chlorococcid; if it exposes yellow, it is a *Trentepohlia*. This is a useful aid to identification in the field. Normally, only a single species of algae acts as a photobiont in a lichen. Cyanobacteria will also house themselves in this layer.

Medulla: Below the algal strata is another layer of fungal hyphae, but in this situation, they have a loose arrangement, with plenty of air spaces between them; a few algal cells or cyanobacteria are found in some of these spaces. The air spaces allow for gaseous exchange to enable metabolic reactions occur, in particular, the movement of oxygen and carbon dioxide for photosynthesis. Sugar produced by photosynthesis is also stored in the medulla.

Lower cortex: This layer is well developed and typical of foliose lichens. It is composed of tightly woven hyphae. Small root-like structures termed rhizines may project down into the substrate from the lower cortex. Rhizines do not specifically absorb water from the substrate; they function to help the lichen adhere to the substrate and increase humidity around the lower surface. This lower layer may be highly modified so that a thick, soft felt-like mat of hyphae form, termed the tomentum. A tomentum may also develop on the upper surface, although it tends to develop there as a very thin membrane, with a cobweb-like white colour. It is an important characteristic in field identification (see *Peltigera membranacea*). If cyanobacteria are present, they tend to gather into wart-like structures called cephalodia.

Some lichens such as the 'jellies' do not display this neat stratified arrangement, but instead are a simple mixture of algal cells and fungal hyphae, living in a gelatinous matrix. This unstratified structure is found in the genus *Collema*. A gelatinous matrix allows the rapid absorption of water, swelling the lichen to its jelly-like appearance. The bulk of the lichen thallus is fungal, with just 5% to 20% composed of algae, however in the case of cyanobacterial photobionts the percentage is usually higher, sometimes reaching 50% of body mass.

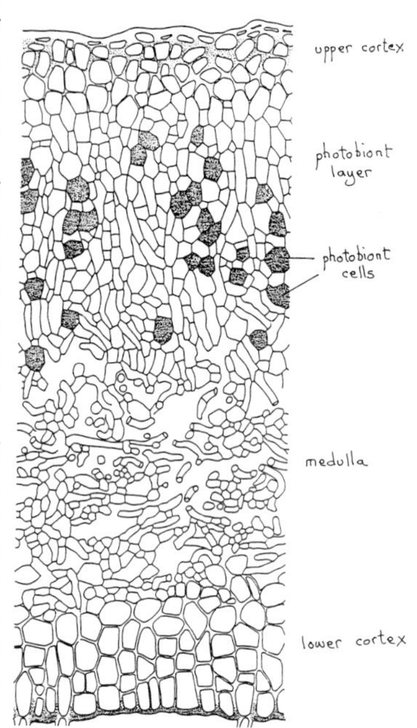

Above: Section through an idealized lichen showing the arrangement of tissue in layers. There is variation on this arrangement through the different groups or genera of lichens. Jelly lichens do not have this high degree of organization.

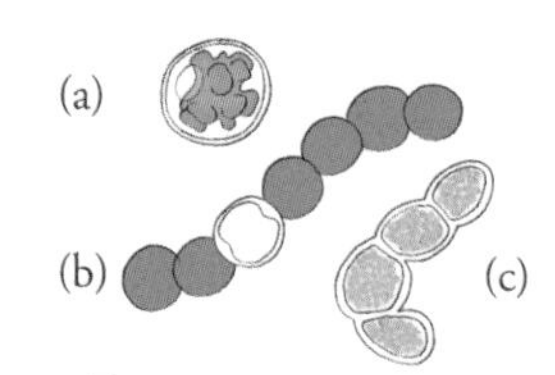

Above: Three common photobionts as seen under a microscope.
(a) *Trebouxia* (b) *Nostoc* (c) *Trentepohlia*

The cobweb-like whitish covering on this lichen is the tomentum (adj. tomentose). When found on the underside, it tends to be black to brown and much more fibrous.

The underside of many foliose or leaf-type lichens have rhizines. These superficial root-like structures function primarily to anchor (velcro effect) lichens to the substrate and to increase humidity levels.

Growth forms and colours

The identification of lichens depends almost solely on looking at thalline structures, sexual reproductive structures, asexual reproductive structures, thalline forms, colours, textures, spores and asci shapes and sizes. Substrate and habitat also contribute to support identification.

Growth forms

The bodies or thalli of lichens occur in several growth forms. This method of grouping lichens is of great value for identification, particularly in the field, although recent genetic analysis demonstrates that the grouping is highly artificial. Four basic growth forms are described below.
Crustose lichens look like a crust sitting on a substrate. They are subdivided into areolate, rimose, placodioid and leprose types.
Foliose lichens have a distinct upper and lower surface. They are subdivided into lobate types, umbilicate forms and jelly lichens.
Fruticose lichens are further subdivided into the cup lichens (e.g. some *Cladonia*), shrubby types (e.g. some *Cladonia*), bearded lichens (e.g. *Usnea*)and hair-like types (e.g. *Bryoria*). They all share lobes or branches that do not have distinct upper and lower sides.
Squamulose lichens are composed of tiny scales or squamules lacking a lower cortex.
As with any classification system, nature will always create some exceptions that invalidate it.

Crustose Lichens

Crustose lichens grow as crusts on the substrate. They may look like dabs of paint on walls and trees. A characteristic feature is their lack of a lower cortex, but the rest of the stratified arrangement of tissue is still intact. Lacking a lower cortex, the fungal hyphae can penetrate the substrate (soil, bark, rock). Consequently, they cannot be separated from the substrate in one piece. Sometimes the thallus is so immersed in the substrate that the only indication that a lichen is present is the appearance of the reproductive bodies, or a faint colouration on the substrate. See *Verrucaria baldensis*.

Many crustose lichens have a prothallus surrounding them. This is a region where the fungal hyphal tissue is exposed (unlichenized). The prothallus runs under the lichen crust forming a carpet of fungal hyphae. Its colour is often an identification aid, as is its absence or presence. Prothalli tend to be black or white, but various other colours exist. Crustose lichens may be further divided into the following types: areolate, rimose, placodioidal and leprose.

Crustose areolate: the surface of the thallus is composed of little islands or areoles that sit on a hyphal base. A characteristic of areolate types is that the cracks reach down through the medulla to the underlying fungal mat (called the hypothallus – 'hypo' means below) and is visible between the areoles. *Acarospora impressula* is a typical crustose areolate lichen.

Crustose rimose: these are superficially like the areolate type, but the thallus forms a smooth surface initially (termed continuous) and as it matures, begins to crack, producing a crazy-paving effect. Cracking is more irregular than in the areolate form and is probably as a result of hydration. This can be seen in *Lecanora carpinea*.

Crustose placodioidal: A prothallus is absent and instead the edges have the appearance of fingers or elongated lobes. It is as though the central area of the thallus is crustose and then becomes foliose at the edges, however the finger-like lobes are tightly attached to the substrate. *Caloplaca thallincola* is a good example.

Crustose leprose: Leprose lichens lack any layering structure. They have no cortex (upper or lower). The body is simply a mass of intermixed algal cells and fungal filaments. Visually powdery in appearance they tend to be light green to creamy white in colour. Leprose lichens like damp and shaded areas and are common in Ireland, particularly the *Chrysothrix* and *Lepraria* groups, specifically *Lepraria incana* and the fine powdered *Lepraria lobificans*.

Crustose leprose lichens are powdery, consisting simply of loose aggregates of hyphal threads and algal cells.

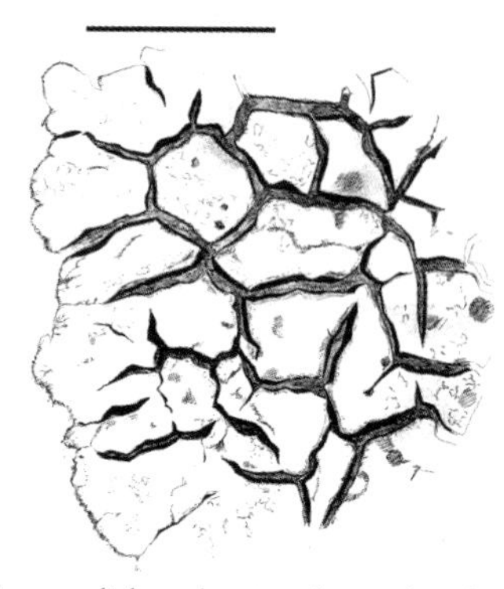

Crustose lichen showing the areolate form. The hypothallus is visible through the cracks.

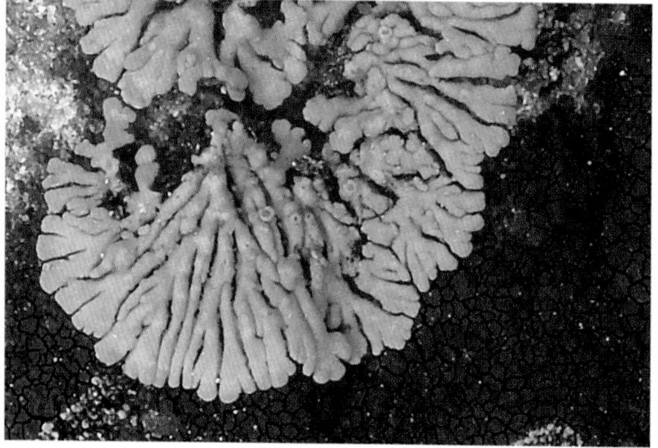

Crustose lichen (yellow) showing the placodioidal form around the edge.

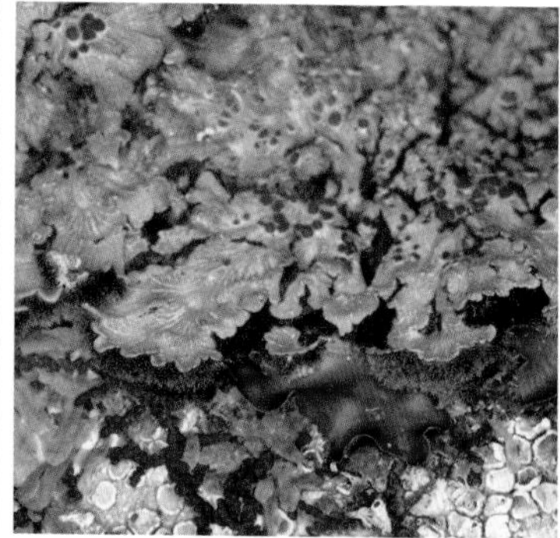

Degelia plumbea showing a dark, furry tomentum on the underside

Foliose Lichens

As the name implies, these are leaf-like, flattened and with a distinct upper and lower surface reflected internally as an upper and lower cortex. Foliose lichens are often loosely attached to the substrate and the underside is easily visible by turning up the lobe edge. Sometimes they may be tightly adpressed to the substrate, or may be loosely attached by root-like rhizines or by a simple fungal hyphal mat (tomentum). Rhizines may be branched dichotomously (Y-shaped) or have perpendicular side branches like a bottle brush. Foliose lichens are further subdivided into the following types:

Foliose lobate: Thalline lobes are frequently important for identification because of their variation, sometimes rounded at the ends, or perhaps a little angular or even spiky. Are the lobes turned up at the end, or do they bend down; are they convex or concave or perhaps flat? The under-surface of lobes may be white or black or perhaps some variation on this. Textures vary from smooth to wrinkled to warty or ridged.

Foliose umbilicate: Some lichens such as *Dermatocarpon miniatum*, or *Umbilicaria polyphylla* are attached by a single stout umbilical-like structure called a holdfast or umbilicus.

Foliose jelly: Usually brittle and black when dry but absorb water, rapidly turning gelatinous, changing colour to olive green or brown when wet. The genera *Collema*, *Leptogium* and *Lichina* are typical jelly lichens, in which the primary photobionts are cyanobacteria. *Collema* species lack a lower cortex while *Leptogium* species retain it. As a general rule, jelly lichens are more common in the west of Ireland (west of the Shannon river) than elsewhere in Ireland.

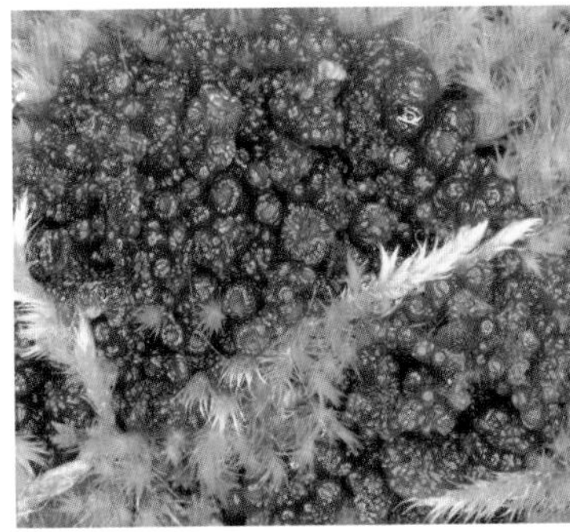

Jelly lichens such as this *Collema* species, contain cyanobacteria and lack a highly organised internal structure. Much of the body is composed of a gelatinous matrix that can absorb water rapidly when it rains.

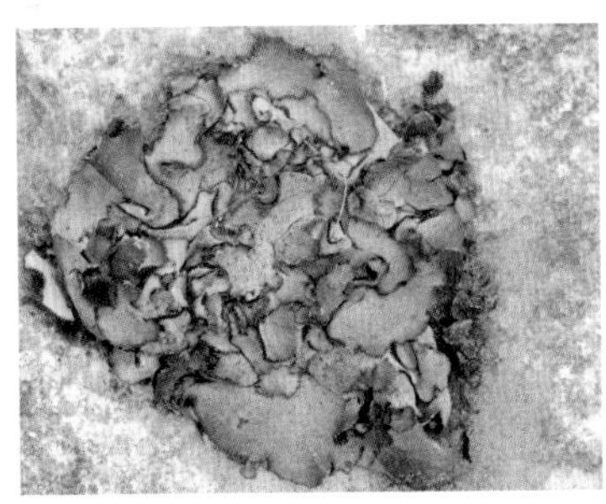

Dermatocarpon attaches to the substrate by a central single stalk, the umbilicus.

Lobaria virens is a lobate foliose lichen. Identification features include the green oily texture, and short unridged incised lobes.

Fruticose lichens

These lichens look like tiny shrubs or tufted vegetation. Some are erect, others pendant. The branches or lobes are either hair-like, strap-like or scaly, with cup-like structures. There is no distinction between their upper and lower sides.

Fruticose 'cup' lichens: Because of the distinctive 'cup' it is easy to recognise the *Cladonia* group in the field, although a much more difficult task to identify them to species level. Technically the group or genus *Cladonia* is a mixture of both the squamulose and fruticose body plans. A typical *Cladonia* consists of a base or primary thallus of squamules and growing from this base is a stalk or secondary thallus, the podetia, with sexual reproductive structures at the top. The stalks can reach a height of 60mm and may open out into cups termed scyphi. See *Cladonia gracilis*.

Fruticose 'shrubby' lichens: Other *Cladonia* species take on a different growth form, developing mats of highly branched thalli. The tips of the spikes contain reproductive structures. *Cladonia portentosa*, found in many Irish bogs, takes on this form.

Fruticose 'beard' lichens: The area of attachment to the substrate is relatively small; often attached at a single or just a few points. Some are fine and hair-like, while others are strap-like. The most important defining characteristic is that there is no distinct upper surface or underside (an exception to this is *Evernia prunastri*). The photosynthetic layer runs the whole way around a section. Inside the algal layer is a medulla and finally at the centre of the thallus is a strengthening cord of connective tissue. In some groups such as *Usnea*, this is an important feature in identification, as it is particularly tough and elastic in some species.

Fruticose 'hair' lichens: These are hair-like, similar to the *Usnea* species, but they lack a central axis or core. *Bryoria fuscescens* is a typical example.

Fruticose 'cup' lichen. *Cladonia* species.

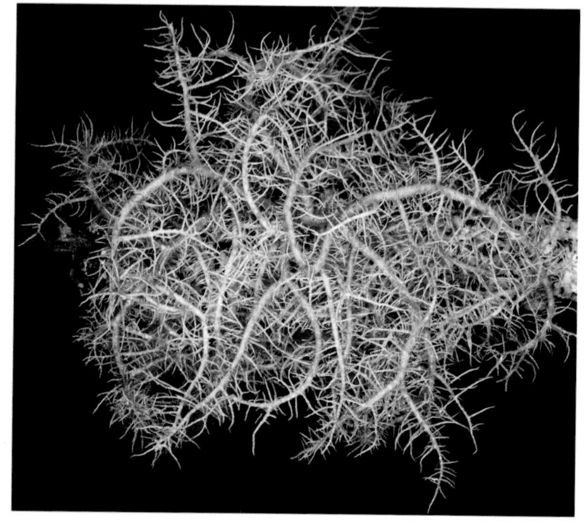

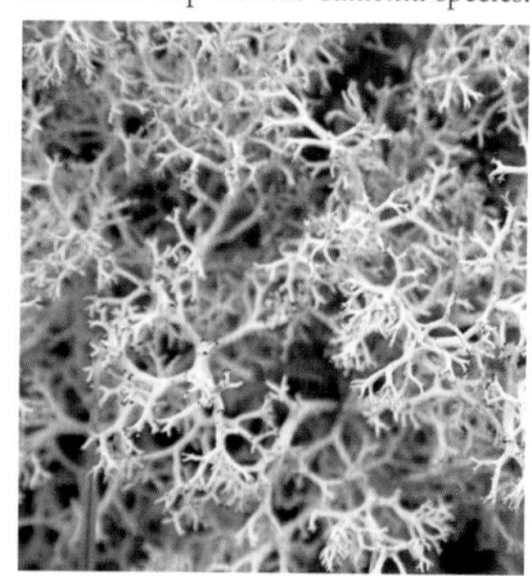

Fruticose 'shrubby' lichen.

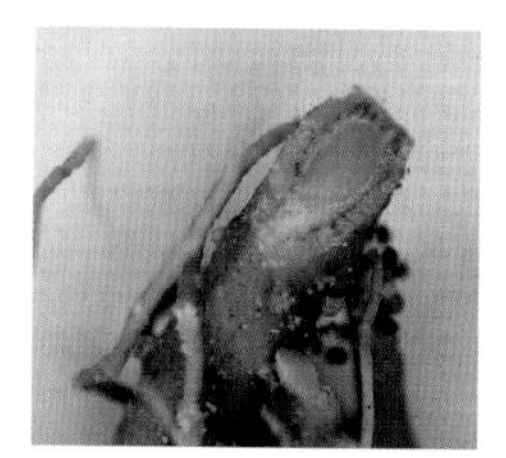

Above: A fruticose 'beard' lichen (*Usnea*). It lacks a distinct upper and lower surface. **Left**: section through an *Usnea* lichen, showing the green algal layer running the whole way around the section.

Hypocenomyce scalaris has large green squamules.

Normandina pulchella has plate-like squamules.

Squamulose Lichens

Squamules are small scales or plate-like structures that are usually anchored along one edge. They frequently lie obliquely, like plates stacked in a plate rack or dishwasher and range in size from 1–15mm in diameter.

An interesting characteristic of squamules is their stratified internal structure, as occurs in fruticose lichens: cortex, photobiont layer, medulla and sometimes lower cortex. Many also hint at the formation of lobes. Technically, squamulose lichens are fruticose, but because of the predominance of squamules, it is more convenient for field lichenologists to place them in a separate group. Sometimes, if the squamules are around 1mm diameter, they are grouped as crustose lichens. In this text they are treated as squamulose lichens. *Placidium squamulosum* is a squamulose lichen found in Ireland on humus-rich soils. Other squamulose lichens common in Ireland are *Normandina pulchella* and *Hypocenomyce scalaris.*

Lichen colours

Lichen colours function to protect the lichen from damaging radiation, or help regulate temperature. Colours are often dramatic and very beautiful when viewed under a hand lens. Lichens lacking pigment in the upper cortex tend to be grey or muddy green grey in colour, particularly when dry. On wetting such lichens, the cortex becomes transparent and the greenness of the algal cells shows through, giving it a greeny grey or olive colour. If a brown pigment, such as melanin, is scattered through the cortex, the lichen will have a characteristic brown colour when dry and turn deep olive green when wet. Usnic acid is responsible for the watery yellow colour of some *Usnea* and *Xanthoparmelia* species. The yellows of the genus *Buellia* are due to xanthones, while anthraquinones produce bright red at the tops of *Cladonia* podetia and on the thalli of some *Caloplaca* and *Xanthoria* species.

Both habitat and substrate may also influence colours. White-grey and yellow-orange lichens tend to be found on calcareous substrates, while acid bark and siliceous rocks attract yellow-green genera. Yellow-orange pigmentation acts to filter out UV light. Frequently a species in this colour range turns more green-grey when shaded. This is noticeable in the common *Xanthoria parietina. Rhizocarpon lavatum* turns from grey to greenish in the shade (or when wet) and *Porpidia flavocruenta* absorbs iron, turning the crustose thallus rust red.

Lichen sexual reproduction

Reproduction in lichens implies that all partners in the symbiotic relationship must reproduce. This problem has been solved by lichens in an admirable way, particularly in relation to asexual reproduction and has also led to a profusion of reproductive parts. Having recognized that the fungal part was 'dominant' and reserves sexual reproduction for itself, it may be suggested that it actively suppresses sexual reproduction in the photobiont. Sexual reproduction involves the fusion of two sex cells. In the case of lichens, the spore is the result of this fusion. Asexual or vegetative reproduction does not require any fusion of sex cells or gametes. Lichens do not have clearly defined periods of growth or reproduction, as found in flowering plants.

Most lichens in Ireland involve fungi from the phylum *Ascomata*. *Ascomycete* lichens form the familiar jam-tart-like reproductive structures. Fewer lichens are formed using the mushroom-like *Basidiomycetes* fungi.

Sexual Reproduction in ascomycete lichens

Sexual reproduction occurs in the fungal partner only and the structures involved are identical to those found in non-lichenized fungi. The organs that produce these spores are what concern us here, as their structure, shapes and colour help in the identification of a lichen.

Life cycle of ascomycete lichens

Gametes are produced in structures called pycnidia and trichogynea. Pycnidia are relatively large and visible with a hand lens. They are used to aid in the identification of lichens. Pycnidia produce the 'male' or '+' gamete which is called a spermatia or a conidia (although this term is usually used for asexual spores in non-lichenized fungi) and sometimes a pycnoconidia. A trichogyne is a single hyphal filament that produces the 'female' or '–' gamete. This is basically a single nucleus at the tip of the trichogyne filament.

Sexual reproduction then, involves the fusion of these two sex cells (haploid genetic make-up). The male sex cell (+) fuses with the female (–) cell or nucleus and the resulting zygote cell (diploid) immediately undergoes meiosis to produce haploid spores (ascospores). Ascospores are subsequently dispersed and if they arrive at a suitable habitat, will germinate. The resulting mass of fungal hyphae captures suitable algae (becomes lichenized) and then proceeds to develop into a new lichen body, taking on the appropriate shape.

The above description is based on what has been observed in ascomycete fungi. It has not been directly observed in lichens.

Ascomycete lichens produce their spores in sacs called asci (ascus = sing.). The sexual reproductive bodies in phylum *Ascomata* are termed ascoma. Lichenologists do not use the term 'fruiting' bodies (or try to avoid the phrase) when referring to lichen reproductive parts.
Lichen ascomata are apothecia (sing. apothecium) and perithecia (sing. perithecium).

Apothecia

Shapes and colours: To the delight (and sometimes despair) of the amateur lichenologist, apothecia come in a great variety of shapes and sizes. Identification makes use of this variation. Some look like small jam tarts, or cups of coffee; others are single strokes as though made by a calligrapher's pen; others again are star-shaped. Many are small dots immersed in the thallus while others sit proudly on short or long stalks. Colour variation is just as wide, ranging from bright crimson through yellows and oranges to greens, greys and blacks.

Structure of an apothecium

There are two types of apothecia, shown on the left and right in the illustration below:

- lecideine
- lecanorine

Lecideine apothecium

Typical of the genus *Lecidella*, the exciple or rim has no algal cells and is frequently black in colour. It is also called a proper margin or rim, as it develops from the tissue of the apothecia.

Lecanorine apothecium

Typical of the genus *Lecanora,* the exciple or rim contains algal cells. When the rim is the same colour as the thallus it is described as a 'thalline rim'.

The hymenium layer holds the asci with the ascospores. Asci are separated by fine hair-like structures and are collectively termed paraphyses. The tips of the asci are collectively termed the epithecium; this is the disc you see from the top. The hypothecium is supportive connecting tissue below. The exciple is sterile (non-reproductive) tissue that holds the hymenium in place. In other words it is the rim or margin around the disc.

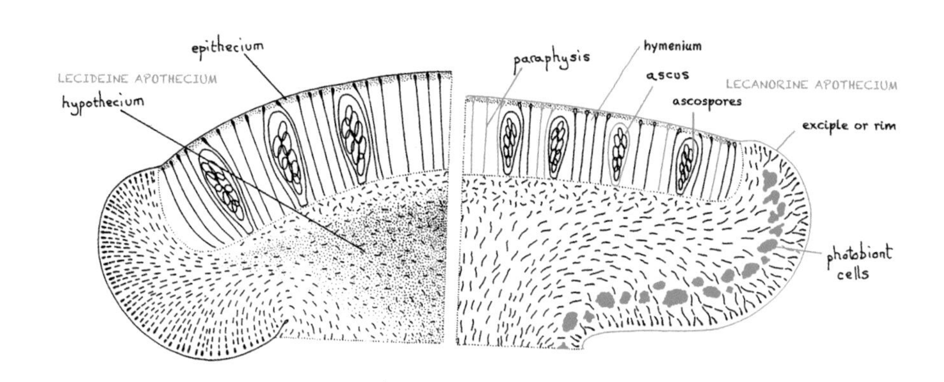

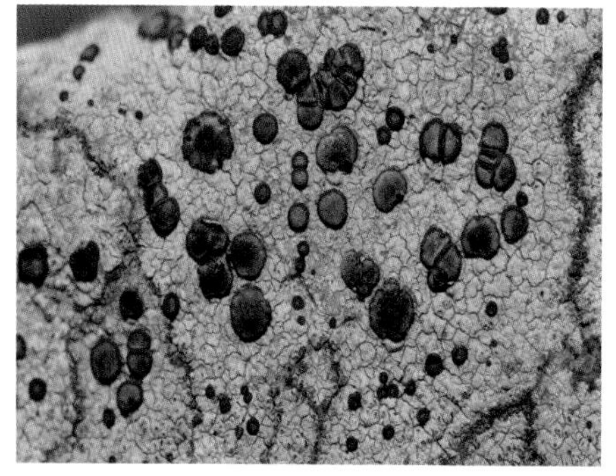

Left: This *Porpidia* species has a non thalline rim.

Right: Lirellate type apothecia of *Opegrapha calcarea*.

Apothecial variations

Apothecia may vary considerably from 'classical' jam-tart shapes. Some of these variations are described below.

(i) **Arthonioid**: flattened, irregular apothecia, sometimes stellate or star shaped. They lack a rim. A classic example is seen in *Arthonia radiata.*

(ii) **Lirellae**: apothecia can be stretched or elongated in some genera such as *Opegrapha* or *Graphis.* In the *Opegrapha* group the rim or margins are proper, having developed from the tissue of the apothecia itself. The disc follows the shape and is consequently elongated also. There is great variation in the types of margins (double or single, for example) and these variations are used to distinguish species. *Opegrapha* and *Graphis* species are frequently found on smooth-barked trees such as birch, hazel and various young twigs.

(iii) **Gyrose**: imagine a lirellae type folded back on itself to form concentric rings. Good examples are seen on *Opegrapha gyrocarp*a and *Umbilicaria cylindrical.*

(iv) **Pin**: the spores are unprotected and form as a mass on the 'head' of the pin. Stalks are variable in length. A common pinhead lichen is *Calicium viride.* See mazaedia, below.

(v) **Podetia**: apothecia develop on the top of large solid or hollow stalks called podetia, typical of genus *Cladonia.*

(vi) **Mazaedia**: In some groups or genera, the walls of the asci dissolve as they mature, leaving an exposed mass of spores and debris from asci and the paraphyses or sterile hairs. This mass of material may protrude above the apothecia in some genera, such as *Calicium* or *Chaenotheca* (pinhead lichens), or lie within the walls of the apothecia as in the genus *Sphaerophorus.* See also *Bunodophoron melanocarpum.*

(vii) **Apothecia** that look like perithecia: Some apothecia have the volcano-like shape of perithecia (they are not perithecia; see below) but they develop from apothecial tissue in various ways. The development of the rim or exciple tissue is important. In the genus *Pertusaria* the wall of the apothecia is of thalline tissue. In *Thelotrema* (see *T. lepadinum*) species two margins are visible (double-walled): the outer margin is thalline and the inner one is the exciple or proper rim. In *Diploschistes* the apothecia also have two margins: the inner one is a well-developed exciple and the outer is a thalline margin.

Perithecia

These are small flask-shaped structures producing spores in a manner similar to the apothecia. They are often black in colour. Perithecia look like tiny pimples or volcanoes. The opening pore at the top is the ostiole; the spores are released through this pore. There is variation in the shape, structure and colour of perithecia that assists identification. For example, the perithecia may be fully or partially immersed in the thallus or not at all, sitting proudly on the surface. In others the ostiole is not at the highest point of the conical shape, often falling to one side. Perithecia may be symmetrical while others take on an asymmetrical appearance. Lichens that reproduce by perithecia are termed pyrenocarpous.

Note: some young developing apothecia may look like perithecia (e.g., *Lobaria virens*), although the opening on the developing apothecia is much larger than the ostiole found on perithecia. Mature spores are released through the ostiole either freely or immersed in a jelly-like material.

Spore size and the micron

The sizes of ascospores within apothecia or perithecia are often critical guides in microscopic identification of lichens to species level.

The unit of measurement used is a *micron*, indicated by the symbol μ. One micron is one millionth of a meter (= 0.000001 metres (m) or 1×10^{-6} metres).

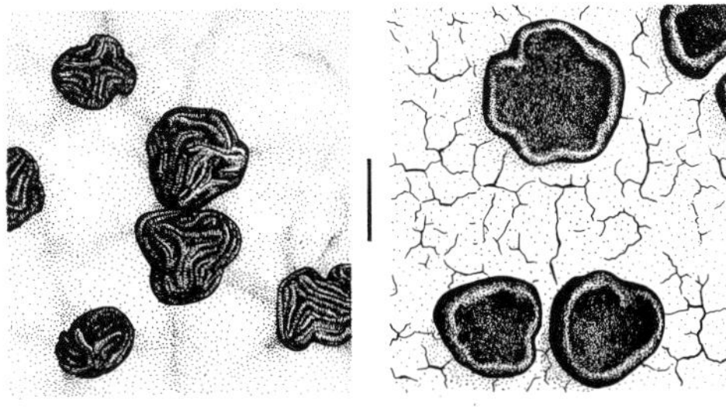

Left: gyrose as in *Opegrapha gyrocarpa*.
Right: lecideine, (lacks a thalline rim or exciple).

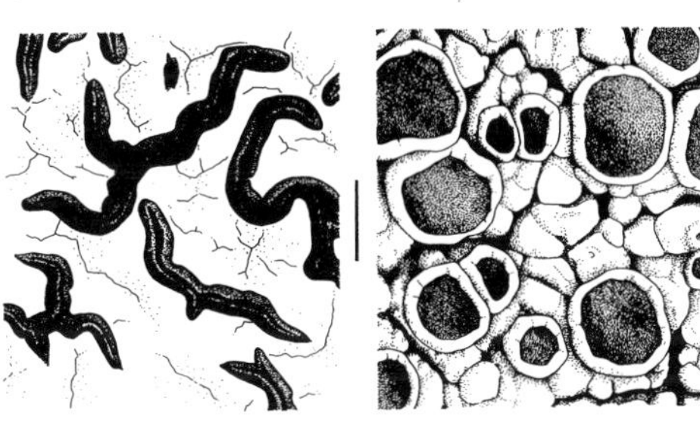

Left: lirellate.
Right: lecanorine with a thalline exciple.

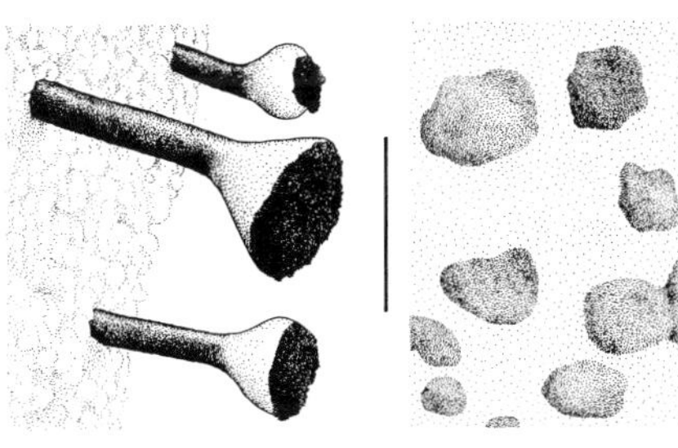

Left: pinheaded or stalked, e.g. *Calicium viride*.
Right: arthoniod.

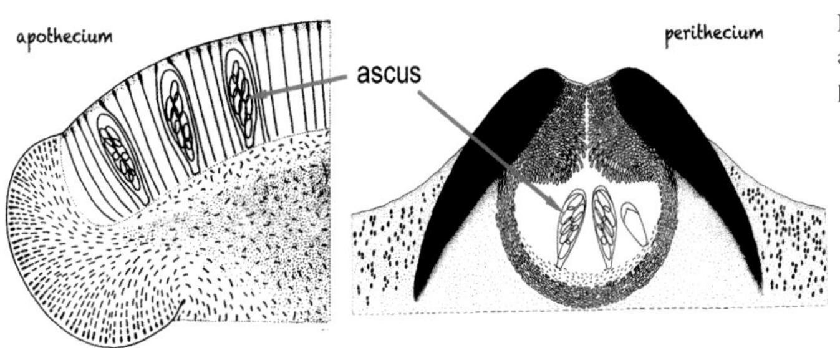

Left: asci location in an apothecium and perithecium

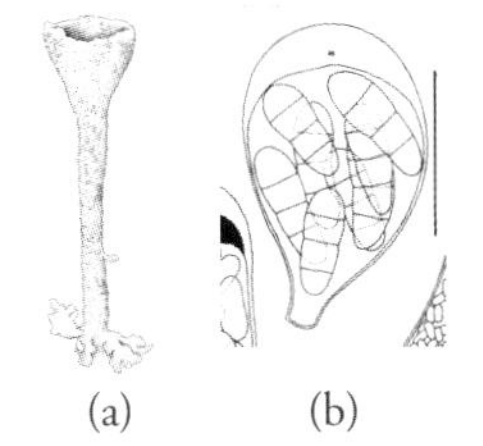

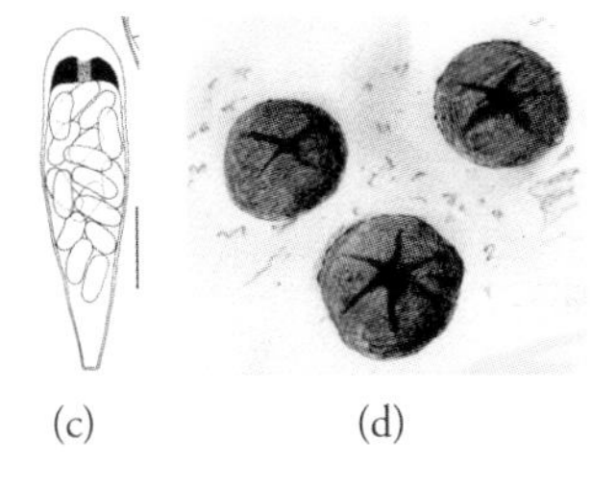

(a) (b) (c) (d)

(a): podetia with a well-developed schypus (*Cladonia coniocraea*).
(b): spores in an ascus (*Opegrapha*).
(c): spores in an ascus (*Xanthoria*).
(d): perithecia of *Verrucaria baldensis*.

In other words there are 1000μ in 1mm. To get a 'feel' for this unit, think about the following:
→ An object 500μ is half a mm or, 500/1000=1/2
→ 825μ is nearly 1mm or 850/1000=85/100 (85% of a mm)
→ 100μ is one tenth of a mm or 100/1000=1/10
As a micron is defined in terms of a meter it is written as μm. Some examples of sizes in microns: yeast cell=3–4μm, human red blood cell=7μm, droplet of fog=10μm, paper thickness=90μm. Lichen spore sizes often falls within a range of values. For example 50–68 x 30–36μm.

Asci tip shapes are also used in identification, although these are beyond the scope of this book.

Basidiomycete lichens

The fungi of *basidiomycete* lichens produce their spores (basidiospores) in groups of four at the top of a structure, the basidium. Being a minority group in Ireland, they are not covered in this book.

Spore Dispersal

Wind can disperse ascospores a great distance. Insects, molluscs (snails and slugs) and other small creatures also play a significant part in dispersal over shorter distances and within a specific habitat. In a study of the faecal pellets of slugs, viable ascospores and potential algal photobionts have been found. The mollusc's faecal pellets bring algal and fungal spores into close proximity, increasing the chances of each discovering the other. This is an important consideration, as the random dispersal of spores in the hope of finding a photobiont and the correct habitat is probably less productive. Habitats, especially for the initial stages in lichenization, need to be rather specific; neither too dry nor too wet. This is often only achieved in crevices or other micro-depressions in the habitat.

The abundance of symbiotic propagules (e.g., isidia and soredia) for asexual reproduction implies that lichens do not depend on sexual reproduction for dispersal or propagation. Sexual reproduction functions primarily to introduce genetic variation into a population.

Left: *Pannaria rubiginosa* with chestnut discs in lecanorine apothecia with crenulate margins.
Right: *Peltigera horizontalis* showing lecanorine apothecia that develop from the upper surface on the lobe margins.

Asexual reproduction (vegetative)

Fragmentation

The simplest form of asexual reproduction is fragmentation; parts of the parent lichen break off and are independent enough to grow into a new lichen. No special reproductive parts are needed. Fragmentation frequently occurs when the weather is dry and the lichen thallus dries out and becomes brittle. Animals such as birds landing on the lichens or squirrels scampering across them are usually enough to break off brittle fragments. *Cetraria*, *Usnea* and *Cladonia* genera are particularly good for fragmentation because of their protruding parts. Birds also collect lichens as nesting material and, of course, drop pieces in flight.

Fragmentation is a quick and easy method of reproduction and highly successful because the fragments are not normally carried too far from the parent material and this increases the chance that a fragment might fall into the same suitable habitat as that of the parent.

Soredia (and soralia)

Soredia are tiny balls or packages of fungal hyphae with a few algal cells (mycobiont and photobiont). When dispersed from the parent lichen, both symbiotic partners are in place to form a new lichen. Soredia develop in the algal or photobiont layer and break through the cortex when they are ready to be released. A good example is found in *Evernia prunastri*, where the soredia can be seen along the edges of the strap-like thallus. Soredia have all the characteristics for success: light in weight and small in size for easy dispersal with both symbionts in a single package.

Soredia form in clusters termed soralia and are easily visible on a lichen with a 10x hand lens as a powdery texture. Their absence or presence and the position they occupy on the lichen play a part in identification, especially in lichens found in damp and/or shady habitats. Soralia may also develop from isidia (see isidia overleaf).

Soralia in various positions on some representative lichens

Laminal soralia: they are found on the open surface of a lobe. They may have either a granular (granulose) or powdery as fine as flour (farinose) appearance, depending on the species.

- Laminal excavate: on the surface in depressions or crevices.
- Laminal hemispheres: on the surface in small hemispheres.

Marginal soralia: these run around the edges of lobes.

- Marginal labriform: sometimes the edge with soralia curls up and back.

Terminal soralia: at the ends or apices of lobes.

- Terminal capitate: at the ends of lobes but spherical and sitting on the upper surface.

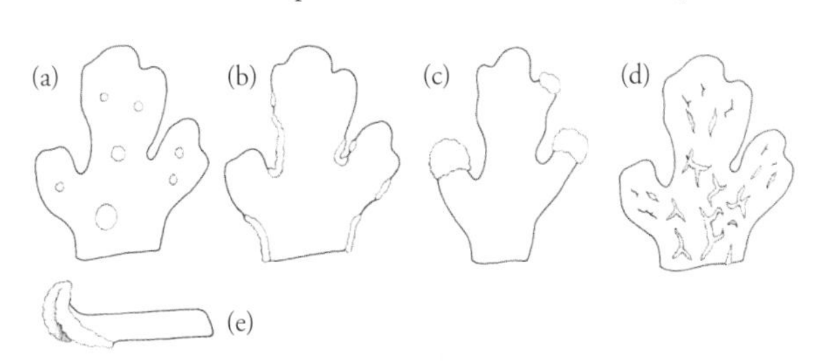

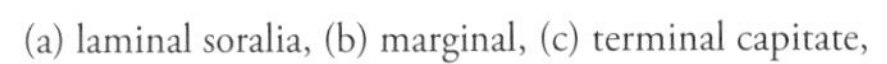
(a) laminal soralia, (b) marginal, (c) terminal capitate, (d) laminal excavate, (e) marginal labriform.

Above: Soralia at the tip of a lobe of *Hypogymnia physodes*: (marginal labriform) sometimes the edge with soralia curls up and back.

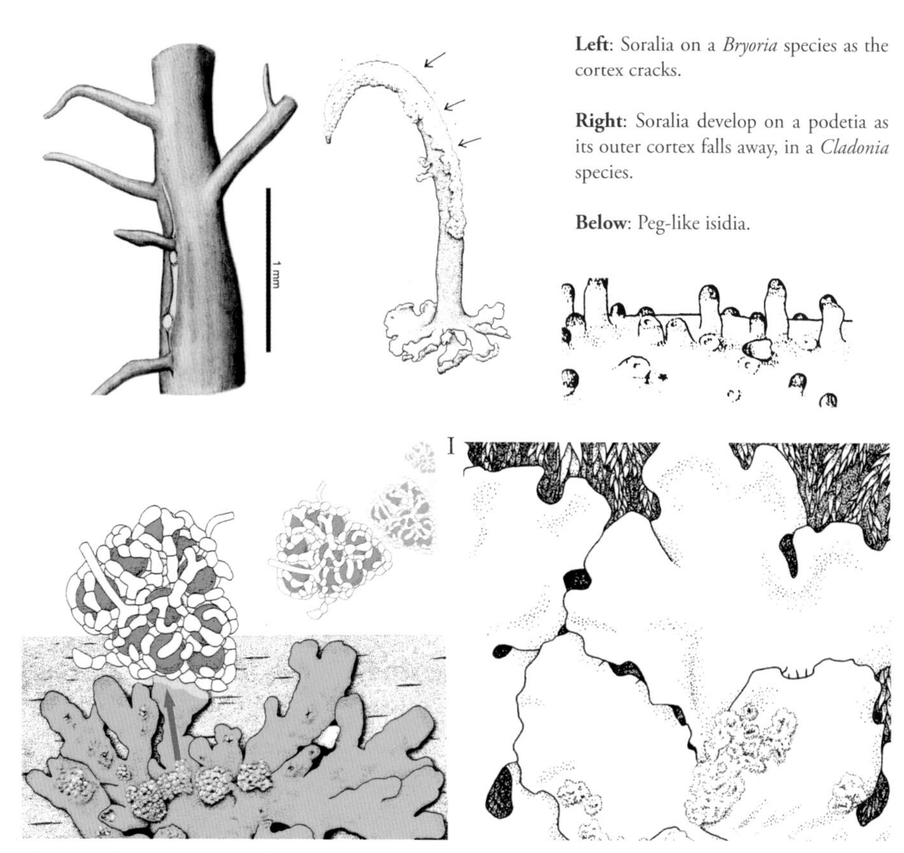

Left: Soralia on a *Bryoria* species as the cortex cracks.

Right: Soralia develop on a podetia as its outer cortex falls away, in a *Cladonia* species.

Below: Peg-like isidia.

Above: Soralia on the surface of *Parmelia* species and detail of a soredium showing the green algal cells wrapped in fungal hyphal filaments. **Right**: Laminal soralia on *Hypotrachyna revoluta*.

Isidia

Similar to soredia in function in that they are also packages of photobiont and fungal cells. They have a different structure, however, developing from the cortex and taking with them an outer layer of cortex tissue. They are generally finger- or peg-shaped, although again there is great variation in their appearance, so much so that at times they seem identical to soredia, especially in lichens that do not have a cortex in the main thallus (for example, genus *Collema*). Some are narrow at the base which encourages them to break off the parent for dispersal by the wind. Isidia tend to develop on lichens found in bright airy, dry habitats.

Schizidia

Scale-like propagules that develop from the upper cortex. When in abundance they can affect the colouration and texture of the lichen. See *Degelia ligulata*.

Pyncidia

A conical or flask-shaped structure that produces conidia ('+' or male gametes). See illustration on the next page.

Blastidia

These are the same as isidia (both symbionts present) but are found in fungi that belong to the group *Basidiomycetes*.

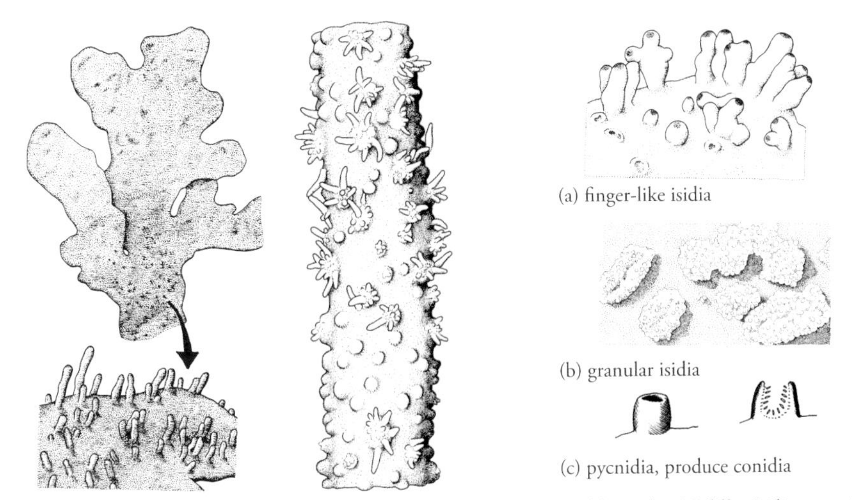

Above left: A full lobe of a *Melanelia* species showing numerous finger-like isidia. **Middle**: Isidia on a side branch of *Usnea subfloridana*. These will break off and frequently leave a sorediate area.
Right: (a) Isidia of *Parmelia saxatilis*. (b) Granular isidia on *Parmelia sulcata*. (c) pycnidia and conidia.

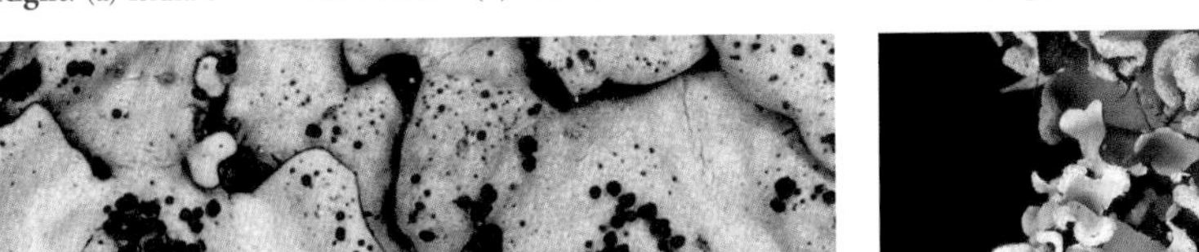

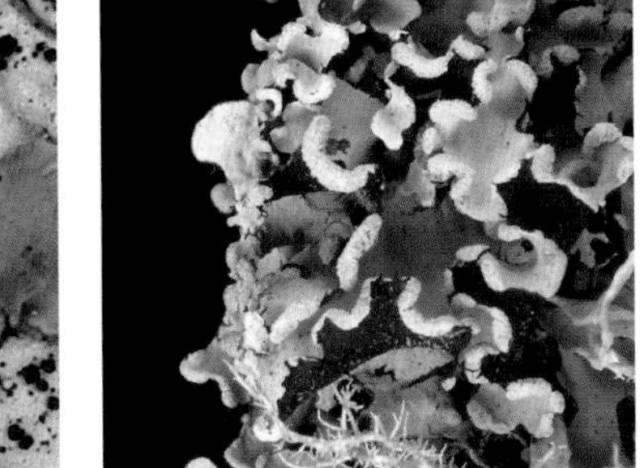

Above: Bun-shaped isidia on *Parmelia pastillifera*. **Right**: Marginal soralia on *Parmotrema perlatum*.
Below: Peg-like isidia on *Parmelia saxatilis*.

Non-reproductive bits

Small growths and depressions on both the thalli and apothecia can act as signposts to the identification of lichens. Some of these are described here.

Cilia: Hair-like structures usually growing around the perimeter of a thallus or reproductive bodies such as apothecia. They vary in colour from black to green to white. Cilia lack a photobiont and so cannot act as propagules. See examples in *Physcia leptalea* and *Teloschistes chrysophthalmus*.

Maculae: The photobiont layer influences the colour of the upper surface of the thallus. When the photobiont is missing from parts of the photobiont layer, its absence is reflected as white patches or blotches on the thalline surface. These areas are termed maculae.

Pseudocyphallae: they look like tiny upside-down bowls or cups. The cortex on the upper or lower sides of the thallus may be very thin or broken, exposing the medulla below. This shows on the thalline surface as white lines or veins and if the cortex is completely ruptured, fungal hyphae may be visible. Pseudocyphallae can also form as small bumps or recesses. They are common on many of Ireland's foliose, crustose and fruticose lichens. See *Parmelia saxatilis*.

Cyphellae: These are similar to pseudocyphellae except that they are found only on the underside of a thallus and only in the genus *Sticta* in Ireland. Whereas pseudocyphellae are frequently just breaks in the cortex, cyphellae are openings that are lined by specialized cells.

Cephalodia: These are either prominent protrusions on the upper thalline surface or buried within the thallus. They have been likened to galls and contain a photobiont, usually cyanobacteria, which is not a primary photobiont of the lichen. Frequently the primary photobiont is algal, while the photobiont in the cephalodia is cyanobacteria. See *Peltigera britannica*.

Pruina: White regions like a frost, generally on the discs of apothecia. On *Physcia aipola* the pruinose discs are the result of the excretion of calcium oxalate crystals.

Several identification features described in the text may be seen on these lichens. For example, the apothecia are thalline and lightly pruinose. The lobes are not tightly attached to the substrate and are covered with a web of white lines or pseudocyphallae.

The rims of apothecia on the Gold Eye (*Teloschistes chrysophthalmus*) lichen are fringed with cilia, adding to the variation in apothecial types.

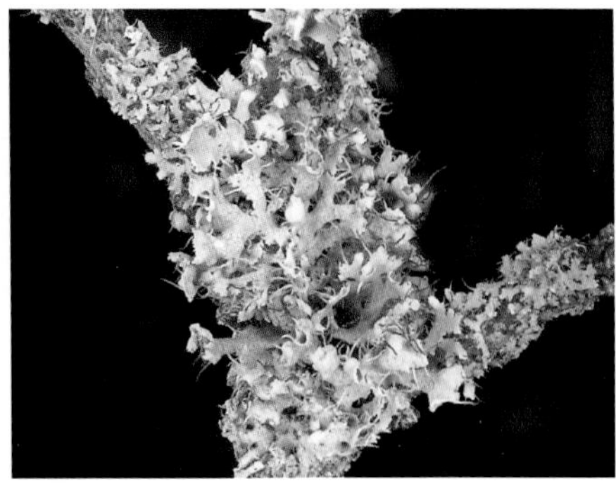

Physcia adscendens with large characteristic cilia protruding from under the lobes.

Physcia species showing cilia and white frost-like pruina on the apothecia discs.

Parmelia saxatilis showing pseudocyphallae lines covering the lobes.

Peltigera britannica showing dark disc shaped cephalodia. Each cephalodium breaks off and becomes an independent lichen with cyanobacteria as the primary photobiont, giving it a different colour (darker) than the parent. Eventually it captures an algae that becomes the primary photobiont and the lichen develops the green colour of its parent. This is an example of a cyanobacterial morph.

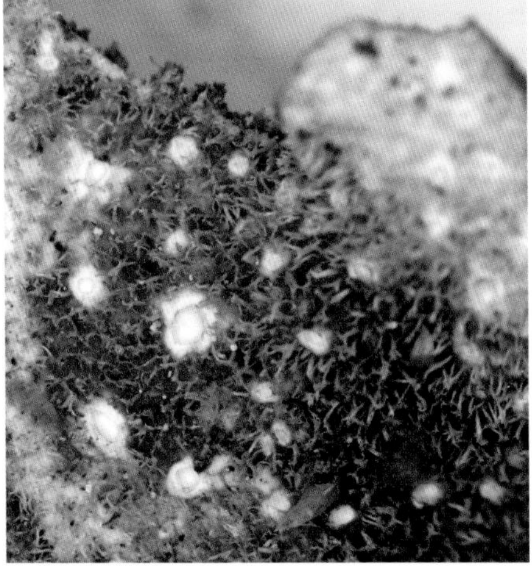

The underside of *Sticta sylvatica* showing regular pale coloured circular cyphellae. This is the only species in Ireland with true cyphellae.

A Practical Approach

A guide to basic equipment

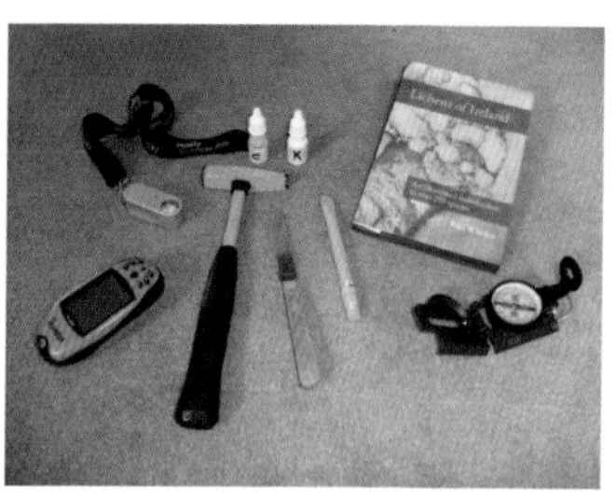

Field equipment: GPS, 10x hand lens, compass, light hammer and chisel, and dropper bottles of C and K chemicals.

Hand lens: Regardless of your level of expertise, a hand lens is a lichenologist's indispensable tool. The most suitable magnification is 10x; more experienced people may carry a 20x lens to help in specific field identification. Some hand lenses have a very useful built-in light.

How to use a hand lens: Hold the lens about 2–3cm from the specimen and then bring your eye down to the lens. This gives maximum magnification and resolution.

Note book: A small, pocket-friendly notebook with attached pencil is also indispensable. Jotting down species names in the field and totting up the list at the end of an outing is very rewarding. Keep note of the following: date, location name, grid reference or latitude/longitude and weather conditions. The latitude/longitude can be read from most in-car GPS SAT NAV devices.

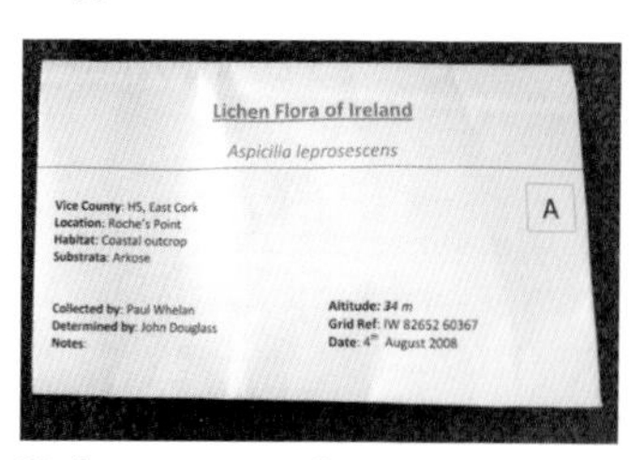

Herbarium envelope constructed from an A4 sheet (acid-free paper is recommended), with information on vice county, location, substrate, etc. clearly written on the front.

Boots: A pair of walking boots is essential, especially those with a good grip on all types of surface, with good ankle support. Do not use wellingtons or other rubber boots.

Knee pads: Wearing knee pads provides more comfort when kneeling and so more time to 'look'. Try to get rubber or waterproof knee pads, as other materials tend to absorb water.

Bag: A waist bag is probably the most convenient, but a light rucksack is also suitable.

Taking samples: Both beginner and specialist need to take samples of lichens for different reasons. A 'collecting code' has developed among lichenologists: never take all of a specimen and never take a specimen that you do not label immediately in the field, with details of location and substrate.

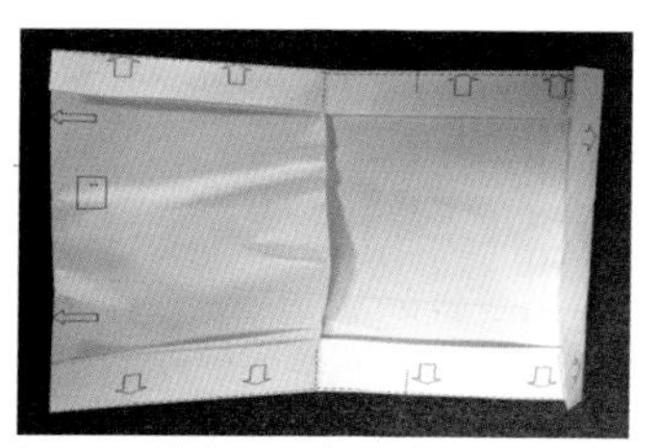

Interior of the envelope showing how it is constructed.

Chisel and hammer: Beginners, or those less experienced in dealing with rock, tend to opt for the heavy lump hammer and chisel. This is not necessary. A small geology hammer, around 454g weight, is adequate when used correctly. A gently tapping action is better than brute force. One or two chisels will suffice. A good working size falls in the range of 10–15mm-wide tips. If the hammer and chisel are not already bright yellow, then paint them so (or use yellow tape). Chisels must be treated as prisoners on a day out; they want to escape. They have a tendency to roll off a rock into the nearest inaccessible crevice. A useful rock-chipping technique is to cup your hand over the specimen you are chipping; this prevents the fragment from flying away when loosened. Or use a handkerchief or other cloth around the point of the chisel to prevent losing the fragment.

Secateurs: A small garden secateurs is invaluable for clipping off small branches.

Knives: A sharp, strong blade that runs directly into the handle is useful for lifting specimens off substrates. Beware of using a penknife as the blades invariably spring back and cut your hand. They are not recommended.

Envelopes: You will need some envelopes to bring the specimens home. Try acquiring small brown paper envelopes used for holding coins. Always label them with the location, substrate and species name (if possible). Lichens stored in plastic will quickly rot.

Camera: The rate of digital camera development is so fast these days that it is an impossible topic to cover in detail. A small pocket camera is an essential tool for any budding lichenologist. The choice is yours, but it is advisable that it (i) has a good macro mode (ii) is good at shooting in low light and (iii) allows spot metering. Digital SLR cameras are far superior for close-up photography once macro lenses are used, however they are more cumbersome to carry. See Thompson, Robert. *Close-up and Macro: A Photographer's Guide*, (2007 edition).

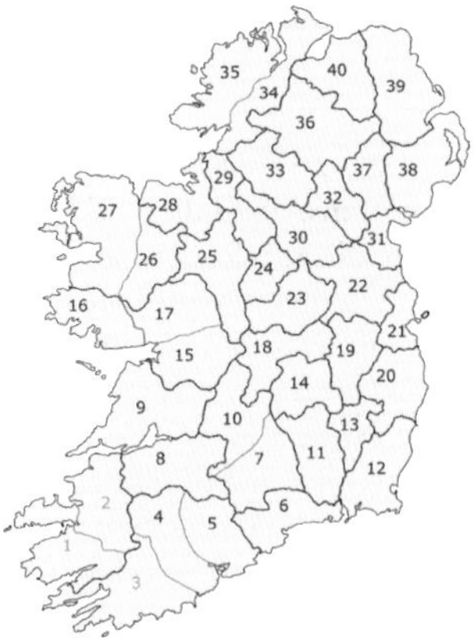

A vice-county distribution map is based on the existing counties but divided (see red boundaries) into 40 areas of approximately equal size.

Setting up your own herbarium

A herbarium is a collection of reference specimens that have been reliably identified. It is an invaluable resource tool that any lichenologist (beginner or expert) can return to. After identifying the specimen (have it verified or determined by another lichenologist if possible), the specimen needs to be dried by either placing it near a heater (but not directly on it) or in a south-facing window that gets plenty of direct sunlight. A specimen should not be dried quickly. A week or so of slow drying is best. Specimens should then be placed in envelopes. Acid-free paper is best, as it reduces deterioration of the lichen. Envelopes can be constructed using A4 pages.

The cover of the envelope should contain the following information: name, vice county, location name, habitat, substrate, altitude, name of the collector, name of the determiner, grid reference using the Irish Grid System, notes and date of collection.

A herbarium of fungi and lichens is housed at the National Botanic Gardens, Dublin.

Vice-county Maps

For the purposes of recording and displaying the distribution of Ireland's biodiversity, a vice-county system was set up by Robert Lloyd Praeger (1901). This divided Ireland into 40 regions of approximately equal area. Each vice county was assigned a number. Some larger counties were divided in two or three. Co. Cork comprises three vice counties: West (3), Mid (4) and East (5). The letter H for Hibernia may be written before a vice county number. In the case of East Cork, this is H5. A vice county is marked even if only a single verified recording for a species is made. Such a broad-wash misrepresents the distribution of some species. However the system is still in use today, as it allows current data to be compared with older records. A paper on vice counties is available in the *Proceedings of the Royal Irish Academy*, Vol. 80B, 179–196 (1980). It may also be downloaded from the Botanic Gardens, Glasnevin, website.

Lichen substances and spot tests

Lichen substances are special chemicals produced by lichens, particularly by the fungal partner. Approximately 700 lichen substances have been identified. They are secreted by the fungal hyphae into the spaces around them. These extracellular compounds (also known as secondary substances) are not secreted evenly throughout a lichen. Some may be concentrated in the cortex or the medulla or in the reproductive bodies. For example, the surface of the disc of apothecia may be coated in fine salt-like granules, termed pruina, which is a lichen substance called calcium oxalate.

Most lichen substances are colourless, however, in the 1860s the Finnish botanist William Nylander discovered that some of them reacted with chemical reagents that he dabbed (or spotted) on the thallus, producing various colours. Since Nylander's time, about one third of known lichen species worldwide (about 5,000 species) have been analyzed for lichen substances. The collected data on colour change in these substances has lead to greater confidence in their use as an aid in lichen identification.

Chemical spot tests are never solely used to identify lichens, but in conjunction with morphological features, such as the type of apothecia or the colour of the underside of the thallus. However, some crustose lichens are so lacking in diagnostic features that the chemical spot test is relied on to a large extent. Over-reliance, however, is to be avoided. The spot tests described here can be used in the field or laboratory, on fresh or herbarium-dried specimens. The majority of reactions occur in the medulla and consequently, it is often beneficial to scrape off a little of the outer cortex before applying the chemicals. Chemicals are carried in the field in small dropper bottles and applied in situ.

Ultraviolet light is also used as an identification aid. Although not in itself a chemical test, it is described here for convenience as it is frequently used in conjunction with chemical spot tests.

Spot Tests and how to apply them

Treat all chemicals as hazardous. Use just a small amount of the chemical, especially on herbarium specimens, as the reagent invariably kills the lichen. One needs only to slightly moisten the tip of the dropper and dab it on the lichen for a reaction to occur. Watch reactions carefully as they can occur quickly and there may be colour changes to observe.

- C is a calcium or sodium hypochlorite solution. Use thin household bleach.
- K (potassium hydroxide) is a solution of 10% sodium hydroxide in water. The typical positive reaction here is crimson red or yellow sometimes changing to red or brown.
- Pd or P, is an abbreviation for paraphenylenediamine. Pd produces yellow/orange/red reactions. It should be used with care as it is a carcinogen and also stains skin, clothes and paper.
- KC describes the application of the K test first and then the C test. Once the K test has occurred, dab the reaction away with filter or tissue paper and then apply the C test on the same spot.
- CK describes the application of the C test first and then the K test. Once the C test has occurred, dab the reaction away with filter or tissue paper and then apply the K test on the same spot.

A positive reaction is indicated by a + symbol and a negative reaction by –. The expected colour is written after the symbol. For example, C+ red means that a drop of C was applied and a red reaction occurred. C– means that no reaction occurred. C+ yellow → red means yellow changing to red.
A variable reaction is shown with ±. Variable reactions can occur in situations where the concentration of the chemical (reagent) is critical or in some lichen species that are subdivided into chemotypes. For example, there are two chemotypes of *Usnea subfloridana*. There is no physical difference between them, just a chemical difference.

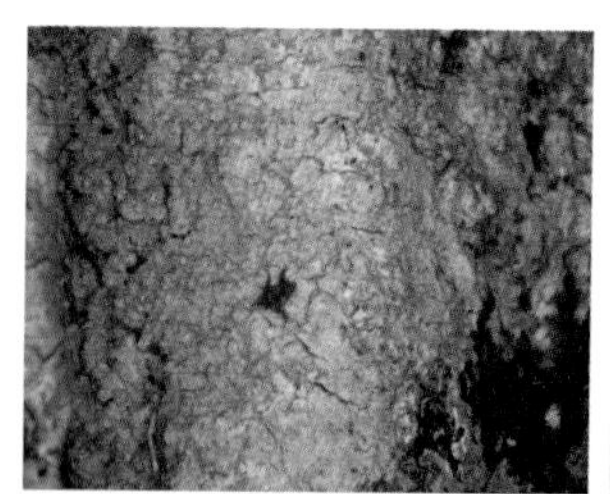

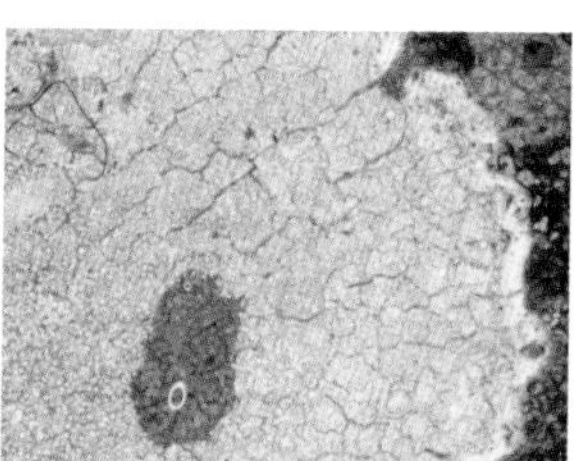

Left: Spot test of K+ yellow turning red, on *Pertusaria coccodes*. **Middle**: K+ yellow, on *Pertusaria corallina*. **Right**: K+ crimson on *Caloplaca*. Nearly all *Caloplaca* species react K+ crimson on either the thallus or apothecia.

Ultraviolet Light (UV)

Some lichens fluoresce a distinctive and characteristic colour under ultraviolet (UV) light, that has a wavelength of about 350μm. This fluoresence may be a valuable identification tool. The UV lamps used by stamp collectors are suitable for use on lichens. Some modern hand lenses have a built-in UV light. UV light is particularly useful in the *Cladonia* and *Lecanora* genera.

Microscopes

Binocular or low-powered microscope: a good low power binocular microscope will allow you to explore the anatomy of a lichen with ease; however, it will not allow you to see spores. It is also useful for making drawings of specimens. Drawing is a wonderful tool in learning, regardless of your artistic skills. Look for a binocular microscope that offers a range from 20x to 40x.

Compound Microscope: a compound microscope is essential for looking at spores. Try to get one that has good resolving power up to about 800x magnification, or higher if you can afford one. Use a compound microscope to look at the asci (spore sacs) and spores. There are plenty of guides on how to do this, but here is a quick outline, which you will perfect with experience.

How to section an apothecium

You will two need glass slides, cover slips, water dropper and a hard-backed blade.

• Select an apothecium from a specimen and place a drop of water on each of the two slides. Have your cover slips ready.

• Place the apothecium for sectioning in the drop of water on one of the slides, for a few seconds, to soften it.

• Use a hard-backed blade to slice through the centre of the apothecium. You will see various tissues in section. Move one half of the apothecium to the second slide and try to slice a paper-thin sliver section off it.

• Once successful, remove the bulky remains of the apothecium. Apply a cover slip over the thin section in the drop of water, leaving it down on the section to remove air bubbles.

• Apply gentle pressure to the cover slip with your finder or an eraser, moving it around a little to rupture the tissues. This action will release asci from their binding tissues and spores from the asci cases. View under the microscope using the lowest power, slowly working up to a higher power.

Spore septa and spore size

Some spores have dividing walls termed septa. Spores with a single septum are written as 1-septate, with 2 septa as 2-septate. Spores with a variable number of septa, say 5, 6 or 7 are written 5–7 septate. The number of septa aid in identification to species level.

To measure the size of spores you will need a graduated eyepiece or slide. These are inexpensive. There are plenty of 10x eyepieces with a micrometer scale etched onto them. You can also purchase a microscope slide with 1cm divided into 100 units. They allow for easy measurement of spore size.

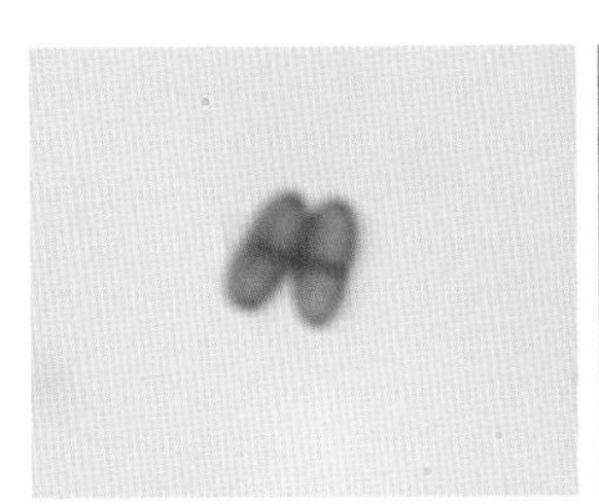

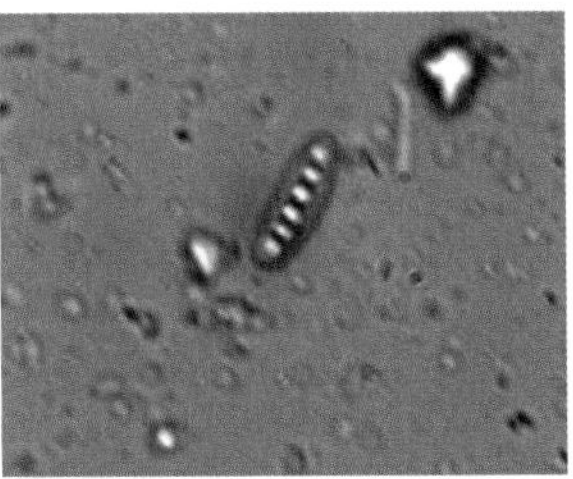

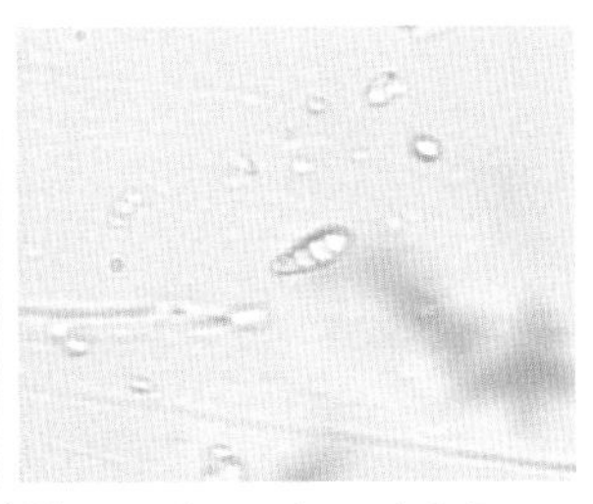

Left: Spores with a single septum, written as 1-septate. **Middle**: Spore of *Phaeographis smithii* with 5–7 septa measuring 30 x 12*u*m. **Right**: Spores of *Opegrapha calcarea* are 3–septate, measuring 14 x 4*u*m.

Ecology of lichens

Ireland's geology

Lichens that grow on rocks have a tendency to show a preference for a particular rock type. One method geologists use to classify rocks is by assessing their silica content. Silica, or silicon dioxide (SiO_2), is found in almost all rocks, excepting the calcareous types such as limestone. Rocks with the highest silica content in Ireland are granite, rhyolite and Old Red Sandstone (ORS), with over 65% silica. Rocks with intermediate levels of silica (50%–65%) include trachyte, andesite and diorite. Silica-poor rocks (45%–50%) include basalt and gabbro. All these rocks, apart from ORS, are igneous, and were produced directly from silica-rich magma below the earth's crust. ORS is a collective title for a variety of sedimentary rocks. The dominant sedimentary rock in Ireland's geology is limestone, produced in a warm sea during the Carboniferous Period 330 million years ago. Limestone is totally devoid of silica, being made up entirely of calcium carbonate in the form of two minerals, aragonite and the more stable calcite. All the above rocks can be changed by heat and pressure metamorphism, giving rise to a complex of rocks such as schists, gneisses, marbles and serpentine. The silica content of a metamorphic rock depends on the silica content of the parent rock. Silica-rich rocks tend to be light coloured. Schists are highly metamorphosed rocks. If formed from slate they are called mica-schists, while if the parent rock is basalt they are termed hornblende schists. Gneisses are metamorphosed rocks that show colour banding of dark and light-coloured minerals, and tend to have the same composition as granite and so are rich in silica. Marbles are metamorphosed limestones, and consequently lack silica. Serpentine (more correctly serpentinite) is green and a rather complex rock, being essentially an unusual silica-containing limestone. Connemara marble is a mixture of white marble and serpentine.

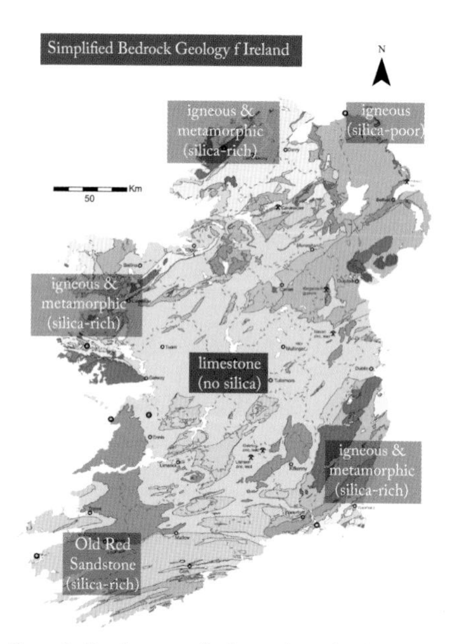

General distribution of silica-rich and silica-poor rocks in Ireland. Note the 'bowl' effect in the distribution pattern: the central plain is limestone and the 'sides' of Ireland are various types of silica-rich rocks. Map available from the GSO Ireland.

Where are these rocks?

The distribution of rocks in Ireland conjures up the image of a bowl, the base being composed of limestone and the edge formed from various silica-containing rocks. In general terms, then, the rocks are distributed in the following manner.

Limestone (no silica): various shade of grey, it covers all of the central plain and pushes out into Dublin in the east and to Galway and Sligo in the west and northwest. Outcrops occur regularly across the country, protruding out through a covering of glacial till left after the last Ice Age. The Burren is Ireland's only upland limestone region.

Old Red Sandstone (silica-rich): a complex set of rocks formed from the erosion of ancient mountains, it is rich in silica. Purple to red-grey in colour, Old Red Sandstone shapes much of the landscape of Kerry and Cork and stretches along the south coast into Waterford.

Granite (silica-rich): a silica-rich, light-coloured rock with medium to large crystals. Principal outcrops are the Wicklow Mountains, stretching into Carlow; Donegal Mountains; a less mountainous area north of Galway Bay and south of a line from Galway to Clifden; much of the Mourne Mountains into which are intrusions of gabbro.

Pertusaria lactescens (white) growing on siliceous sandstone, refuses to grow on the dark band of a silica-poor rock.

Quartzite (silica-rich): a hard, brittle rock of pure sand (silica). Often white or orange-white, it forms cone-shaped hills and mountains. The most famous Irish outcrop is Mount Leinster near Bray, where its conical shape has the geologically challenged convinced it is an extinct volcano. Quartzite also runs through Co. Wexford.

Serpentine (silica-poor): as for marble below, although a particularly good outcrop of serpentine can be found at Lissoughter, after Maam Cross in Co. Galway.

Gneiss (silica-rich): metamorphosed rocks with the same composition as granite, that display colour banding of dark and light-coloured minerals. They occur in Mayo and Galway.

Schist (depends on parent rock): highly metamorphosed rock. If formed from slate they are termed mica-schists. When created from basalt, they are called hornblende schists. It is difficult to know the silica content of schists. They occur in abundance in Mayo and Galway.

Marble (no silica): occurs in areas that have been metamorphosed, usually among schists. Outcrops occur on the south side of the Twelve Bens, at the foot of Errigal and in Donegal near Portnoo.

Rhyolite (silica-rich): a fine-grained glassy rock of almost pure silica with a flint-like appearance. It is found in small amounts thoughout the silica-rich band of rock around Ireland. Veins of it have been found as far apart as Skellig Michael (World Heritage site) off the southwest coast and the Antrim plateau in the northeast.

Basalt (silica-poor): the most extensive outpouring of this rock (it forms on the surface) is the Antrim Plateau. It is a dark coloured rock composed of small crystals (too small to see with a hand lens), low in silica. Contains many small cavities or vesicles.

Gabbro (silica-poor): a coarse-grained, dark-coloured rock, though not as dark as basalt. Large outcrops of gabbro can be seen in the Mourne mountains.

Climate and substrates

The richness of Ireland's lichen flora is due to a combination of factors. Overall, the climate is oceanic, providing both mild winters and summers and a consistently high humidity. Ireland has a great variety of topography, a dauntingly long coastline and an euoceanic (eu=true or good) climate west of the Shannon river, which, very appropriately, is also home to a rich and varied geology. Lichens are found in all our habitats, from the lowest part of the seashore, through grassland, woodlands, towns and villages, graveyards, megalithic tombs, freshwater streams, and uplands regions. All are tightly woven into our ecology, the richest biodiversity occurring on native trees, in particular ash, oak and hazel. The dominant rock types in Ireland are limestone in low-lying areas and siliceous rocks such as granites and sandstones in coastal and upland areas. Rainfall is highest west of the River Shannon, where a high proportion of cyanobacteria photobiont lichens are found.

There are threats to our lichen biodiversity. Ireland is a rather cloudy country, and climate-change scientists think this may increase further over the next 100 years or so. Persistent cloud cover has reduced the biodiversity of light-loving lichens to much lower levels than would be expected for an island of its latitude. Shade-loving *Enterographa crassa* is found in a wide variety of habitats including well lit areas. Continuity of habitat or the need for undisturbed habitats, is an important factor for all lichen types, but particularly the old woodland species. Much habitat destruction occurred in Ireland during the years 1995 to 2007.

Oceanic Climate

Ireland lies on the northwest of the European mainland and experiences an oceanic climate. Parts of the west of Ireland, in particular west Cork and Kerry (Iveragh and Dingle Peninsulas), west Galway (Connemara) and Mayo (north and south of Clew Bay), experience a hyper-oceanic climate. Such a climate provides high humidity and rainfall, mild winters and summers, persistent cloud cover and frequent fog, often rolling in from the sea. The duration of time over which conditions of high humidity and rainfall occur are significant. The Gulf Stream and general proximity to the Atlantic Ocean are responsible for the mild winters and high humidity. The jet stream, never too far away, feeds in low-pressure systems across Ireland all year roud.

Oceanic climatic conditions are found in other countries. Parts of North America and our nearby neighbour Scotland have areas of hyper-oceanic climate. Interestingly, the same lichens often turn up in these hyper-oceanic regions. For example, we share *Nephroma laevigatum* with the hyper-oceanic areas of both North America and Scotland. Hyper-oceanic areas of Scotland and Ireland share species such as *Thelopsis rubella*, *Pseudocyphellaria intricata*, *Pyrenula hibernica*, *Leptogium hibernicum*, *Leptogium juressianum* and *Leptogium coralloideum*.

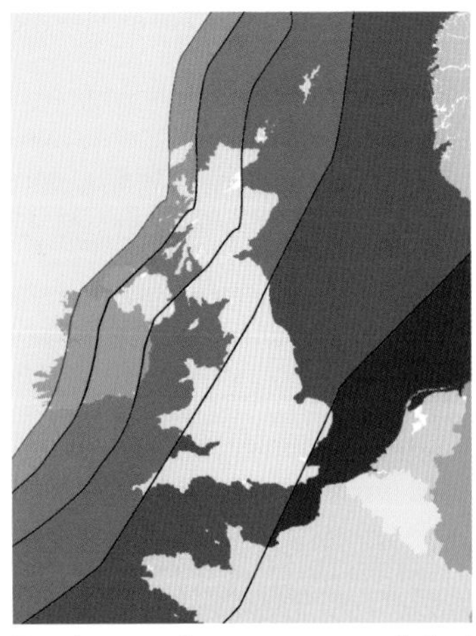

Distribution of oceanicity across Ireland (simplified from Gilbert 2004). Lightest blue colour is hyper-oceanic climate. It passes through parts of west Cork, west Kerry and west Mayo. This type of climate has a major influence on the distribution and biodiversity of lichens in Ireland.

Both woodland and saxicolous lichens flourish in this climate. Little winter snow ensures the lichens are exposed to light all year round and rocks are kept continually damp, enhancing the growth of many saxicolous lichens. Bogs with their associated lichen flora also benefit.

The climate's high humidity enhances growth for many foliose species, as they have the ability to take water from the air directly, rather than wait for direct external water in the form of rainfall. In general, humidity is highest in the early morning, just after sunrise, and it is between this time and 9am or 10am that lichens are thought to do most growing (metabolism).

Lichen Substrates

Lichens grow on a great variety of substrates, including rocks, bark, dead wood, and worked timber. Less obvious substrates include bones, and many man-made substrates such as mortar, cement, asbestos, plastic and glass. The first recording of a lichen growing on glass dates back to 1831, when *Xanthoria parietina* was noticed growing on a church window in Sweden. *Collemopsidium foveolatum* grows on the shells of barnacles around the coast. Bark-loving lichens are described as corticolous and rock-loving as saxicolous. The value of a knowledge of substrates can be illustrated

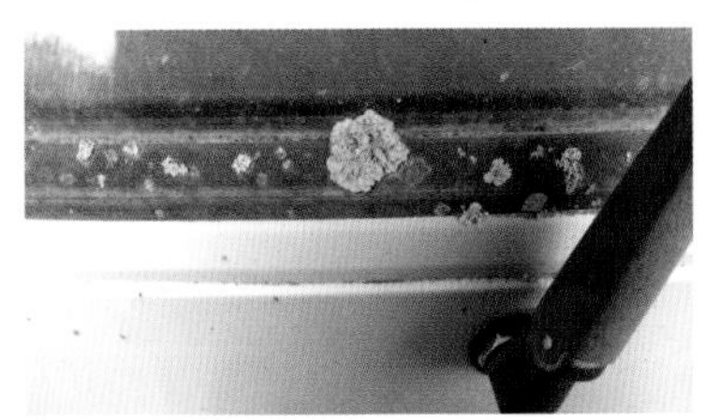

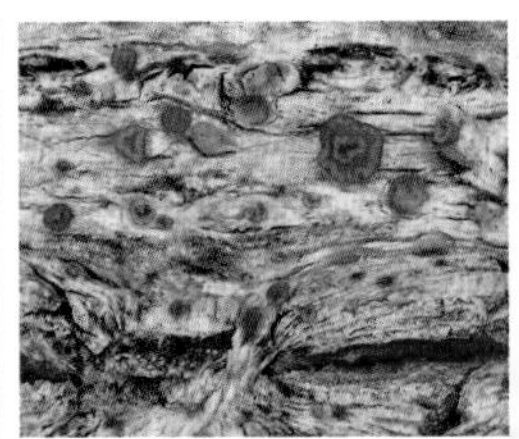

Left: Lichens (*Xanthoria* and *Physcia* species), growing on the rubber seal around a car window.
Middle: *Caloplaca crenularia* grows on rock only. **Right**: *Caloplaca ferruginea* grows on bark only.
Both *Caloplaca* lichens look identical in the field. An awareness of substrate can help with identification.

by examining *Caloplaca ferruginea* and *Caloplaca crenularia*. Both look identical in the field, but one is saxicolous and the other corticolous.

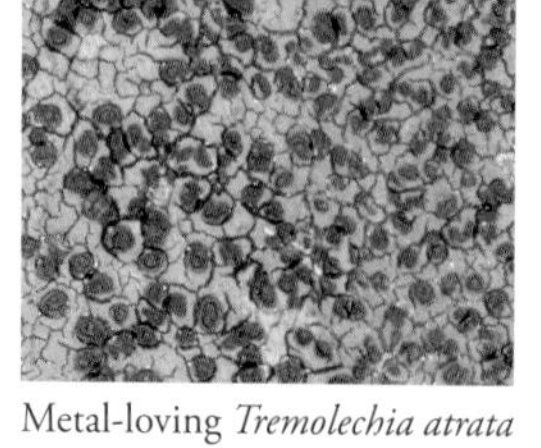

Metal-loving *Tremolechia atrata* stores iron in its cortex as an oxide, producing this dramatic rust colour.

Saxicolous lichens – rocks

The lichen flora on rocks that contain lime or calcium carbonate is very different from the lichen flora on rocks that contain little or none, the siliceous rocks. For example, *Placynthium nigrum* will only inhabit a calcareous substrate such as limestone, mortar or cement, and never a substrate lacking calcium carbonate. Alternatively, *Umbilicaria cylindrica* or *U. polyphylla* will only live on a silica-rich substrate. Silica-rich granitic boulders, similar to those at Carnsore Point, Co. Wexford, may be covered in just one silica-loving species such as *Ramalina siliquosa*. Rocks rich in metals such as iron (Fe) and magnesium (Mg) frequently have their own specific lichen flora. *Stereocaulon vesuvianum* grows on such metal-rich rocks in the west of Ireland. Some metal-loving species (see *Tremolecia atrata*) retain the metals as oxides, storing them in the cortex and producing a rust red thallus. *Porpidia flavocruenta* typically has a yellowish orange thallus, but absorbs iron when available and becomes rust coloured.

The pH of rocks and their associated soils plays a considerable part in the lives of saxicolous lichens. While a rock itself does not have a pH (measure of acidity) value, when wetted, the water reacts with the rock and takes on a pH value. Assuming the rain is not itself an acid, then the pH value of rain will adjust to take on a value related to the rock type. The hypothallus of many crustose lichens penetrates rock, the hyphae weaving around crystals in search of mineral nutrients.

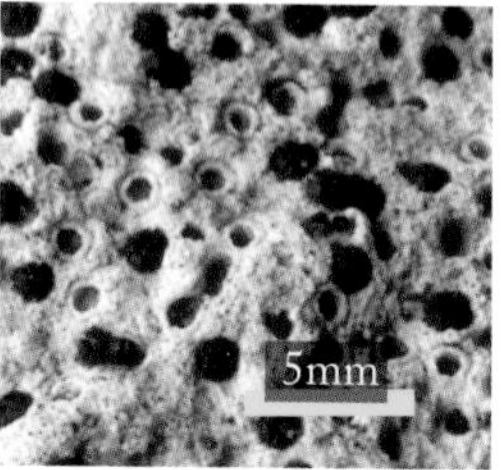

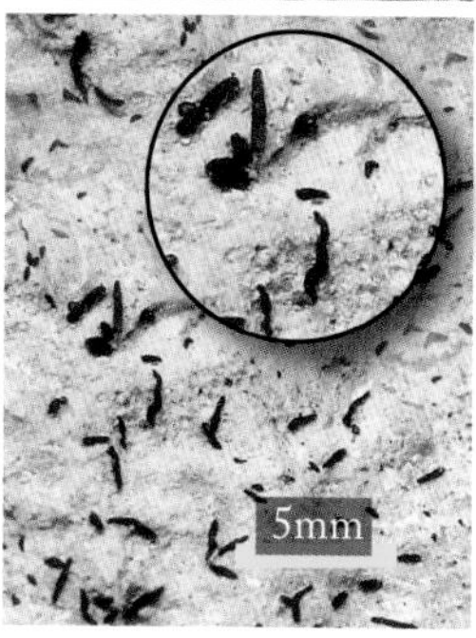

Top: Some of the perithecia of this *Verrucaria* species growing on limestone have fallen out revealing the extent to which they had dissolved the limestone to 'fit' in.
Above: The thallus of this tiny lichen (*Opegrapha mougeotii*) of limestone regions is invariably immersed in the rock, leaving only the apothecia visible.

Lichens dependent on cyanobacteria, such as the genera *Leptogium* and *Collema*, have a preference for silica-poor or calcareous substrates such as limestone or mortar. One possible reason for this is that cyanobacteria's ability to fix nitrogen is inhibited in an acid environment. *Nostoc* functions best in an alkaline environment. The relationship between rock surface water pH (including the rock's associated soil types) and lichen distribution is so strong that some lichens can be used to determine the wetted rocks/soil pH.

For example, *Cladonia coccifera* indicates a pH=3 (very acid) while *Rhizocarpon geographicum*, typically found on granites and slate, indicates a pH=4. *Ochrolechia parella* common on ORS and basalts, points to a pH=5. The tiny ruby-red *Protoblastina rupestris*, indicates a pH=7. *Verrucaria baldensis*, common in the Burren, stipulates an alkaline pH=8. (*Lichens: Oliver Gilbert, 2000*).

Rock porosity and water-holding properties also influence lichen flora. Old Red Sandstone is relatively porous and slow to dry out. This increases the humidity of the microclimate across the rock surface, allowing not just crustose species to gain a foothold, but also some foliose species. Seepage tracks often ensure a continual source of water, encouraging localised lichen communities. *Dermatocarpon miniatum* may be found in abundance on a single seepage track, and then not again for many kilometers, despite the rock type being similar. Isolated boulders or old standing stones are always worth examining. Their location often ensures that they have a sharp wetting/drying cycle and are exposed to all the sunlight that is available. As Ireland was glaciated, it is strewn with a healthy number of erratics as the ice retreated, their geology often being considerably different from the local bedrock. Quartzites are hard, silica-rich and lack nutrients, consequently their lichen flora is poor and often particularly difficult to identify. Granite serves as a good all-round substrate for lichens but its hardness and lack of cleavage make it particularly difficult to take voucher samples away. Your efforts will ensure a blunt and useless chisel at the end of the day. Be prepared to get your identification correct in the field. Basalt is also difficult to chip, as it fractures irregularly. Work with your chisel and hammer carefully, using goggles, as basalt sends splinters flying in an unpredictable manner.

Ireland's limestone was deposited in the Carboniferous period. Its flat surface often appears devoid of lichens (apart from the obvious white extensive splashes of *Aspicilia calcarea*), but on close examination it may be seen to be home to many very tiny, pale-coloured, paper-thin lichens. The thalli of many limestone crustose lichens are totally immersed in the rock, leaving tiny reproductive parts as the sole aid to identification. Other limestone lichens may further embed themselves by dissolving holes for their reproductive structures. This can be seen in several species of *Verrucaria*, whose perithecia leave tiny holes in limestone, after they have died and fallen out. Lichens that integrate into rock to this extent are termed endolithic. Epilithic limestone lichens, such as *Collema auriforme* (page 82), have thalli visible.

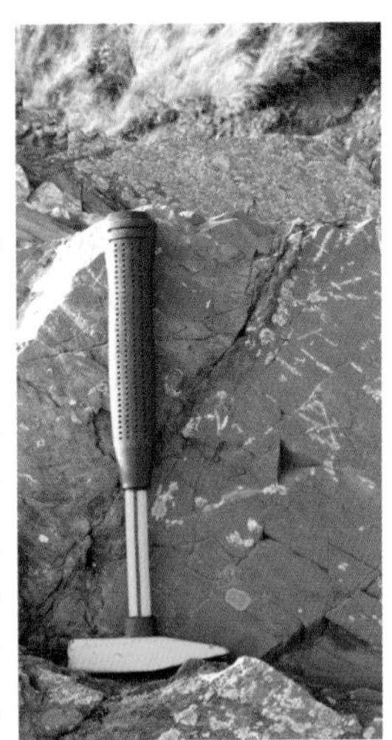

Fracture lines on Old Red Sandstone in Co. Cork hold on to rainwater a little longer than the smooth rock face. These, in conjunction with providing a foothold, are enough for the white lichen (*Lecanora helicopis*) to move in. At the bottom of the picture are some orange/yellow *Caloplaca* species, also taking advantage of the rock's drainage system.

Corticolous Lichens – bark and sawn wood

Assemblages of lichens found on bark are determined by many factors, including light intensity, degree of wetness, humidity, bark texture, canopy density, direct competition with bryophytes (mosses) and bark pH.

Bark is a complex material and varies considerably from species to species and particularly between coniferous and deciduous trees. Coniferous trees tend to produce resins and gums, giving barks a higher acidity than deciduous trees. Light intensity is directly influenced by leaf density and proximity to other trees. Deciduous trees lose their leaves for winter, exposing the bark to more light. Often, lichen growth will become more pronounced during winter. The bark of trees on the edge of woodlands or wayside trees also receives more light than those in denser plantations.

Ireland's southwest prevailing winds, directing the soft Atlantic rains over the country, ensure that many trees receive a good supply of rainwater on their southwest-facing bark. Coniferous trees such as larch, have branches that drop down and away from the tree bole, directing the rain away from the trunk. On the other hand, trees such as native ash and oak have branches that grow from the tree at acute angles and so channel water to the centre of the tree and down the trunk. Frequently, such water also contains nutrients, such as bird droppings and dead insects, from the surface of leaves. Some of Ireland's thirstiest and largest lichens such as *Lobaria pulmonaria* and

An ash tree with rainwater channelled down the bark supports *Lobaria virens* and *Lobaria pulmonaria.*

Lobaria virens are found on the trunks or large horizontal branches of ash and oak. Inevitably, parts of a tree's bark will remain sheltered and dry, particularly on rough-barked trees such as mature oak. These hidden, dry crevices harbour a specific lichen flora, like tiny pin-headed lichens, including *Calicium viride* or the crustose *Pyrrhospora quernea*. Many dry-bark lichens are shared between woodlands and wayside trees. The appearance of lichens on one side of a tree as opposed to another is often due to competition between light intensity, wetness, other competing lichens and epiphytes such as mosses and ferns. Bark pH plays a major role in a lichen's ability to take up nutrients. Depending on soil type or age, some trees may be slightly basic or acidic, often moving between one pH and another, particularly hazel, ash, elm and willow. **Very Acid bark**: oak, birch, alder. **Mildly Acid bark**: hazel, ash, elm, rowan, willow, old oak. **Basic bark**: hazel, ash, elm, willow, poplar, elder, field maple, sycamore.

The rough bark on the northeast side of this tree provides a dry habitat for some lichens such as *Chrysothrix candelaris*.

Twigs that have fallen to the ground show a changing pH over time, as they decay. Consequently, its initial lichen flora will change as the twig's pH changes and the twig dies. Eventually the lichen flora is replaced by non-lichenized fungi.

Wood, or lignin, often attracts a different lichen assemblage from bark, although a considerable number of lichens share both substrates. Some species specialize in soft decaying wood, while others prefer hard, dry and well-weathered wood.

Bryophytes and dead vegetation

Some lichens are habitually found growing among mosses, where they are enveloped in a microclimate of high humidity and a continual or reliable supply of direct external water. Examples include the diminutive *Normandina pulchella* and *Dimerella lutea*, the foliose *Sticta limbata* or *Peltigera praetextata*. Decaying vegetation, such as dead stems of Sea Pink (*Ameria maritima*) are frequently home to the beautiful *Lecanora zosterae*.

Lichen habitat types in Ireland

Habitats are areas that a species inhabits. They are composed of an abiotic element (the physical environment and climatic conditions), and a biotic element (plants and animals around it). The following habitat classification will help in your search for and identification of lichens.

'Ordinary' mixed woodlands

Mixed woodlands are relatively new and include dead wood and clear-felled trees. Bark types tend to be both acid and basic and generally smooth, as the trees are not yet mature. Typical lichen species include *Amandinea punctata, Calicium viride, Hypogymnia tubulosa, Lecanora carpinea, Lecidella elaeochroma, Parmotrema perlatum*, *Pertusaria leioplaca, Enterographa crassa,* and several *Cladonia* and *Graphis* species. Undisturbed rotting tree trunks often house good communities of *Cladonia* species. Smooth barked young trees are a good place to look for 'background' species such as *Lecidella elaeochroma* and *Lecanora chlarotera*. Lichens found here are also found in other habitats.

Old woodlands

The phrase 'old woodlands' describes woodlands that have been uninterrupted since the 1830s and show a possible link to ancient woodlands. In the past, they were exploited as a source of timber and for charcoal kilns. At the time of writing, there are just 12,500 Ha. of old woodland left in Ireland and these tend to be in very remote areas or in association with large houses. Lichens specific to this type of woodland require a stable, unchanging environment such as constant humidity and levels of

Left: Old woodlands are among the richest lichen habitats in Ireland, rivalled only by our Atlantic hazel woods. They provide constant levels of humidity and light intensity but unfortunately they are now rare. **Right**: Trees in open areas receive plenty of sunlight. Their lichen flora may be dictated by nitrogen enrichment from farms.

light intensity. Stability of environment is also important for the completion of their reproductive cycles. Lichen literature refers to these as 'old woodland species'. Example species include *Degelia plumbea, Leptogium brebissonii, Leptogium lichenoides, Leptogium teretiusculum, Lobaria virens, Pannaria conoplea,* and various *Peltigera* and *Lobaria* species.

Limestone, Mortar and Concrete

Limestone is the most common rock type in Ireland. Much of it can be found in lowland areas, but covered with glacial till, being exposed here and there as rocky outcrops. Limestone lichen flora is frequently also found on mortar and concrete and includes *Aspicilia calcarea, Acrocordia conoidea, Agonimia tristicula, Caloplaca decipiens, Diplotomma alboatrum* and *Toninia aromatica.*

Silica-rich rocky outcrops/boulders

Upland regions of Ireland tend to consist of siliceous rocks such as granite (Donegal and Wicklow). Siliceous rock also occurs as boulders strewn across the country from the last Ice Age. Many of these boulders are found in mountain streams. Silica-loving lichens include *Lecidea lithophila, Parmelia saxatilis, Pertusaria pseudocorallina, Porpidia hydrophila* and *Rhizocarpon lavatum.*

Open areas with remnant trees in pasture

These trees receive plenty of sunlight and usually have a rich lichen flora, although this may be dictated by pollution levels in the surrounding countryside. Lichens found here may be occur in other woodland types. Typical species include *Acrocordia gemmata, Bryoria fuscescens, Melanohalea exasperata, Physcia tribacioides, Pyrenula macrospora, Ramalina fastigiata* and *Usnea subfloridana.*

Uplands (bogs and heaths) terricolous areas

Upland areas in Ireland are often covered in bog or heathland. Lichens here are frequently terricolous (ground dwelling) and are typical of upland bogs and heaths. Species of this habitat include *Cetraria islandica, Cladonia bellidiflora, Cladonia fimbriata, Cladonia floerkeana, Cladonia gracilis, Cladonia polydactyla,* and *Cladonia squamosa.*

Coastal–Terrestrial (on trees, rocks, old walls & buildings)

Lichens of this habitat are found from the coast to as far inland as is under the influence of the sea. This varies from region to region depending on the type of landscape and its exposure to wind. Consequently the distance inland cannot be stated in kilometres. These lichens are found in woods, fields, wayside trees and rocky outcrops. In general they are salt tolerant. Species include *Acarospora impressula, Anaptychia ciliaris, Anaptychia runcinata, Caloplaca ceracea, Caloplaca marina, Caloplaca verruculifera, Catillaria chalybeia, Lecanora zosterae, Leprocaulon microscopicum, Ramalina cuspidata* and *Solenopsora holophaea.*

Mountain streams (left) and ravines (right), with their gushing waters, shrubby vegetation, shelter and high humidity provide for rich pickings of both saxicolous and corticolous lichens.

Coastal–Submerged (submerged by the tide)

Lichens here are covered by the tide each day. They are habitat specific and rarely overlap with other habitats. They are tolerant of both salt and fresh water (rain). These are further subdivided into the black zone, yellow zone and grey zone. Examples include *Lichina confinis* and *Lichina pygmaea.*

Coastal–splash, but never submerged

Lichens in this zone are just above the high-water mark. They are exposed to sea spray. Some may be found inland, but generally they are quite specific to the splash-zone habitat. Species include *Anaptychia runcinata, Caloplaca marina,* and *Caloplaca thallincola.*

Urban/Farm 'yellowing'

This habitat refers specifically to lichens growing in towns and villages and in or near farms, where there may be a high nitrogen content in the air. Such areas are dominated by 'yellow' lichens of the Xanthorian community, and also by species from the Physcia community. Expect to find *Acarospora fuscata, Caloplaca decipiens, Catillaria chalybeia, Lecanora campestris, Lecanora muralis, Parmelina pastillifera, Xanthoria calcicola, Physcia adscendens* and *Physcia tenella.*

Fresh water

Streams, particularly mountain streams and lakes, have lichens that are frequently covered by water. Ravines with turbulent freshwater streams running through them also experience high humidity, under which many lichens flourish. Species include *Porpidia hydrophila* and *Ephebe lanata.*

Trees in parklands, hedgerows, by rivers, etc.

Generally these trees are well lit, being in gardens, orchards, along old roads, by rivers and hedgerows. Representative species are *Bryoria fuscescens, Cladonia pyxidata, Parmelia pastillifera, Parmotrema perlatum, Peltigera hymenia, Physcia tribacioides* and *Punctelia borreri.*

Sawn wood and worked timber, old fences, gates, etc.

Some lichens are specific to worked timber or sawn-wood substrate. They tend to be 'early colonisers'. Because sawn wood/worked timber is associated with human activity, you will find that many of the lichens are both urban (town) and/or rural (fencing on farms). Expect to find *Amandinea punctata, Bryoria fuscescens, Cladonia fimbriata, Cladonia polydactyla, Lecanora pulicaris, Lecanora varia, Melanohalea exasperata, Parmelia saxatilis* and *Usnea subfloridana.*

Graveyards (headstones, tombs, walls and old churches)

Headstones in Ireland tend to be made from limestone, reducing graveyard lichen biodiversity to those that prefer this substrate. Traditionally, graveyards have offered a stable unchanging environment allowing development of lichens. Graveyard species include *Ochrolechia parella, Toninia aromatica,* various *Pertusaria* and *Lecanora* species and usually some members of *Collema.*

Lichens and Pollution

Lichens traditionally have been associated with a clean or unpolluted environment. This is a simplistic view. Some lichens only survive in a clean environment, while others flourish in polluted areas. For example, some species of the genus *Xanthoria* establish and grow abundantly in nitrogen-rich areas, such as near farms or chemical factories. Some species of the genus *Usnea* are sensitive to sulphur dioxide levels in the air and will only grow in areas where its concentration is negligible or non-existent. So the idea that lichens only live in an unpolluted environment is untrue.

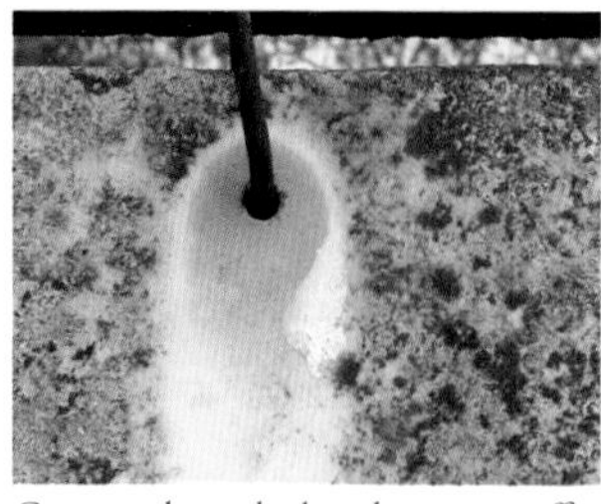

Graveyards and churches may offer an opportunity to see the effect of metals on lichens. **Above**: Few lichens will grow over copper or zinc or in the run-off area below them.
Below: Lead is less toxic, as can be seen from this headstone inscription. Lichens refuse to grow over the lead lettering, but will tolerate the run-off residue around and below them.

Lichens are unable to 'refuse' entry to many chemicals into their bodies. This implies that chemicals can freely invade them and interfere with their metabolic processes, often killing the lichens, but sometimes increasing their growth rate. Also, lichens are unable to excrete or secrete these chemicals and so they accumulate within the thallus, sometimes changing their colour (see *Tremolechia atrata*). Lichens are excellent bioaccumulators. Lichenologists use these lichen properties to monitor pollution levels, particularly levels of sulphur, nitrogen (their oxides, SO_2 and NO_2) and heavy metals. A study into the effect of air pollution on lichens was carried out by Hawksworth and Rose (1970) and Gilbert (1970). They divided lichen sensitivity to airborne SO_2 into 10 zones. This 10-zone system is still in use today, although it has been modified and developed since its creation. With reference to moderately acid barked trees, lichens such as *Lecanora conizaeoides, Lepraria incana, Hypogymnia physodes,* and *Parmelia saxatilis* can tolerate high levels of SO_2, while moderate levels are acceptable to *H. physodes, P. saxatilis, Calicium viride, R. farinacea, E. prunastri* and *Platismatia glauca.* Less tolerant species include *Parmelia caperata, Graphis elegans, Pseudevernia furfuracea, Parmelia caperata, Usnea subfloridana, Parmelia perlata* and *Normandina pulchella.* The most sensitive species include *Lobaria pulmonaria, Dimerella lutea, Sticta limbata* and *Usnea articulata.* (Based on the Ten Point Hawksworth-Rose SO_2 Pollution Scale).

Importance of lichens in an ecosystem

Lichens contribute to the flow of energy through an ecosystem. As a source of nutrition, they are high in carbohydrate and poor in protein. The diet of some large mammals, such as caribou in North America, is largely composed of lichen flora. In Ireland there is little evidence that mammals use them as a source of nutrition; however, it would not be surprising if squirrels and other small

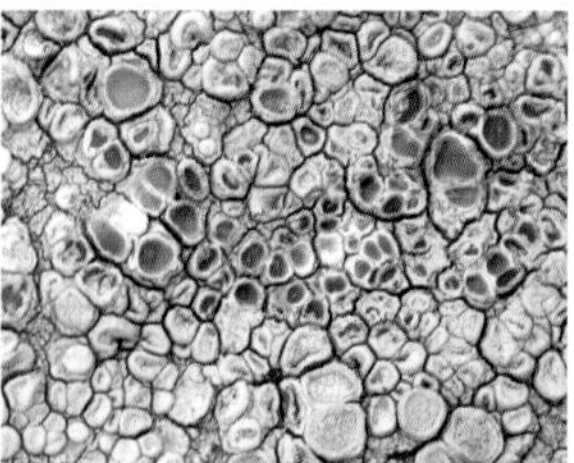

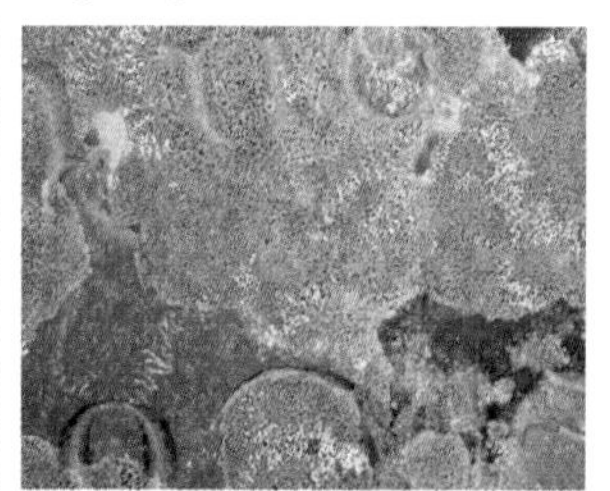

Left: Apothecia of this *Ochrolechia parella* have been grazed away by a slug. **Middle**: A slug feeding on lichens. **Right**: Rasping marks over *Rhizocarpon reductum* on a headstone are typical of slug feeding.

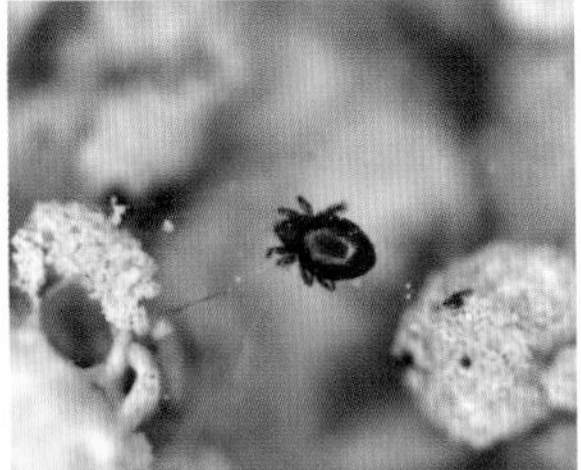

Left: A bird's nest made mostly from moss, lined with feathers and clad on the outside with the following lichens: *Parmotrema perlatum, Xanthoria parietina* and *Physcia adscendens*. Interestingly, two of these lichens have cilia or rhizines that give the lichens a 'velcro' property for attachment. Lichens act to camouflage the nest.
Middle: An oribatid mite on a lichen (15x), moving across from one cluster of soredia to another.
Right: A November moth (*Epirrita dilutata*) blends in with both the substrate (limestone) and crustose lichens.

mammals living in our few remaining old woodlands have incorporated some *Usnea* and *Bryoria* species into their diet. Squirrel nests have been found lined with these species, where the lichens are abundant. Evidence of invertebrates both sheltering among and feeding on lichens is common. Scanning tree trunks and twigs with a hand lens regularly brings you face to face with tiny grubs, mites, silverfish, springtails, some in the act of eating soredia. Take a voucher sample home and you will soon see them scurrying out of the envelope. Lichens are regularly scarred by the feeding marks of snails and slugs. Lichens are also used as camouflage. Moths, such as the Peppered moth, *Biston betularia*, with its white speckled wings, blends in seamlessly with many corticolous lichens. Some caterpillars have markings, such as the Brussels Lace moth (*Cleorodes lichenaria* – common in Ireland), that mimic lichen shapes and colouration. Many birds use lichens as a nesting material.

Algal photobionts produce oxygen (by splitting water molecules) and use carbon dioxide to manufacture sugars (photosynthesis). These sugars are shared with the saprophytic fungal partners. Cyanobacteria take free nitrogen, N_2, from the air and convert it ('fix' nitrogen) into a form, usually a nitrate, that the algae can use. Hence they play a critical role in the nitrogen cycle. Nitrogen is needed by all living things to create protein molecules. Soil-dwelling lichens (e.g., *Trapeliopsis pseudogranulosa*) add nitrates to the soil directly. Reflection on the above chemical procedures will soon lead one to see a lichen as a miniature ecosystem in itself. The gifted lichenologist Oliver Gilbert studied ash trees and outlined the flow of energy (food chain) on tree trunks as follows: ***1/ algae and lichens (primary producers) → 2/ herbivores (mainly bark lice – Psocids) → 3/ omnivores and decomposers (earwigs, woodlice, beetles → 4/ carnivores (harvestmen, spiders and lacewings, for example) → 5/ birds***. A study in Sweden (Petterson *et al.* 1995) showed that there were nearly five times more invertebrates per branch in a lichen-rich woodland than in a managed one (See *Lichens* – Oliver Gilbert).

Some conservation pointers

Ireland is home to many lichens of international importance. Conservation must focus on their habitats, be they graveyards, woodlands or mountain ravines. The threat from sulphur dioxide pollutants has receded in recent years with the installation of 'scrubbers' in many industrial plants. There is, however, a new threat from excess production of nitrogen, which either kills lichens or strengthens the 'weed' species. A few guidelines for conservation/biodiversity aware communities are outlined below. Remember that wildlife needs wild places.

- Remove ivy from headstones and monuments (it causes limestone to crumble). Avoid needlessly removing lichens from headstones; just clean the lettering or just one side. Don't paint headstones. Try to avoid using polished headstones (if the choice is yours) as lichens cannot get a foothold.
- Leave rotting logs and fallen trees in a woodland.
- When replacing old wooden fencing, leave the old fence to 'infect' the new one.

• Resist power-hosing roofs or walls needlessly.
• When cleaning or pointing old buildings such as outhouses, abbeys, churches, etc., there is no need to clean the stone. Carry out the pointing in stages, so lichens on old mortar can move to the new mortar. If mortar was used on old walls, then use mortar to repair them, and not cement.
• If there is a hedgerow in front of your house, then leave it there. Don't replace it with a fence.

Left: This west Clare graveyard has a wonderful lichen flora that adds interest to the landscape. Headstones are made all the more interesting in both colour and texture. **Middle**: *Xanthoria* species add visual interest to this house in Co. Mayo. **Right**: Of the two houses in the photo, the near one had its roof power hosed, removing all the lichens. A needless exercise in habitat destruction.

Left: A headstone cleaned and painted. Paint will soon fade leaving the headstone looking drab and lichenless.
Middle: This headstone was photographed during a survey in 2009. The lichens added an aesthetic quality of natural colours and textures to it and other similar headstones in the graveyard.
Right: The headstone in 2011, cleaned of lichens (as were all the other headstones in this graveyard), not only decimated the graveyard's lichen biodiversity, but removed the 'old' feeling from the graveyard.

Left: New fencing was added around this west of Ireland field, while leaving the old fencing in place. Practice like this, (intentional or otherwise) is good, as it allows lichens on old posts to transfer to the new.
Middle: A National Monuments wall being pointed. The unpointed part of the wall is on the left. The right of the image shows the wall was cleaned first, then an effort to repoint was made, using cement instead of mortar.
Right: The Rock of Cashel has a limestone lichen flora that enhances the buildings aesthetically.

Lichen Communities and habitats

A community, in ecological terms, is a group of organisms that interact with each other and the immediate environment around them (trees, rocks, etc.). An ecosystem is made up of many communities of organisms. In terms of lichens, a community is an assemblage of lichens. Defining lichen communities means that it is easier to talk about groups of lichens in an ecosystem, without having to name all the species. Communities define habitats and are named after the dominant or common species in the group, such as Lobarion, Graphidion, Parmelion, Usneion and Xanthorion. Of special significance in Ireland are the Lobarion, Parmelion and Graphidion communities. Here is an outline description of these three types.

Lobarion community – also called *Lobarion pulmonariae* or 'lungs of the forest'
Members of this community include loose foliose lichens, belonging to the genera *Lobaria, Nephroma, Peltigera, Pseudocyphellaria* and *Sticta,* and more tightly adpressed members of the genera *Collema, Degelia, Pannaria, Parmeliella, and Leptogium.* They are typically found on deciduous trees in old woodlands, in oceanic climates and like a pH of 5 or greater. Many Lobarions have cyanobacteria as their primary photobiont, or as a secondary photobiont packed into cephalodia. In other words, they are important nitrogen fixers and considered to be the climax community.

Graphidion community – also called Graphidion scriptae or 'pimples and wrinkles'
This group is found on smooth-barked trees, where the Lobarion community cannot occur or has not yet occurred, for various ecological reasons. Their photobiont is invariably a *Trentepohlia* algae. Graphidions are found on young smooth-barked ash, oak, rowan, holly and are at their best on hazel. They are a difficult group to identify (about 60 are recognized). Examples are *Graphis scripta, Pyrenula macrospora, Thelotrema lepadinum, Pyrenula hibernica* and *Pyrenula dermatoides.*

Parmelion community
Occurs on very acid-barked trees such as alder, birch and oak. Species include *Ochrolechia androgyna, Menegazzia terebrata, Hypotrachyna laevigata, H. sinuosa, Parmelia saxatilis, Parmotrema crinitum, P. perlatum, Cetrelia olivetorum, Platismatia glauca* and the coral-like lichens *Sphaerophorus globosus* and *Bunodophoron melanocarpum.*

Left: Members of the Graphidion community on a smooth barked tree.
Right: Members of the Lobarion community in the Atlantic woodlands of Killarney National Park.

The Burren Limestone

The Burren district in Co. Clare, is Ireland's only upland limestone region that runs down to sea level. The limestone is a little alkaline (pH 7.8), nutrient poor, and well grazed by snails. It is soluble in water, but free draining and exposed to sun, wind and frost. Differing lichen communities are found on the hostile open limestone (clints), in the grikes (fissures), around the turloughs and in its unique hazel woods. You will be sure to find species of *Acrocordia, Aspicilia, Caloplaca, Protoblastina* and *Verrucaria* on the open paving. The 'solution' hollows or kamenitzas are home to cyanobacteria of the genus *Nostoc* and lichens of the genera *Collema* and *Leptogium*, all of whom tolerate regular wetting and drying. Grikes experience greater humidity and less extreme conditions, where a build-up of pockets of soil leads to the development of a different lichen flora than on the paving clints (and a sure place to find the Burren's wildflowers, lizards, slow worms, snails, ferns and mosses).

The Burren is sprinkled with silica-rich granite boulders, left after the last Ice Age, with their own lichen assemblages. Similarly, Burren walls contain silica-rich rocks dispersed among the predominant limestone, harbouring a different lichen flora than the calcicole species. Monuments also contain both siliceous and calcareous rock, consequently species such as *Rhizocarpon geographicum* (silica loving) may lie a stone or two from a calcareous species such as *Aspicilia calcarea*. Some of the large granite erratics contain *Acarospora impressula, Buellia aethalea, Caloplaca crenularia, Fuscidea cyathoides, Lecanora gangaloides, Pertusaria pseudocorallina, Physcia adscendens* and *Ramalina siliquosa*. The limestone seashore is often difficult to access, but expect to find *Caloplaca marina, Caloplaca thallincola, Ramalina siliquosa* and *Xanthoria aureola*. Turloughs surround themselves with a great variety of habitats such as open pavement, hedgerows, trees and walls. The largest Burren turlough is at Carran. Expect to come across a host of species, too many to suggest even a few. Stone walls are host to many *Leptogium* and *Collema* species and notables such as *Caloplaca alociza* and *Caloplaca variabilis*. The Burren's hazel woods are exceptional in places.

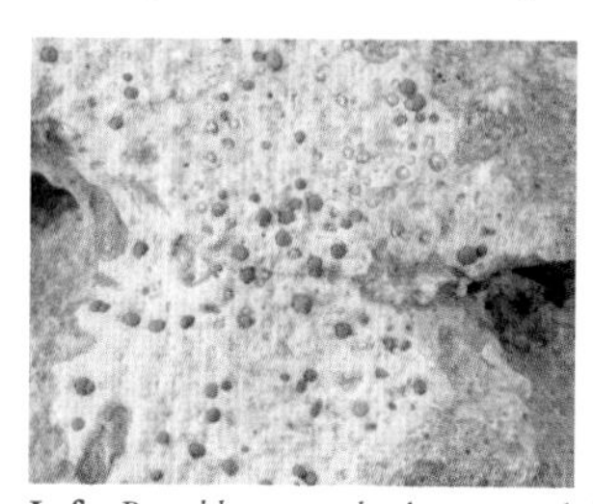

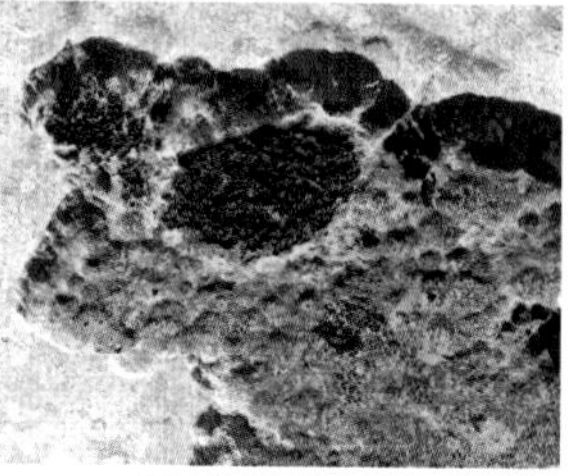

Left: *Protoblastina calva* has an endolithic thallus and occurs on open limestone at Black Head, Fahee North, and around Carran Turlough. **Middle**: Limestone paving showing deep grikes. These have higher humidity, less wind and are home to lichens that could not survive the open pavement. **Right**: Solution hollows regularly contain jelly lichens such as *Collema auriforme, Collema fragile, Leptogium gelatinosum,* and *Leptogium schraderi.*

Left: Stone walls at Fahee North contain many *Collema* and *Leptogium* species and also the genus *Caloplaca* such as *C. cirrochroa*. **Middle**: Many siliceous erratics were left scattered through the Burren after the last Ice Age. They contain lichens not found on the limestone pavements. **Right**: Carran Turlough is the largest in the Burren and offers a range of habitats for lichens, such as walls, hedgerows, trees and open paving.

Atlantic Woodlands – Killarney

The National Park at Killarney is composed of old woodland. The oaks around Dogarry townland, above 200m may be the last relict of 'ancient' undisturbed woodland. Because of Killarney's close proximity to the Atlantic, its hyper-oceanic climate and the influence of the Gulf Stream, it is further classified as 'Atlantic Woodland'. Old woodlands can reside outside hyper-oceanic areas, whereas Atlantic woodlands must lie within them. Further, representatives of three lichen communities are present in Atlantic woodlands: Lobarion, Parmelion and Graphidion. Killarney National Park's geology is divided between lowland Carboniferous limestone to the north (around the lakes) and ORS mountains to the south. The potential for both silica-loving and calcareous species has been fully realized. Killarney also has an ideal undulating topography, with woods covering many sheltered valleys, exposed rocky outcrops and ridges of both limestone and ORS. Over 20% (conservative estimate) of Ireland's lichens are found in Killarney, and many are of international importance. *Fuscopannaria sampaiana* is a key indicator species of Atlantic woodlands and occurs on hazel. Other indicators species include *Pseudocyphellaria crocata* and *Hypotrachyna taylorensis.*

Parmelion species in the National Park include *Hypotrachyna laevigata, H. sinuosa, Parmelia saxatilis, Parmotrema crinitum, P. perlatum, Cetrelia olivetorum, Platismatia glauca* and the coral-like lichens *Sphaerophorus globosus* and *Bunodophoron melanocarpum.*

Lobarion species at Killarney National Park include *Degelia atlantica, Leptogium brebissonii, Parmeliella testacea, Pseudocyphellaria intricata, Pseudocyphellaria norvegica, Lobaria pulmonaria, Lobaria virens, Lobaria amplissima* and *Lobaria scrobiculata.*

Graphidion species at the National Park include *Graphis scripta, Pyrenula macrospora, Thelotrema lepadinum, Pyrenula hibernica, Pyrenula dermatoides* and *Melaspilea atroides.*

A major threat to the lichens at Killarney is *Rhododendron ponticum.* It decreases light dramatically, edging out lichens and substrate species such as hazel and holly.

Left: Killarney has a hyper-oceanic climate. Regular soft rain and mists enable the Lobarion, Parmelion and Graphidion communities to flourish. **Middle**: *Lobaria pulmonaria* is an old woodland species that rarely produces apothecia, however, this specimen photographed in Killarney, illustrates that the hyper-oceanic climate suits it well. **Right**: Two trees with a profusion of Lobarion community species.

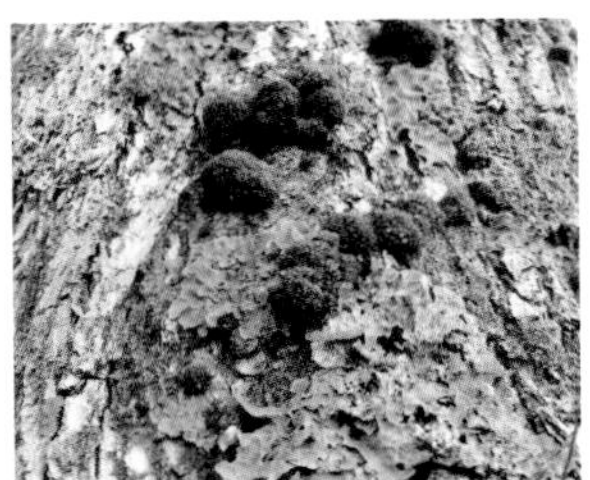

Left: A fallen log with *Lobaria virens,* on the left and *Degelia cyanolomma* on the right. **Middle**: Ivy, seen here over-running a Lobarion community, is a major threat to lichens, . **Right**: A Killarney ash tree with over 40 species including *Collema furfuraceum, Degelia atlantica, Fuscopannaria sampaiana, Leptogium lichenoides, Lobaria amplissima, Lobaria pulmonaria, Lobaria virens, Pannaria conoplea,* and *Pannaria rubiginosa.*

Atlantic Hazel Woods

Several of Ireland's hazel woods are goldmines of lichen biodiversity, in particular the large tracts of hazel in both the Burren, Co. Clare and in Co. Fermanagh. The Burren hazel is climatically euoceanic, its lichen biodiversity is of international importance and must be protected. Hazel has been in Ireland for at least 9,000 years, but was considered sadly by many in derogatory terms such as 'scrub' and part of the understory (with holly) of oak woodland. Ecologists now consider hazel 'scrub' as mature woodland in itself, its small stature dictated by its habitat, occurring on slopes, in shallow soil and facing the strong Atlantic winds. Burren hazel is categorised as 'Atlantic hazel', and left to its own ways, develops initially as a single stem for about 5 years, and then becomes multi-stemmed. Their initial stems are smooth and host Graphidion species on their mildly acidic bark. Later, the stems mature and become fissured and rough, allowing the Lobarion community to take hold. Indeed the Lobarion and Graphidion communities lay testament to hazel's ancientness. Graphidion species are developed to their finest in euoceanic hazel woods.

Many unique unlichenized fungi also establish in hazel wood, including the eerie 'hazel gloves' (*Hypocreopsis rhododendri*) that characterize the Burren hazel. Parts of the Burren have a rich Graphidion community such as *Pyrenula hibernica, Graphis scripta, Lecania naegelii, Lecanora albescens, Lecidella elaeochroma,* several *Opegrapha species, Pertusaria albescens* and other *Pertusaria* and *Phaeographis lyelli.* Disappointingly, there are as yet no Burren records of *Thelotrema macrosporum* or *Thelotrema petractoides.* Lobarion representatives in the hazel woods include *Lobaria scrobiculata, Pseudocyphellaria crocata, P. intricata, Degelia plumbea, Pannaria rubiginosa* and *Leptogium cochleatum.*

The principal threats to the Burren hazel come in the form of coppicing and overgrazing. Coppiced hazel has a dramatically lower lichen biodiversity, preventing the Graphidion community reaching maturity. Overgrazing prevents the Lobarion community from establishing itself.

Left: Multi-stemmed young hazel in the Burren is host to a rich Graphidion community including the rare *Pyrenula hibernica.* **Middle**: the eerie 'hazel gloves' (*Hypocreopsis rhododendri*) fungus, grasping a hawthorn in the Burren. **Right**: Dense hazel woodland interior makes it difficult for light to penetrate in the summer.

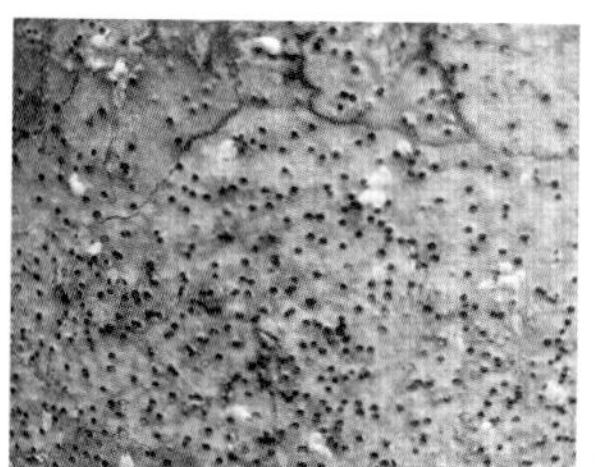

Left: Burren Atlantic hazel (in April), once considered 'scrub' is now appreciated as a climax woodland of international importance. Threats come from coppicing and overgrazing. **Middle**: *Pyrenula macrospora,* a member of the Burren's hazel Graphidion community. **Right**: *Leptogium cochleatum,* a member of the Lobarion community found in the Burren hazel woods, probably because of the persistent moist Atlantic winds.

Rocky Seashores

Ireland's coastline runs for an estimated 7524km, taking in sand dunes (Donegal and Wexford), machair (west coast) and rocky shores of both siliceous and limestone rocks. Machair (flat calcareous grassland on top of acid peaty bog) is one of Europe's unique habitats and Ireland has several instances of it along the west coast. Rocky seashore lichens have to contend with a wide range of stresses as their habitat changes twice a day (tidal). Some can tolerate being covered by the tide for longer than others. More can only tolerate heavy sea spray and yet others, found at the top of the shore can only tolerate fine sea mist and salty air. The external manifestation of these tolerances is the zonation of sea shore organisms.

The first person to recognise lichen zonation on rocky seashores was the Frenchman H. A. Weddell in 1875. He defined three zones: one covered by the tide; one influenced by wave splash; one beyond the direct splash of the waves.

Matilda Knowles (National Museum of Ireland) further defined the zonation in 1913, when she recognized three colour zones; grey (terrestrial zone), orange (heavily influenced by sea spray) and black (intertidal zone). She applied names to the lichens found in these zones as follows.

Terrestrial – 'grey' zone, richest in species (runs inland but with tolerance of a little sea spray): *Anaptychia ciliaris subsp. mamillata, Collema furfuracea, Degelia ligulata, Flavoparmelia caperata, Leprocaulon microscopicum, Parmelia saxatilis* and *Toninia aromatica.*

Supralittoral – 'orange' zone, tolerant of sea spray (very rarely swamped by seawater): *Anaptychia runcinata, Ramalina siliquosa, Rhizocarpon richardii, Xanthoria aureola, Xanthoria parietina, Caloplaca marina, C. thallincola, C. verruculifera, Lecanora actophila* and *Lecanora helicopis.*

Littoral – Intertidal or 'black zone': *Collemopsidium foveolatum, C. sublitorale, Lichina confinis, Verrucaria maura, V. mucosa* and *V. striatula.*

Left: Matilda Knowles (1864–1933) assigned species names to the colour banding seen on rocky seashores. **Middle**: Knowles' banding: black at sea level through orange to grey at the top.
Right: A rocky seashore assemblage, *Ramalina* and *Xanthoria* species found in the 'orange' band.

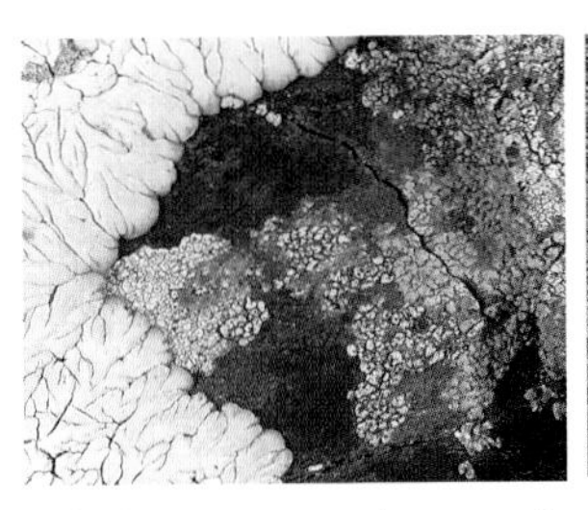

Left: Competition on the upper shore where *Diplocia canescens* is growing directly over several other maritime species. **Middle**: Skellig Michael has over 128 species of maritime lichens, including the only known recording of *Lecania poeltii* in Great Britain and Ireland. **Right**: Ireland's sand dune flora needs further exploration. Dunes are home to many calcareous loving species such as *Fulgensia fulgens.*

Part II – Species Descriptions

A total of 258 lichens are described in part II, in alphabetic order. Descriptions include a photograph typical of each specimen. A magnified area on the photographs of many species illustrates some important or identifying feature of a species. The scale bar on photographs is provided to give a general sense of scale, particularly on very small specimens. Spot tests symbols: '+' indicates a positive result, '–' a negative result and '±' is a variable result. Symbol '→' means turning as in colour change, e.g. K+ orange → red. Nature notes describes a preferred habitat of the species, The 'confusion' heading lists obvious similar species, where relevant. Not all similar species are described in this book. Descriptive words highlighted in green are a visual aid to guide you to diagnostic parts. Below is a complete list of all species described in part II, catagorised according to body plan.

Crustose *Acarospora fuscata*
Crustose *Acarospora impressula*
Crustose *Acrocordia conoidea*
Crustose *Acrocordia gemmata*
Crustose *Acrocordia macrospora*
Crustose *Acrocordia salweyi*
Crustose *Amandinea punctata*
Crustose *Arthonia cinnabarina*
Crustose *Arthonia pruinata*
Crustose *Arthonia punctiformis*
Crustose *Arthonia radiata*
Crustose *Arthopyrenia analepta*
Crustose *Arthopyrenia punctiformis*
Crustose *Arthopyrenia salicis*
Crustose *Aspicilia calcarea*
Crustose *Aspicilia contorta subsp. contorta*
Crustose *Aspicilia contorta subsp. hoffmanniana*
Crustose *Aspicilia leprosescens*
Crustose *Bacidia laurocerasi*
Crustose *Bacidia rubella*
Crustose *Bacidia scopulicola*
Crustose *Belonia nidarosiensis*
Crustose *Blarneya hibernica*
Crustose *Buellia aethalea*
Crustose *Buellia subdisciformis*
Crustose *Calicium viride*
Crustose *Caloplaca arnoldii*
Crustose *Caloplaca aurantia*
Crustose *Caloplaca britannica*
Crustose *Caloplaca ceracea*
Crustose *Caloplaca citrina*
Crustose *Caloplaca crenularia*
Crustose *Caloplaca ferruginea*
Crustose *Caloplaca flavescens*
Crustose *Caloplaca littorea*
Crustose *Caloplaca marina*
Crustose *Caloplaca microthallina*
Crustose *Caloplaca ochracea*
Crustose *Caloplaca saxicola*
Crustose *Caloplaca thallincola*
Crustose *Caloplaca verruculifera*
Crustose *Candelariella coralliza*
Crustose *Catinaria atropurpurea*
Crustose *Dimerella lutea*
Crustose *Diplotomma alboatrum*
Crustose *Enterographa crassa*
Crustose *Fuscidea cyathoides*
Crustose *Graphina anguina*
Crustose *Graphis elegans*
Crustose *Graphis scripta*
Crustose *Gyalecta jenensis*
Crustose *Herteliana gagei*
Crustose *Icmadophila ericetorum*
Crustose *Ionaspis lacustris*
Crustose *Japewiella tavaresiana*
Crustose *Lecanora albescens*
Crustose *Lecanora carpinea*
Crustose *Lecanora chlarotera*
Crustose *Lecanora gangaleoides*
Crustose *Lecanora muralis*
Crustose *Lecanora poliophaea*
Crustose *Lecanora pulicaris*
Crustose *Lecanora stenotropa*
Crustose *Lecanora sulphurea*
Crustose *Lecanora varia*
Crustose *Lecanora zosterae*
Crustose *Lecania aipospila*
Crustose *Lecidella asema*
Crustose *Lecidella elaeochroma*
Crustose *Loxospora elatina*
Crustose *Mycobilimbia pilularis*
Crustose *Mycoblastus sanguinarius*
Crustose *Ochrolechia androgyna*
Crustose *Ochrolechia parella*
Crustose *Ochrolechia tartarea*
Crustose *Opegrapha atra*
Crustose *Opegrapha calcarea*
Crustose *Opegrapha gyrocarpa*
Crustose *Opegrapha vermicellifera*
Crustose *Ophioparma ventosa*
Crustose *Pertusaria albescens*
Crustose *Pertusaria amara*
Crustose *Pertusaria aspergilla*
Crustose *Pertusaria hymenea*
Crustose *Pertusaria multipuncta*
Crustose *Pertusaria pertusa*
Crustose *Pertusaria pseudocorallina*
Crustose *Phaeographis dendritica*
Crustose *Phaeographis smithii*
Crustose *Porpidia cinereoatra*
Crustose *Porpidia crustulata*
Crustose *Porpidia flavocruenta*
Crustose *Porpidia hydrophila*
Crustose *Porpidia tuberculosa*
Crustose *Protoblastenia rupestris*
Crustose *Pyrenula dermatodes*
Crustose *Pyrenula macrospora*
Crustose *Pyrrhospora quernea*
Crustose *Rhizocarpon geographicum*
Crustose *Rhizocarpon lavatum*
Crustose *Rhizocarpon petraeum*
Crustose *Rhizocarpon reductum*
Crustose *Tephromela atra*
Crustose *Thelotrema lepadinum*
Crustose *Toninia aromatica*
Crustose *Tremolecia atrata*
Crustose *Verrucaria baldensis*
Crustose *Verrucaria macrostoma*
Crustose *Verrucaria maura*
Crustose *Verrucaria mucosa*
Crustose to foliose *Leptogium brebissonii*
Crustose to foliose *Leptogium cochleatum*

Crustose to foliose	*Leptogium diffractum*
Crustose to foliose	*Leptogium gelatinosum*
Crustose to foliose	*Leptogium hibernicum*
Crustose to foliose	*Leptogium lichenoides*
Crustose to foliose	*Leptogium schraderi*
Crustose to foliose	*Leptogium teretiusculum*
Crustose, placodioid	*Caloplaca decipiens*
Crustose, placodioid	*Candelariella medians*
Crustose, placodioid	*Diploicia canescens*
Crustose, granulose	*Chaenotheca furfuracea*
Crustose, squamulose	*Candelariella aurella*
Crustose, squamulose	*Candelariella vitellina*
Crustose, squamulose	*Pilophorus strumaticus*
Crustose, squamulose	*Placynthium nigrum*
Foliose	*Anaptychia ciliaris subsp. mamillata*
Foliose	*Anaptychia runcinata*
Foliose	*Candelaria concolor*
Foliose	*Dermatocarpon miniatum*
Foliose	*Flavoparmelia caperata*
Foliose	*Flavoparmelia soredians*
Foliose	*Hypogymnia physodes*
Foliose	*Hypogymnia tubulosa*
Foliose	*Hypotrachyna laevigata*
Foliose	*Hypotrachyna revoluta*
Foliose	*Hypotrachyna sinuosa*
Foliose	*Lobaria amplissima*
Foliose	*Melanelixia subaurifera*
Foliose	*Melanohalea exasperata*
Foliose	*Menegazzia terebrata*
Foliose	*Nephroma laevigatum*
Foliose	*Nephroma parile*
Foliose	*Parmelina pastillifera*
Foliose	*Parmotrema crinitum*
Foliose	*Parmotrema perlatum*
Foliose	*Peltigera britannica*
Foliose	*Peltigera collina*
Foliose	*Peltigera horizontalis*
Foliose	*Peltigera hymenina*
Foliose	*Peltigera membranacea*
Foliose	*Peltigera praetextata*
Foliose	*Platismatia glauca*
Foliose	*Punctelia borreri*
Foliose	*Punctelia jeckeri*
Foliose	*Punctelia subrudecta*
Foliose	*Sticta canariensis*
Foliose	*Sticta dufourii*
Foliose	*Sticta fuliginosa*
Foliose	*Sticta limbata*
Foliose	*Sticta sylvatica*
Foliose	*Tuckermanopsis chlorophylla*
Foliose	*Umbilicaria cylindrica*
Foliose	*Umbilicaria polyphylla*
Foliose	*Xanthoria aureola*
Foliose	*Xanthoria parietina*
Foliose	*Xanthoria polycarpa*
Foliose, appears fruticose	*Evernia prunastri*
Foliose, (lobate)	*Parmelia omphalodes*
Foliose, (lobate)	*Parmelia saxatilis*
Foliose, (lobate)	*Parmelia sulcata*
Foliose, (lobate)	*Physcia adscendens*
Foliose, (lobate)	*Physcia aipolia*
Foliose, (lobate)	*Physcia leptalea*
Foliose, (lobate)	*Physcia tenella*
Foliose, (lobate)	*Physcia tribacioides*
Foliose, (lobate)	*Physconia distorta*
Foliose, (lobate)	*Physconia grisea*
Foliose, crustose	*Collema auriforme*
Foliose, crustose	*Collema crispum*
Foliose, crustose	*Collema cristatum*
Foliose, crustose	*Collema fasciculare*
Foliose, crustose	*Collema flaccidum*
Foliose, crustose	*Collema furfuraceum*
Foliose, crustose	*Collema fuscovirens*
Foliose, crustose	*Collema multipartitum*
Foliose, crustose	*Collema nigrescens*
Foliose, crustose	*Collema polycarpon*
Foliose, crustose	*Collema subflaccidum*
Foliose, crustose	*Collema tenax*
Foliose, fruticose	*Cetraria islandica*
Foliose, fruticose	*Cetrelia olivetorum*
Foliose, squamulose	*Parmeliella parvula*
Foliose, squamulose	*Degelia atlantica*
Foliose, squamulose	*Degelia cyanoloma*
Foliose, squamulose	*Degelia ligulata*
Foliose, squamulose	*Degelia plumbea*
Foliose, tomentose	*Lobaria pulmonaria*
Foliose, tomentose	*Lobaria scrobiculata*
Foliose, tomentose	*Lobaria virens*
Fruticose	*Bryoria fuscescens*
Fruticose	*Bunodophoron melanocarpum*
Fruticose	*Lichina confinis*
Fruticose	*Ramalina calicaris*
Fruticose	*Ramalina cuspidata*
Fruticose	*Ramalina farinacea*
Fruticose	*Ramalina fastigiata*
Fruticose	*Ramalina fraxinea*
Fruticose	*Ramalina lacera*
Fruticose	*Ramalina siliquosa*
Fruticose	*Sphaerophorus globosus*
Fruticose	*Teloschistes chrysophthalmus*
Fruticose	*Usnea articulata*
Fruticose	*Usnea esperantiana*
Fruticose	*Usnea florida*
Fruticose	*Usnea subfloridana*
Fruticose, filamentous	*Ephebe lanata*
Fruticose, squamulose	*Cladonia bellidiflora*
Fruticose, squamulose	*Cladonia coccifera*
Fruticose, squamulose	*Cladonia coniocraea*
Fruticose, squamulose	*Cladonia diversa*
Fruticose, squamulose	*Cladonia fimbriata*
Fruticose, squamulose	*Cladonia floerkeana*
Fruticose, squamulose	*Cladonia foliacea*
Fruticose, squamulose	*Cladonia furcata*
Fruticose, squamulose	*Cladonia gracilis*
Fruticose, squamulose	*Cladonia macilenta*
Fruticose, squamulose	*Cladonia pocillum*
Fruticose, squamulose	*Cladonia polydactyla*
Fruticose, squamulose	*Cladonia portentosa*
Fruticose, squamulose	*Cladonia pyxidata*
Fruticose, squamulose	*Cladonia ramulosa*
Fruticose, squamulose	*Cladonia rangiferina*
Fruticose, squamulose	*Cladonia rangiformis*
Fruticose, squamulose	*Cladonia squamosa*
Fruticose, squamulose	*Cladonia squamosa var. subsquamosa*
Fruticose, squamulose	*Cladonia subcervicornis*
Fruticose, squamulose	*Cladonia uncialis subsp. biuncialis*
Leprose	*Chrysothrix candelaris*
Leprose	*Chrysothrix chlorina*
Leprose	*Lepraria incana*
Leprose	*Lepraria lobificans*
Leprose	*Leprocaulon microscopicum*
Lichenicolous	*Arthonia varians*
Squamulose	*Fuscopannaria sampaiana*
Squamulose	*Hypocenomyce scalaris*
Squamulose	*Normandina pulchella*
Squamulose	*Placidium squamulosum*
Squamulose	*Solenopsora holophaea*
Squamulose	*Solenospora vulturiensis*
Squamulose	*Stereocaulon vesuvianum*
Squamulose, crustose	*Agonimia tristicula*
Squamulose, crustose	*Pannaria conoplea*
Squamulose, crustose	*Pannaria rubiginosa*
Squamulose, crustose	*Protopannaria pezizoides*
Squamulose, granulose	*Trapeliopsis flexuosa*
Squamulose, granulose	*Trapeliopsis pseudogranulosa*

Acarospora fuscata – crustose

DESCRIPTION: Thallus has the appearance of dried encrusted cow dung or snakeskin due to its irregular areolate-squamulose crazy-paving pattern. Colour varies from dark oak brown to reddish brown to yellow-brown. The areoles are angular with a variable gap between them. Edges may lift slightly, revealing a dark underside (use 10x hand lens). Margins of the areoles are usually dark. The dark discs of the apothecia also have an angular appearance; often several (1–5) are found on a single areole. They are either slightly sunken into an areole or are flush with its surface. Spores elipsoidal, size range 4–6 x 1–1.5μm.

SPOT TESTS: K–, KC+ pink, C+ pink, Pd–. Tests difficult to see against the brown thallus.

NATURE NOTES: Typically on silica-rich rocks (granite) on the tops of walls or south facing ledges. Enjoys direct sunlight. Tolerant of nutrient rich areas and so is found near farms or bird perches.

CONFUSION: With *Acarospora impressula* and *Acarospora smaragdula*.

Acarospora impressula – crustose

DESCRIPTION: Thallus formed of small interlocking angular areoles that are smaller near the edge of the thallus. Colour varies from red-brown to dark brown. There tends to be just one apothecium per areole (check against *Acarospora fuscata*). Discs show a great variation in shape, from angular to circular with colours similar to the thallus. Areoles are small, reaching a maximum size of just 2mm and apothecia reach a maximum diameter of 0.5mm. Overall it looks like dry snakeskin. Spores 3–4 x 2–2.4μm.

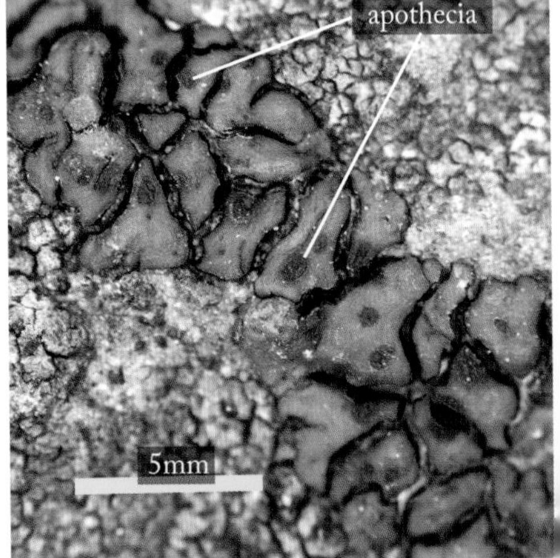

SPOT TESTS: Negative.

NATURE NOTES: A rather rare lichen in Ireland and confined to exposed rocky coastal regions Occurs on silica-rich rocks. Shows a preference for sunlit granite where it grows among feldspar and quartz crystals. The south and southwestern distribution tends to be along coastal exposed Old Red Sandstone. While its presence in the Burren may initially seem rather odd, it is on some of the granite erratics that were left on the limestone paving after the last Ice Age.

CONFUSION: Similar to *Acarospora fuscata*.

ACROCORDIA – 4 SPECIES RECORDED IN IRELAND.

Acrocordia conoidea – crustose

DESCRIPTION: Recognized as black dots on a pinkish immersed thallus. The black dots are the perithecia which look like miniature (0.5–1mm diam.) gently sloping volcanoes, half immersed in the thallus. Examination with a hand lens will reveal a tiny pore or ostiole at the top with projecting papillae. Perithecia drop out leaving empty sockets. Pycnidia (0.14–0.2mm) are very small and numerous. Spores, 12–19 x 6–9μm.
SPOT TESTS: Negative.
NATURE NOTES: Found on hard limestone in shaded places (north side of walls). Occurs on dolomite and calcareous outcrops in woodlands.
CONFUSION: With *Acrocordia salweyi*, but the gently sloping perithecia separate them.

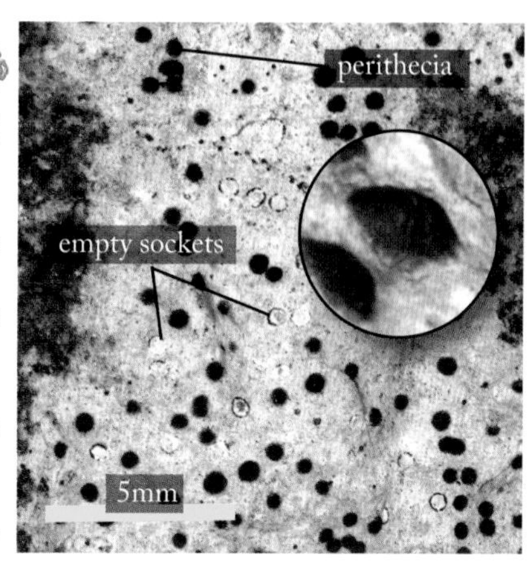

Acrocordia gemmata – crustose

DESCRIPTION: Perithecia appear as large black hemispheres (≤1mm diam.) that are slightly immersed in the thallus. The ostiole of a perithecium may be off centre. The thin thallus is matt in texture and varies from white to grey. Spores, 8 per ascus, 1–septate colourless, ellipsoidal, 18–30 x 6–9μm.
SPOT TESTS: Negative.
NATURE NOTES: Found on rough bark, especially ash and oak. Occurs in mature parklands and on wayside trees. Does not occur on rock.
CONFUSION: Similar to *Anisomeridium biforme* but has smaller perithecia and larger ostioles.

Acrocordia macrospora – crustose

DESCRIPTION: The large black dots are perithecia which range in size from 0.8–1mm in diam. They appear flattened or spread out. Perithecial pores are prominent and circular. Thallus is immersed but when visible is grey to light brown. Spores are colourless and 1–septate, 19–26 x 9–12μm. SPOT TESTS: Negative.
NATURE NOTES: This is a coastal lichen found in sheltered and shaded areas of the shore. Its substrate tends to be silica-poor to calcareous rocks.

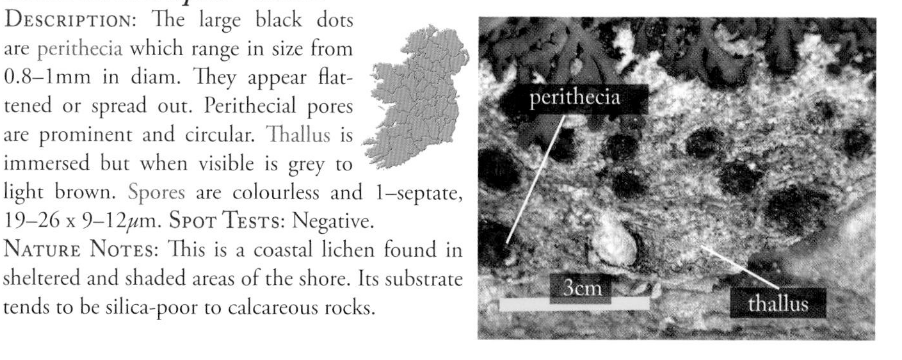

Acrocordia salweyi – crustose

Description: Thallus is off-white to light brown, and frequently immersed. Usually smooth to granular, and may show cracking. Large flat-topped spherical perithecia are semi-immersed. Some fall out leaving a black-rimmed socket.
Spores, 20–35 x 10–15μm.
Spot Tests: Negative.
Nature Notes: Found on soft calcareous rock and mortar, especially on old walls.

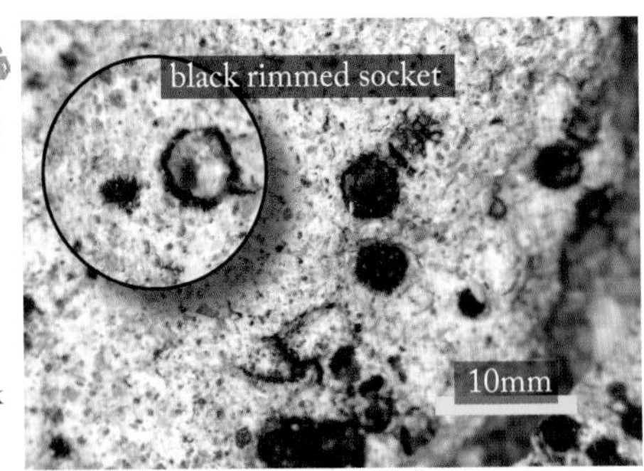

Agonimia – 4 species recorded in Ireland.

Agonimia tristicula – squamulose, crustose

Description: Thallus is composed of squamules, pale green to brown when dry and bright green when wet. They are crowded and variously shaped, including nodular or finger-like. Barrel-shaped perithecia (0.24–0.5mm) are found scattered among the squamules. The upper cortex is characteristically papillate.
Spores, 57–120 x 26–50μm.
Spot Tests: None.
Nature Notes: Found on walls in crevices, particularly with moss. Occurs on a range of rock types such as basalt, limestone, mortar, soil and dunes.

Confusion: with *Agonimia octospora*.

Amandinea – 3 species recorded in Ireland.

Amandinea punctata – crustose

Description: Lumpy to thin thallus but sometimes smooth and varies in colour from light to dark grey with a green tint, especially when wet. Prothallus rarely present. Thallus is highly populated with small matt textured apothecia (≤0.6mm). Discs are flat to convex with rims and discs the same colour. Spores are elipsoidal and olive brown, 10–18 x 5–10μm.
Spot Tests: K–.
Nature Notes: Occurs on fence posts, rocks and bird perches. Tolerant of air pollution (SO_2) and very tolerant of farm fertilisers.

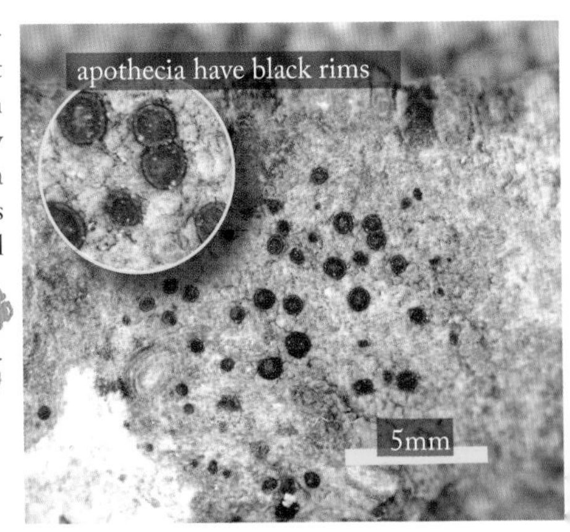

Anaptychia – 2 species recorded in Ireland.

Anaptychia ciliaris* subsp. *mamillata – foliose

Description: Irregular branching of the narrow thalline lobes give it an untidy appearance. It spreads horizontally over the substrate, with edges just turning up. The ends widen and are decorated with large marginal cilia. Apothecia are rare, but when present show a rim similar in colour to the thallus. The upper surface is tomentose, while the under-surface lacks rhizines and is light brown to cream in colour. Spores, 40–45 x 18–24μm.
Spot Tests: Negative.
Nature Notes: Of very limited distribution in Ireland, found on coastal silica-poor or calcareous rocks. Common on Skellig Michael, the Blasket Islands and Inishvickillane. It was first recorded in 1850 on Tearaght Island (Inishtearaght) where is still has a foothold.

Anaptychia runcinata – foliose

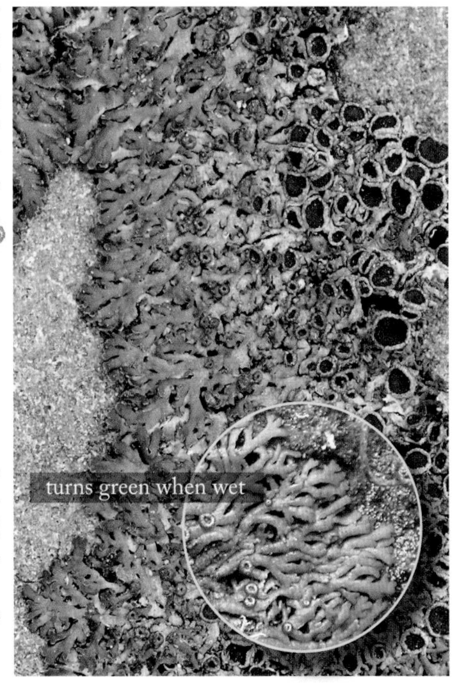

Description: The thallus is bulky, tightly adpressed and characteristically radiating. Lobes overlap and give a crowded appearance. In dry weather they appear pruinose. They have a slightly convex appearance, although frequently flat, and often widen towards the apices. Colour varies from dark brown when dry to dark olive green when wet. The under-surface is dark in colour and contains rhizines. Apothecia are large. Discs are brown to black with crenulate thalline rims. Spores are large (33–36 x 18–21μm), thick-walled, brown and ornamented.
Spot Tests: C+ watery yellow.
Nature Notes: Found along the coast, especially on hard silica-rich rocks on gentle slopes. Forms part of coastal *Ramalina* communities. Occurs inland on old ruins and trees and on turf in undisturbed bogs or on dead Sea Thrift.
Confusion: Looks similar to *Physconia distorta* which usually lives on bark.

Arthonia cinnabarina – crustose

DESCRIPTION: Apothecia are white pruinose and often tinted a cinnabar colour, hence its name. They are variable in shape, sometimes round or even polygonal, sometimes linear and branched. Mature apothecia are brown. Thallus is immersed and has a dull white colour with a delimiting prothallus that varies considerably in colour from dark brown to almost white. Spores, 3 to 5–septate, 20–28 x 7–10μm, wider at one end and sometimes turning brown as they mature.

SPOT TESTS: K+ purple.

NATURE NOTES: Avoids direct sunlight. Common on trees with smooth bark but may also appear on rough bark, particularly in old woodlands when the thallus takes on a powdery texture.

CONFUSION: None to be concerned about as the cinnabar colour is distinctive.

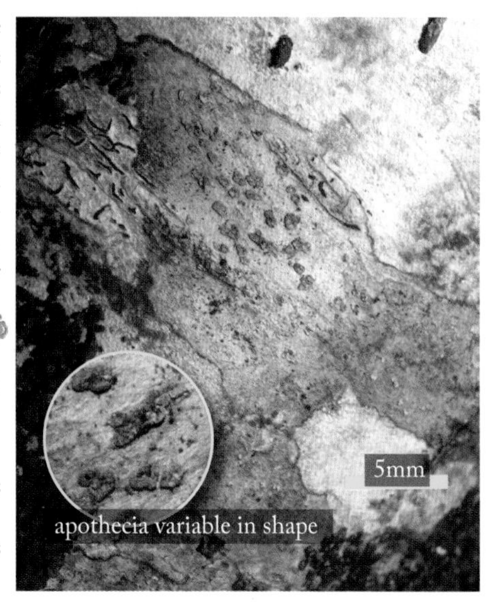

Arthonia pruinata – crustose

DESCRIPTION: Thallus is usually matt and powdery white when dry and grey or brown in colour. It also varies in thickness from thin to thick and may spread extensively across the bark, sometimes being immersed. Apothecia vary in shape from angular or star shaped to round and are often heavily pruinose or powdery. Normally they are brown but may become pink. Spores are 3 to 5–septate, 10–22 x 5–8μm.

SPOT TESTS: Pd–, C+ red for both the thallus and apothecia. UV–.

NATURE NOTES: Found typically on dry bark, specifically on the sheltered side of trees such as acer and oak. Can dominate the side of a tree.

Arthonia punctiformis – crustose

DESCRIPTION: Thallus is immersed in the substrate and is identified only by the clear patch it creates on the bark. Apothecia are small and vary in shape from round to stellate, frequently elliptical with a hint of stellate. There are black, never pruinose and as small as 0.2mm in diameter. Edges of discs may show a lip of bark (as though the tree bark has been pushed back). Overall the apothecia look like little flecks of black. Spores are colourless, septate (2-celled), oblong or elliptical with

a 'waist', 13–23 x 5–7μm.
SPOT TESTS: None.
NATURE NOTES: Common on small twigs and the smooth branches of trees and shrubs. It is one of the first lichens to colonise bark. Tends to avoid direct sunlight.
CONFUSION: may be similar to *Arthonia radiata* if the apothecia are stellate (as they tend to be in *A. radiata*).

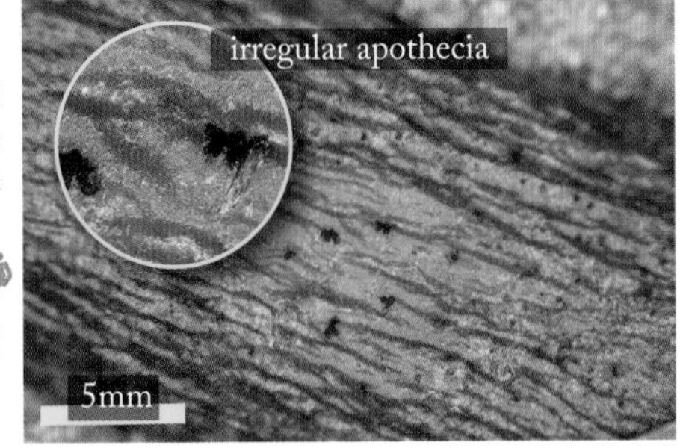

Arthonia radiata – crustose
DESCRIPTION: Pale grey to white thallus lies immersed in the bark of smooth twigs. May form complex mosaics (with a brown prothallus) on twigs or small isolated colonies among other lichens. Apothecia are plentiful and often crowded, black in colour and variable in shape, ranging from fuzzy star-like shapes to circular or linear forms. They are flat to slightly convex, and never pruinose. Pycnidia are rare, black and immersed in the thallus. Spores, 15–20 x 5–7μm.
SPOT TESTS: Pycnidia: K+ light green.
NATURE NOTES: A pioneer lichen, being one of the first to appear on twigs and smooth bark of narrow branches in pollution free areas. Host to the fungal parasite *Stigmidium arthoniae*.
CONFUSION: With *Arthonia punctiformis* but *A. radiata* tends to have crowded apothecia that are also highly branched or stellate.

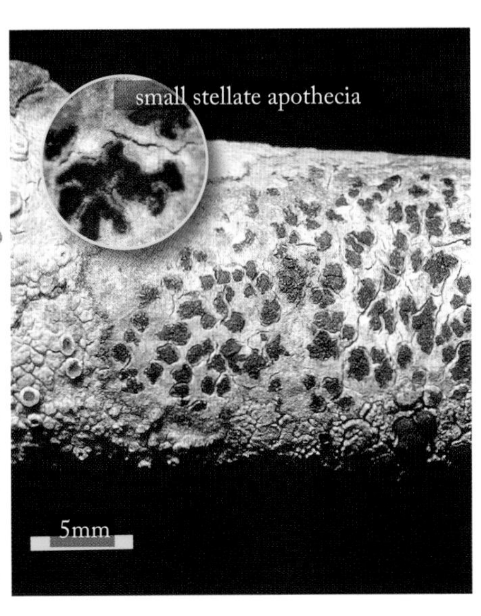

Arthonia varians – lichenicolous
DESCRIPTION: This is a parasitic lichen (lichenicolous) typically found on *Lecanora rupicola* and *Lecanora sulphurea*. It lacks a thallus of its own and manifests itself as black blotches on the discs of the apothecia. The black blotches are the reproductive structures of *Arthonia varians*. Its colourless spores are 2 to 3-septate and range from ovoid to ellipsoid, 10–17 x 5–7μm
SPOT TESTS: None.
NATURE NOTES: Typically found in seashore areas, infecting the apothecia of *Lecanora sulphurea* and *Lecanora rupicola*.

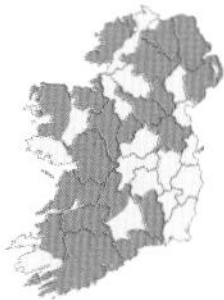

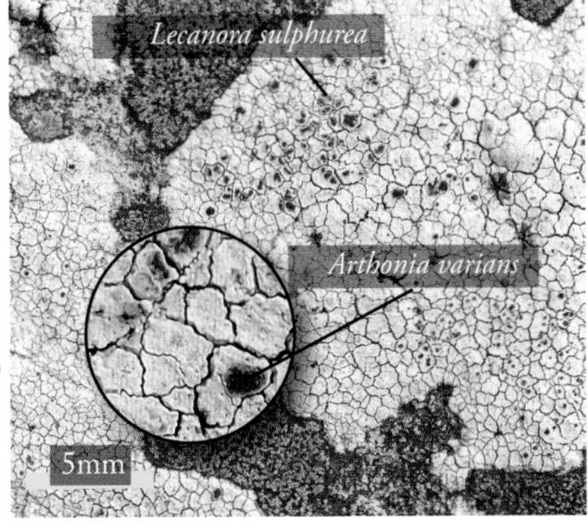

Arthopyrenia analepta – crustose

DESCRIPTION: The thallus is thin, immersed and has a glossy varnish-like appearance. Pycnidia may be present. Gently sloping perithecia give it a pimply appearance. An important characteristic is the shadow ring or halo around the 'pimple' base. Spores are 1–septate, 15–23 x 5.5–9μm.
SPOT TESTS: Negative.
NATURE NOTES: Found on smooth barked twigs and sometimes mature trees such as oak and hazel. Its glossy appearance and 'halo' make it relatively easy to identify. No photobiont present. Likes humid conditions.

Arthopyrenia punctiformis – crustose

DESCRIPTION: The thallus is hardly visible. Perithecia are particularly small, being about 0.3mm diameter with a circular to oval base. They occur scattered rather than in clusters. Pycnidia are unknown. Spores are 1–septate, colourless and 16–20 x 4.5–5μm in size. Some spores may be yellow and 3–septate.
SPOT TESTS: Negative.
NATURE NOTES: Occurs on smooth bark of both trees and shrubs. A pioneer species. Often associated with *Arthonia punctiformis*.
CONFUSION: With *A. salicis* (larger perithecia).

Arthopyrenia salicis – crustose

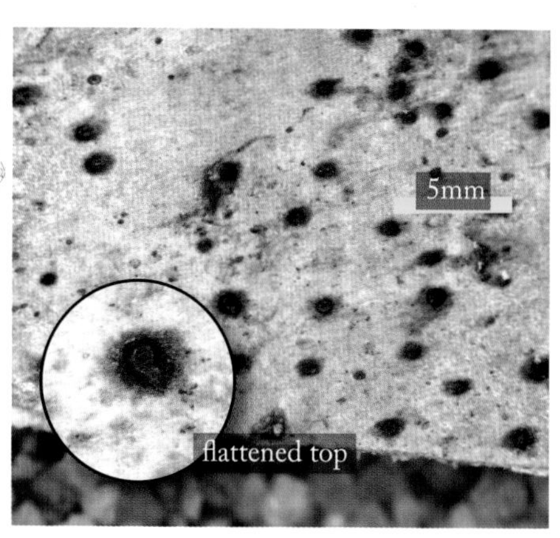

DESCRIPTION: The black pimples are perithecia with a circular or ellipsoidal shape. They have a characteristic flat top (flattened ostiole). Thallus is inconspicuous to invisible. When visible it has a brownish tint due to the brown hyphae. Spores are 14–17 x 4–4.5μm and 1–septate. The lower cell is hour-glass shaped.
SPOT TESTS: Negative.
NATURE NOTES: Occurs on smooth barked trees, particularly common on hazel.
CONFUSION: With *A. punctiformis*. *A. salicis* is browner. Spores need to be examined.

Aspicilia calcarea – crustose

DESCRIPTION: The thallus is frequently very bright white, giving it the appearance of bird droppings, especially when seen on the tops of walls. It may also, however, be off-white or buff coloured. The thallus has a cracked or areolate appearance similar to crazy-paving. The black apothecia are slightly depressed into the thallus and are frequently pruinose, making them difficult to see. They are irregular in shape. Thallus grows in a circular pattern when unimpeded and the prothallus may show radiating lobes. Photobiont is a unicellular chlorococcoid green algae. Apothecia are lecanorine. Microscopic examination shows the top half of the paraphyses look like a string of beads. Spores (spherical or ellipsoidal) are colourless and single celled. Asci contain 4 to 8 spores, 18–30 x 14–27μm.

SPOT TESTS: K–.

NATURE NOTES: *Aspicilia calcarea* is a saxicolous calcicole species and is common on hard limestone (never found on mortar), especially on walls, gravestones and rocky outcrops, particularly around lakes in the centre of Ireland. It is also common along the river Shannon where it grows in a circular pattern at a rate of about 2–3mm a year. Using these figures some specimens have been estimated to be about 800 years old. *Aspicilia calcarea* is a good source of food for snails, especially in limestone areas such as the Burren.

CONFUSION: Similar to *Aspicilia contorta subsp. hoffmanniana* which can grow on mortar.

Aspicilia contorta subsp. contorta – crustose

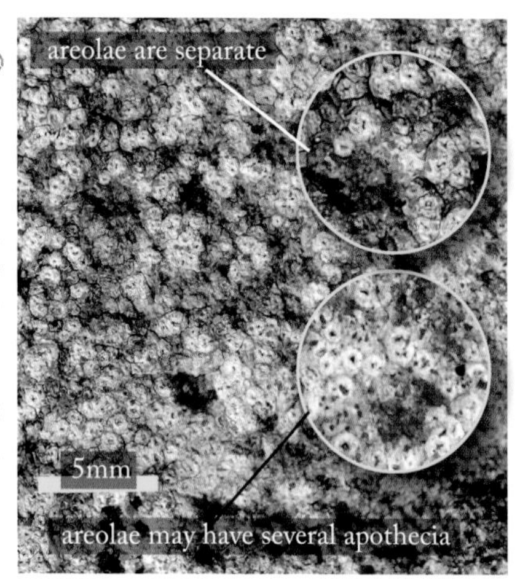

Description: Thallus varies from white through grey to a greenish colour. It is composed of matt areoles (like paving) that are less angular and more separated than *Aspicilia calcarea*. They appear like miniature fossilized vertebrae. There is normally one immersed apothecium per areole, but sometimes two or three may be present. The prothallus is ill-defined and difficult to see. Spores, 18–30 x 15–25μm.

Spot Tests: Thallus: K–. Apothecia: K+ yellowish.

Nature Notes: Found on hard calcareous rocks and man-made paving and concrete. Common on pathways and in gardens.

Confusion: Similar to both *A. calcarea* and *A. contorta subsp. hoffmanniana*.

Aspicilia contorta subsp. hoffmanniana – crustose

Description: Thallus varies from white through grey, but is generally darker than *Aspicilia contorta subsp. contorta*; it may be pruinose. It is composed of matt areolae that are angular and fit together tightly. There is normally one apothecium per areole, but sometimes two or three may be present. The prothallus is white and difficult to see.

Spot Tests: K–. Apothecia: K+ yellow → orange.

Nature Notes: Apothecia not as immersed as in *Aspicilia contorta subsp. contorta*.

Confusion: With *Aspicilia calcarea*. Found on soft limestone.

Aspicilia leprosescens – crustose

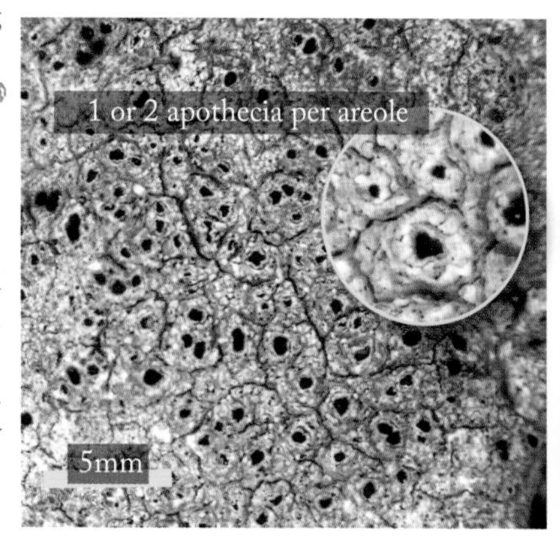

Description: This is a crustose sickly looking lichen. The thallus is off-white to a dull blue-grey. A prothallus, if present, is dark in colour. The thallus is cracked (areolate). Apothecia are rare, but if present one or two are found on the areoles. They are very small with dark steeply convex discs and narrow rims. Rims and discs are different colours. Spores, 14–30 x 7–16μm.

Spot Tests: Pd–, K–.

Nature Notes: A coastal lichen, being found on rocky seashores in the splash zone and occasionally inland on bird perches and silica-rich rocks.

Bacidia laurocerasi – crustose

DESCRIPTION: Thallus is usually smooth and shows some cracking (may also be warted) and always lacks granules. Colour varies from pale grey to green-grey. Pycnidia are present and immersed in the thallus. Apothecia tend to be frequent, lack a thalline margin, with discs flat to convex. Discs are black to brown and take on a reddish brown colour when wet. Spores show 7–16 septate and are long and narrow 34–7 x 2.4–4μm.

SPOT TESTS: K+ purple for the apothecia in section.

NATURE NOTES: Generally found on basic to neutral bark, in nutrient rich regions. Occurs on both coniferous and deciduous trees and is common on ash and sycamore.

CONFUSION: has larger discs than *Bacidia arceutina*.

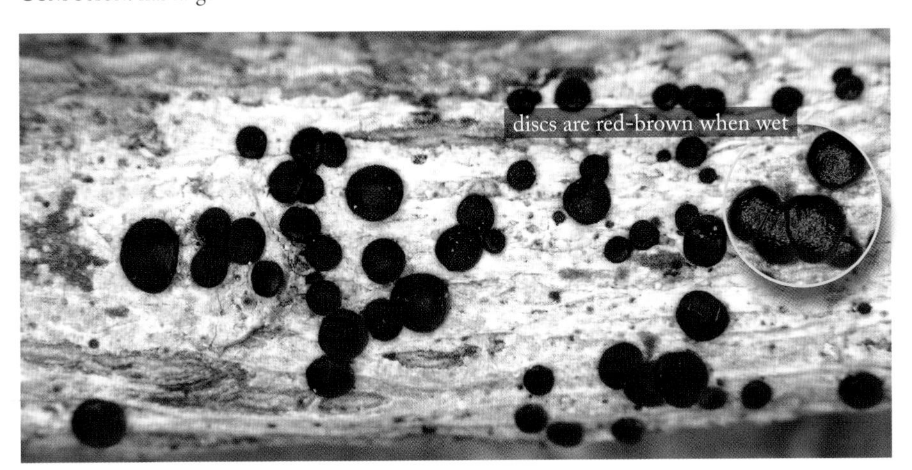

Bacidia rubella – crustose

DESCRIPTION: The generally pale grey-yellow to grey-green thallus has a granular isidia-like appearance. Apothecia are rare and small (≤1.3mm), but when present are an attractive reddish brown to pink colour. Discs range from flat to convex, some being highly convex. Margins of apothecia are often made more visible by being white pruinose. Pycnidia present (pink to reddish brown). Spores are needle-like, both straight and curved, 3–7 septate 40–70 x 2.5–3.5μm.

SPOT TESTS: Apothecia: K+ yellow. UV–.

NATURE NOTES: Occurs on basic bark (elm, plane and ash especially) of mature trees in parklands. Also occurs on smooth calcareous rock, but this is rare. Does not tolerate pollution. Apothecia may be infected with the black perithecia of *Muellerella hospitans*.

CONFUSION: easy to identify when fertile; sterile specimens can be confused with *Bacidia biatorina*.

Bacidia scopulicola – crustose

Description: Thallus granular, appearing loose and crumbly. Colours vary from light tan to dark brown and light to dark green with a strong yellow tint. Apothecia are rare, up to 1.3mm in diam. and show a great variability in shape and colour with red to brown discs. Isidia are present. Brown pycnidia are immersed in the thallus. Spores are 29–45 x 1.7–2μm. Spot Tests: None.
Nature Notes: Found in coastal areas on siliceous rocks away from direct rainfall, generally in damp overhangs. May be found on Sea Pink.
Confusion: With *Bacidia sipmanii* which has abundant apothecia, and a thinner thallus.

Belonia – 1 species recorded in Ireland.

Belonia nidarosiensis – crustose

Description: It has a thin effuse thallus ranging in colour from pink through orange to rusty red. Could be mistaken for *Trentepohlia* algae. Perithecia are very rare, globose shaped and with a central pore. Ascospores are muriform. Spores, 40–60 x 10–15μm.
Spot Tests: None.
Nature Notes: Occurs on hard dry calcareous rocks that are sheltered from the rain or on the north side of churches or even gravestones. Common throughout Ireland.

Blarneya – 1 species recorded in Ireland.

Blarneya hibernica – crustose

Description: The compact cotton-like thallus is pinkish white with a green tinge. Sometimes sprinkled with crystals. Tiny filamentous threads give it a diffuse perimeter. Apothecia and perithecia are absent. Small pale yellow convex powdery structures that look superficially like soralia (C–) are in fact sporodochia (C+) that produce conidia.
Spot Tests: C± red (fleeting), K–, KC± red, Pd–. UV+ powdery bloom.
Nature Notes: Typically found growing in old woodlands near the base of sheltered dry oak and holly. Recorded in Killarney National Park.

Bryoria – 4 species recorded in Ireland. Known as 'horse-hair' or 'tree-hair.

Bryoria fuscescens – fruticose

Description: The pendulous thallus can be as long as 30cm, although typically it falls within the range of 5–15cm. Branching is irregular, with the tube-like branches twisting. Branches are generally dark golden brown with diameters of 0.3mm to 0.4mm. White soralia are common (wider than branch diameter). Pseudocyphellae are absent.

Spot Tests: Thallus, K–, C–, KC–, Pd+ red for soredia.

Nature Notes: Prefers coniferous woodlands that are free from pollution of farm fertilizers (rich in ammonia), hence it is difficult to find in Ireland. It may be found on birch trees also.

Buellia – 11 species recorded in Ireland.

Buellia aethalea – crustose

Description: Thin to thick areolate thallus, varying from white to grey or brown. Areoles are small, generally ≤1mm diam. Apothecia are small and buried in the thallus. Discs are flat and reddish black. Apothecial rim is non-thalline. Pycnidia are rare. Spores, 12–18 x 6–10μm.

Spot Tests: K± yellow → red, C–, Pd+ yellow/orange. UV–.

Nature Notes: Forms mosaics on well lit, smooth, silica-rich rocks. Occurs in coastal areas. It is a pioneer species.

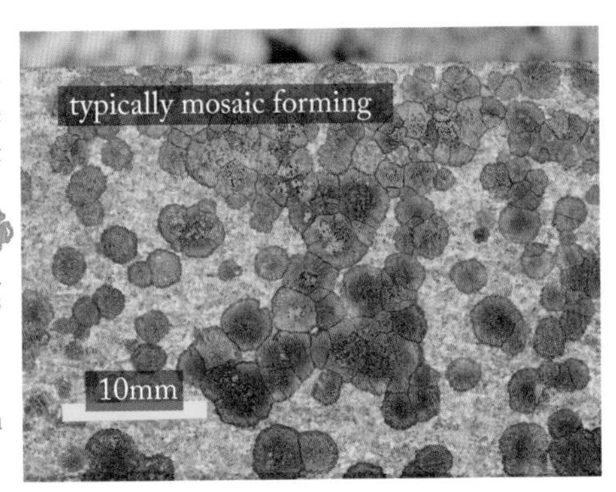

Buellia subdisciformis – crustose

Description: Cracked areolate thallus, cream to light grey. Varies from thin to thick, sometimes lumpy or wart-like. Frequently bordered by a black prothallus. Apothecia are small and abundant. Discs are black and slightly convex, frequently becoming pruinose (white) when juvenile; rims are also black.

Spot Tests: K+ yellow → red, Pd+ yellow-orange, C–. UV–.

Nature Notes: Grows on silica-rich rocks often forming mosaics.

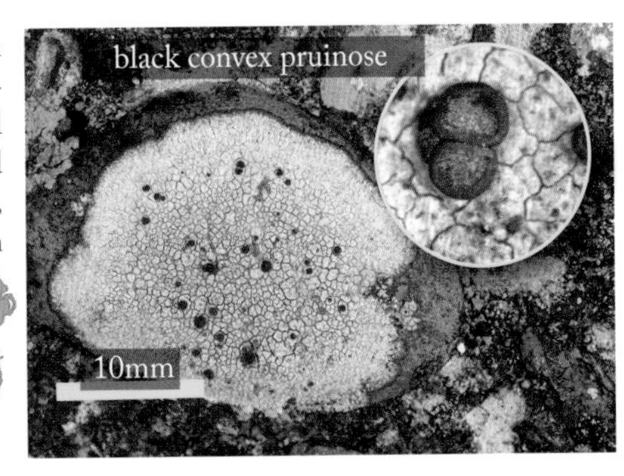

Bunodophoron – 1 species recorded in Ireland.

Bunodophoron melanocarpum – fruticose

Description: Thallus is composed of short sterile branches. Thalline colour varies from grey to dirty grey with blotches of green. Branches are fertile and may reach heights of 3–5cm, often flattened, especially near the base, with a diameter of about 3mm. Short brittle isidioid protrusions develop on the fertile stems. Apothecia are rare and have the appearance of ventilation funnels on ships as they develop at the top of the stalks (on the ventral aspect) but open out laterally. The rim tissue breaks down exposing the dark and dusty soot-like spores (mazaedia). Spores are globose with a diam. of 5.5–8μm. 8 per ascus.

Spot Tests: Medulla: K+ yellow, Pd+ orange.

Natures Notes: Enjoys the company of mosses in sheltered habitats and is found on mossy tree trunks (acidic bark) and silica-rich rocks. Apothecia very rare in Ireland.

Confusion: Similar to *Sphaerophorus globosus* but the flattened stalks and non-terminal apothecia of *Bunodophoron melanocarpum* distinguish them.

Calicium – 6 species recorded in Ireland.

Calicium viride – crustose

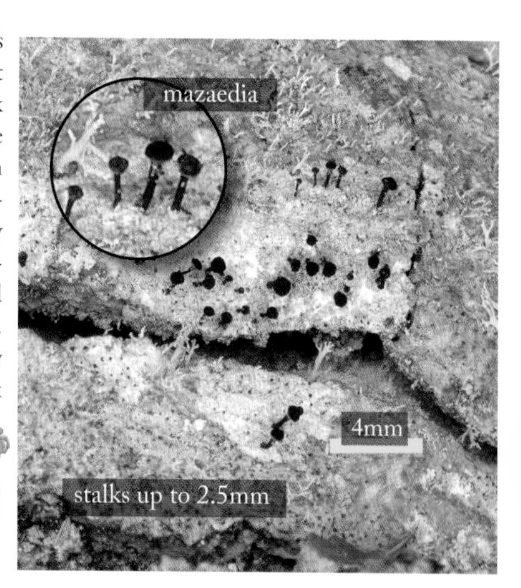

Description: This is the largest of Ireland's pinheaded lichens, the stalks reach a height of 2.5mm. The heads or apothecia are black and contain a loose mass of spores termed the mazaedium. Thallus is bright yellow-green (viridian green), sometimes with a sulphurous tint. The underside of the apothecia may be red-brown pruinose, although this is difficult to see. Thallus may be partially immersed in the substrate. When visible it is smooth. Microscopic examination will frequently show it to be granular or powdery. Spores, 11–14 x 4–5μm. Spot Tests: Negative. UV+ bright orange.

Nature Notes: Found in dry crevices on acidic barked trees such as conifers and oak.

Caloplaca arnoldii – crustose

DESCRIPTION: The yellow-orange thallus is finely textured with tiny parallel lobes at the margins. The prothallus is weakly defined or absent, especially in mature specimens. Apothecia are common and have a red-yellow disc with a yellow rim. Spores, 9–12 x 4–6μm with wide septum.
SPOT TESTS: K+ crimson.
NATURE NOTES: Occurs on smooth silica-rich coastal rocks, particularly on vertical faces that dry quickly.
CONFUSION: With *Caloplaca saxicola*, confined to calcareous and cement substrates.

Caloplaca aurantia – crustose

DESCRIPTION: Forms distinctive yellow patches, with some orange, lighter at the lobe tips. Thallus adpressed, especially at lobe ends. Central region often densely cracked (sometimes with the substrate visible) areolate and darker than the rest of the thallus. Apothecia occur in the central area. Discs are flat to convex and brown-orange in colour. Rims are paler. Spores, 10–13 x 8–10μm.
SPOT TESTS: K+ crimson.
NATURE NOTES: Occurs on hard well lit calcareous rocks (limestone).
CONFUSION: With *Caloplaca flavescens*, with which it often grows.

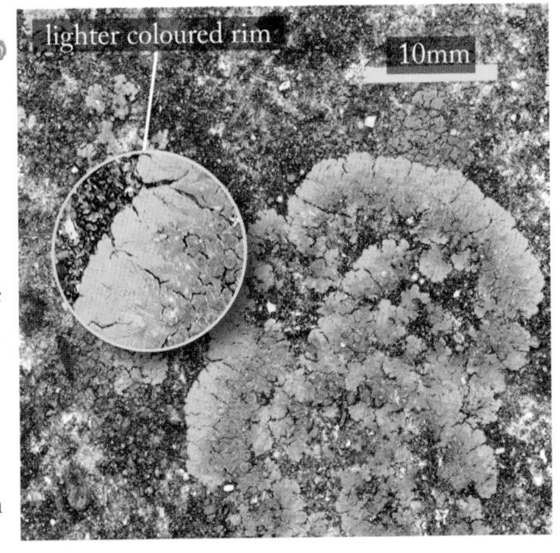

Caloplaca britannica – crustose

DESCRIPTION: Thallus is pale yellow to orange and squamulose-like. Squamules are convex. Looks untidy due to small mounds of isidia and soralia. Apothecia (size ≤0.5mm) have a yellow disc with a paler rim. The prothallus is very pale creamy yellow. Spores,11–14 x 4–6μm. SPOT TESTS: K+ crimson.
NATURE NOTES: Occurs in dry dusty crevices on vertical siliceous rock in coastal areas, often close to bird perches. Nitrogen-loving.
CONFUSION: Like a brighter *C. littorea* when weathered.

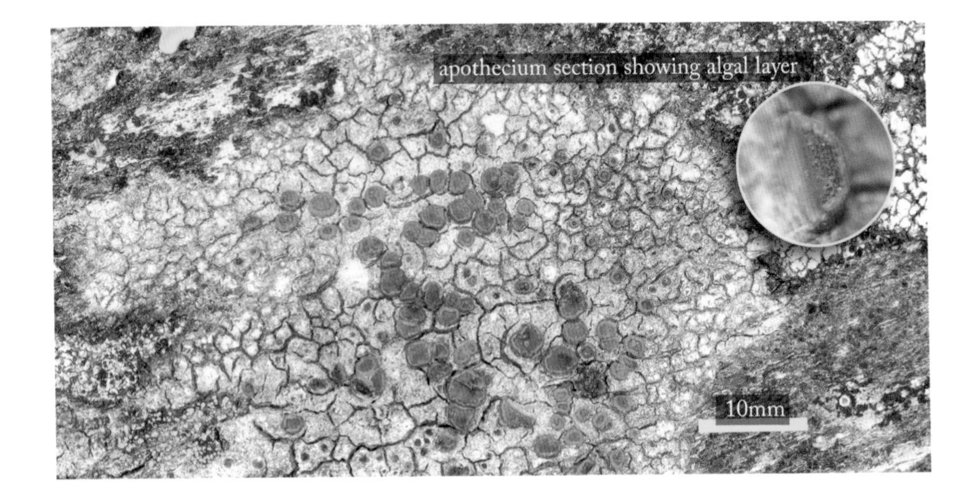

Caloplaca ceracea – crustose

Description: Apothecia are small with flat to convex discs, rusty brown in colour with pale orange wavy rims which may be pruinose. Overall the apothecia look waxy when wet and the discs take on a green tint. Rims or exciples are matt when dry. Thallus is pale coloured and lacking a distinct prothallus. Spores, 13–15 x 8μm with a septum (3–5μm wide) about a third of the way up its length.

Spot Tests: Discs: K+ purple. Thallus: K–.

Nature Notes: Found on silica-rich coastal rocks in the mid to upper shore. Rare inland.

Confusion: With *Caloplaca crenularia.* Apothecia have a layer of green algal cells under the disc; section with finger nail to check. Also, its discs do not change colour when wet.

Caloplaca citrina – crustose

Description: The thick to thin granular thallus is variable in colour, ranging from watery green to yellow to orange. Irregular distinctive areoles are covered with small squamules that in turn are covered in orange coloured soredia. Apothecia are common, (≤1.5mm). Discs are yellow-orange with a pale rim that is granular-sorediate. The prothallus, if present, is white. Spores, 10.5–15 x 5–8μm. Spot Tests: K+ crimson.

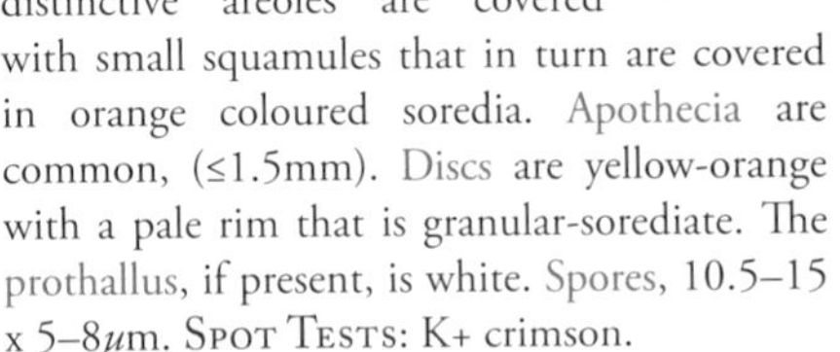

Nature Notes: Occurs on well lit calcareous rocks and sometimes on basic bark (in crevices) or mortar. A very common species.

Confusion: *C. flavocitrina* squamules smaller and apothecia lack soredia. The K+ test distinguishes it from genus *Candelariella*.

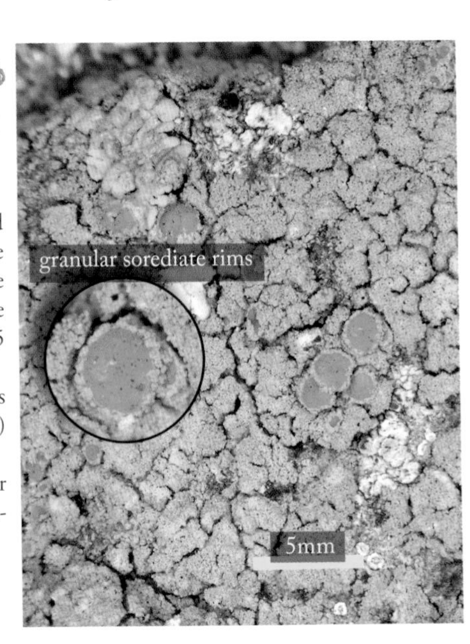

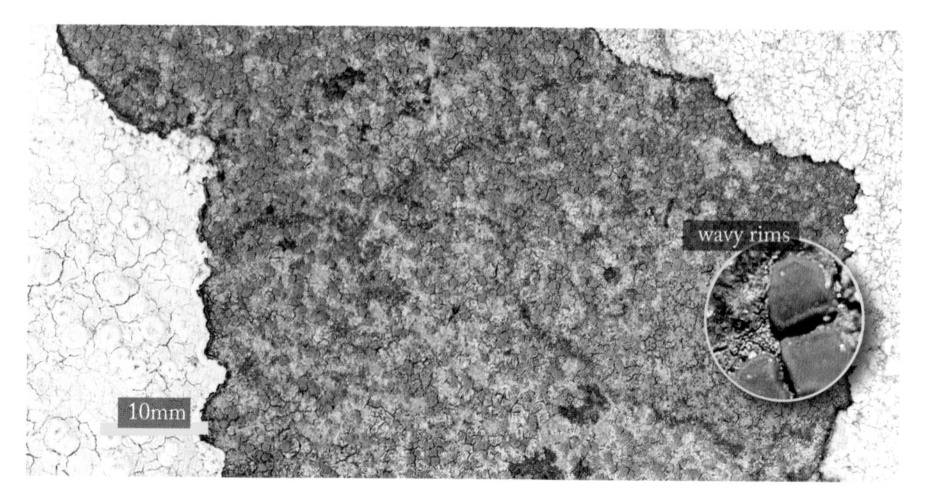

Caloplaca crenularia – crustose

Description: Small (≤1mm) rusty red apothecia are characteristic of this species. They are scattered evenly throughout the grey thallus. Discs are flat to concave and the rust red colour can darken to red-brown. The rim is lighter in colour than the disc and is either narrow and circular or wavy. Red pycnidia are present in large numbers. The thallus itself varies from mouse grey to creamy white with the surface cracked in an irregular fashion. Spores are ellipsoidal with a thick septum; 12–14 x 6–8μm.

Spot Tests: K–.

Nature Notes: It has a preference for silica-rich rocks in damp sheltered locations. Frequently found in sheltered coastal areas and inland on siliceous outcrops. Sometimes it will occur on silica-poor rocks (gabbro). Occurs along the top of undisturbed walls, often with *Protoblastenia rupestris*.

Confusion: With *Caloplaca ceracea* whose discs turn green when wet. Also, it is never found on trees or wood, where its place is taken by an almost identical *Caloplaca ferruginea*.

Caloplaca decipiens – crustose, placodioid

Description: Thallus forms small circular shapes ≤3cm in diameter, yellow to orange in colour although green to light yellow when shaded. Central region is darker in colour, often brown, areolate and with many lip-shaped soralia. It breaks up with age, leaving the substrate visible. Thallus is usually heavily pruinose (white) and the margins are marked by fine crenulate convex lobes. Apothecia are rare, ≤1mm in diameter, with orange concave discs and thalline rims. Spores, 10–15 x 5–8μm. Spot Tests: K+ purple.

Nature Notes: Found in nutrient rich urban areas on mortar, limestone and bird perches.

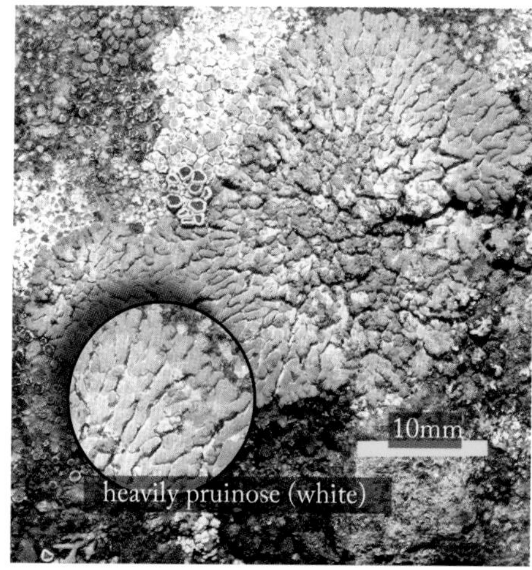

Caloplaca ferruginea – crustose

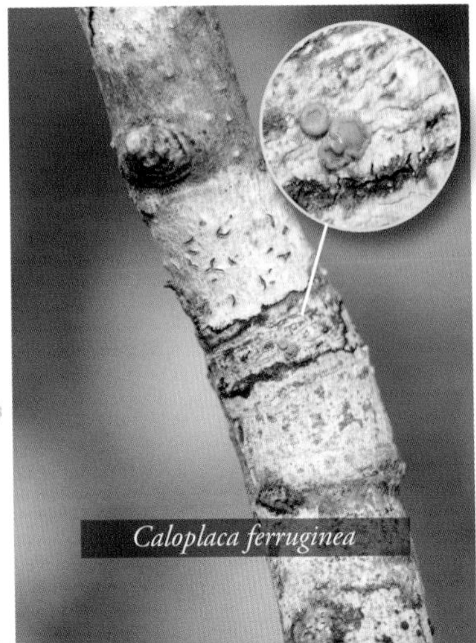

Description: Apothecia are characteristically deep red in colour with a flexuose or uneven rim. The thallus is white to grey in colour and may be immersed in the substrate. Usually found on the bark (neutral to basic) of mature trees (hawthorn and ash especially) and on twigs. When the apothecia are cut in section there is rarely any photobiont present (in the hymenium). Spores, 13.5–15 x 6.6–8.5μm.

Spot Tests: Thallus: K–. Apothecia rims: K+ purple.

Nature Notes: This species is becoming rare in Ireland due to the lack of suitable substrate (*Corylus, Populus tremula, Fraxinus, Sorbus*). Superficially, it looks similar to *Caloplaca crenularia*, however *C. crenularia* is only found on rock.

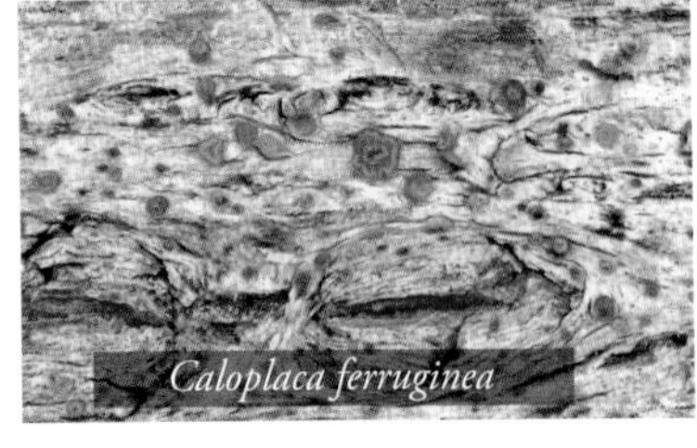

Caloplaca flavescens – crustose

Description: The thallus forms neat circles sometimes reaching 12cm in diameter. The centre is frequently missing; it falls out as the specimen matures exposing the substrate. The overall matt colour is pale to rich orange with a white or non-pigmented area behind the orange edge of the thallus. The centre becomes lumpy and areolate before falling off. Edge lobes are rather narrow and convex and do not widen towards the apex. Apothecia are common. Discs are orange and the margins lighter in colour. It lacks soralia and isidia. Spores, 12–15 x 8–10μm. Spot Tests: K+ purple.

Nature Notes: Found on hard calcareous rocks, especially in nutrient rich areas such as near farms. Frequently seen on the vertical aspect of pillars, walls, old headstones and statues.

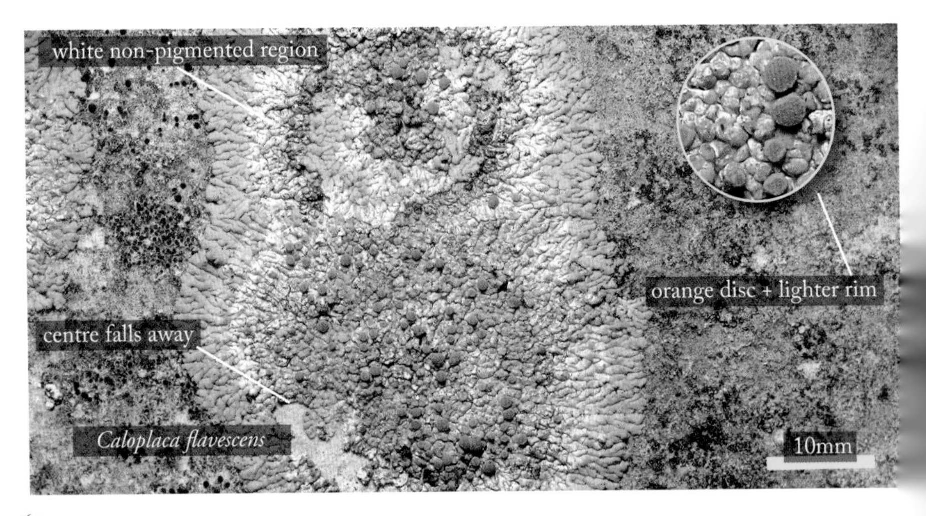

Caloplaca littorea – crustose

Description: Thallus has a distinctive rich orange colour due to abundant orange finger-like isidia. The prothallus, if present, is poorly defined and pale yellow in colour. Apothecia are rare and ≤0.8mm in diameter. They are either distinctly scattered throughout the thallus or in groups. Discs are pruinose. Margins are proper and sometimes excluded. Spores, 11–14 x 5–7μm, ellipsoidal with a wide septum.
Spot Tests: K+ purple.
Nature Notes: Found on silica-rich rocks in dry conditions such as those found under large overhanging rocks and cliffs. Can develop as many small patches or single extensive sheets. The dense population of orange finger-like isidia help in its identification.
Confusion: similar to but readily distinguishable from *C. britannica* and *C. citrina*.

Caloplaca marina – crustose

Description: Thalli orange or orange-red in colour. They may be continuous or fragmented. When fragmented a thallus looks lumpy under magnification. When continuous it appears areolate and the edges may be ill-defined with almost no lobes. It is never powdery or pruinose. A light coloured prothallus may be visible in well developed specimens. Apothecia are small and either scattered though the thallus or grouped in small clusters, with diameters rarely greater than 0.8mm. The orange discs (a deeper colour than the thallus) are concave initially but mature to become convex. Rims become narrow giving the effect that the convex disc is spilling over it. Spores, 11–15 x 4–8μm.
Spot Tests: K+, violet-red for both apothecia and thallus.
Nature Notes: Found on coastal rocks from calcareous to silica-rich types. It is characteristically found in the mesic supralittoral zone or above *Verrucaria maura*.
Confusion: *Caloplaca marina* can be distinguished from the superficially similar *Caloplaca thallincola* by its lack of well defined thalline lobes.

Caloplaca microthallina – crustose

DESCRIPTION: Thallus is a scattering of tiny isidia-like squamules. Dispersed throughout the squamules are apothecia with crenulate or notched rims. Generally ≤1mm in size, they have distinctive convex (sometimes flat) orange discs. A prothallus is absent, but the squamules sometimes form lobate edges. Spores, 12–15 x 6–8μm. SPOT TESTS: K+ purple.

NATURE NOTES: A coastal species that frequently grows over *Verrucaria maura*. Seen in crevices as tiny yellow lines on both siliceous rocks and calcareous substrate. It is the only coastal *Caloplaca* without isidia.

CONFUSION: With *C. marina*, which lacks scattered thallus or crenulate apothecial rims.

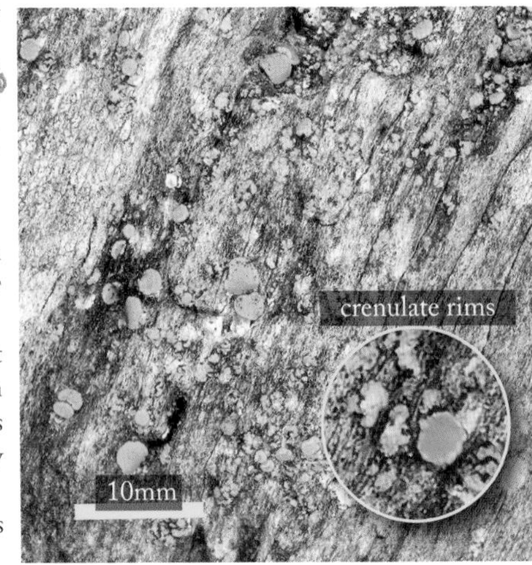

Caloplaca ochracea – crustose

DESCRIPTION: The thallus is a whitish yellow to gold colour, sprinkled with some grey patches. It has a distinct thin black prothallus. Apothecia are abundant, small, ≤1mm, and well scattered across the thallus. Flat to concave discs are deep yellow with a glossy texture. Rims are thick and lighter in colour. Spores, four celled 12–15 x 5–7μm. SPOT TESTS: K+ purple.

NATURE NOTES: Forms mosaics. Found along the coast and inland on sunny hard limestone outcrops and ruins. Common in the Burren.

Caloplaca saxicola – crustose

DESCRIPTION: Forms small, ≤3cm diam., closely adpressed rosettes. Thallus has a dull yellow to orange colour with convex pruinose lobes. The lobes show furrowing in places. Central area is darker than the edges. Granulose and crowded with apothecia ≤1mm in diameter. Discs are flat and have a dull orange tint with lighter coloured rims. Spores, 9–12 x 4.5–7μm.

SPOT TESTS: K+ purple (apothecia and thallus).

NATURE NOTES: Found in dry shaded sheltered habitats on hard calcareous rocks. Avoids direct sunlight. Common throughout Ireland.

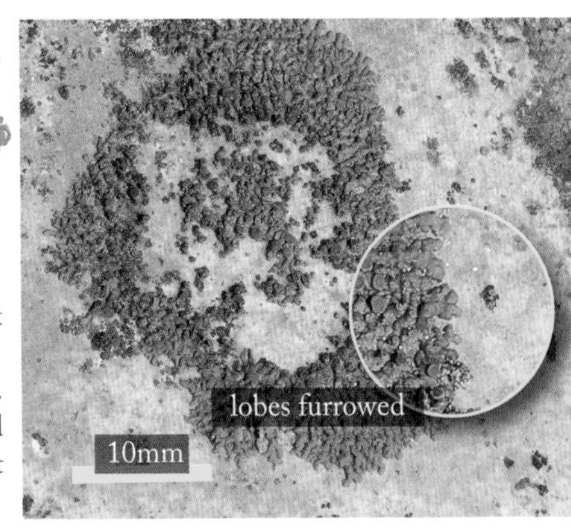

Caloplaca thallincola – crustose

DESCRIPTION: Thallus is adpressed, yellow-orange in colour and forms circular or arc shaped patterns. The fringe of the thallus has a finger-like or placodioid pattern that is well defined. Lobes are long and convex with distinct furrows between. Apothecia normally populate the central area of the thallus which is lumpy or convex areolate. The rims of apothecia have the same orange colour as the thallus. Discs have a brownish-orange colour and are flat in juveniles. Apothecia becoming convex with age. Spores, 10–15 x 8–12μm.
SPOT TESTS: K+ crimson.
NATURE NOTES: Found on seashores in sheltered locations (facing away from direct wave action). Often grows over *Verrucaria maura* where its bright orange colour becomes even more striking. Grazed by molluscs such as limpets, whelks and periwinkles. Occurs on siliceous rocks (rarely on limestone).
CONFUSION: With *Caloplaca flavescens* (*C. thallincola* is brighter).

Caloplaca verruculifera – crustose

DESCRIPTION: Thallus is watery lemon yellow through yellow to almost orange. Forms distinctive convex radiating lobes (placodioid) which are long (6–8mm) and widen slightly towards the tips. Sometimes the lobes are branched. The thalline central region is areolate granulose and covered in an abundance of isidia. Apothecia are rare. Discs are flat and orange coloured with a relatively thick rim. Spores, 10–15 x 5–6μm.
SPOT TESTS: K+ purple for all parts.
NATURE NOTES: Exclusively a coastal lichen found on both siliceous and calcareous rocks, especially in nutrient rich areas such as near bird perches. Rarely found on wood. Sometimes parasitized by *Diplotomma vezdanum*.
CONFUSION: With *Caloplaca thallincola*, which is brighter yellow.

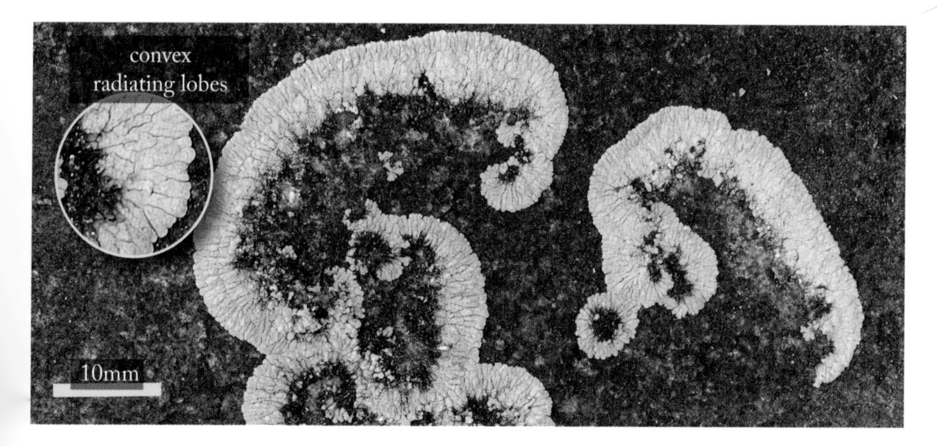

Candelaria concolor – foliose

DESCRIPTION: The yolk yellow thallus consists of minute incised lobes and forms small separate bushy patches. It is tightly attached to the substrate. The lobes are small (≤1mm in length), often sorediate and project upwards making a coral-like statement. Soralia may cover the whole thallus, but this is not common. Pycnidia are rare. Apothecia are rare and have dirty yellow to orange discs less than 1mm in diameter. Rims are rough and the same colour as the thallus. The thallus underside is matt white with simple scattered rhizines. Spores, 6–15 x 4–6μm.

SPOT TESTS: K– , C–, KC–, Pd–. UV–.

NATURE NOTES: Found on basic bark of deciduous trees in open areas such as parks and hedgerows. Favours nutrient rich bark. May occur on fences and other sawn wood structures. Can also occur on rocks. Sensitive to SO_2 pollution Becoming widespread again, possibly due to a drop in SO_2 levels countrywide.

CONFUSION: With *Xanthoria ulophyllodes.*

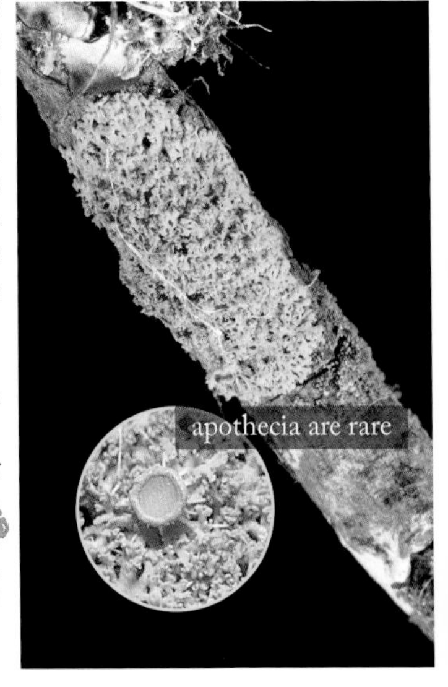

Candelariella – 6 species recorded in Ireland.

Candelariella aurella – crustose, squamulose

Description: Thallus lies either within the substrate or as scattered gold coloured granules on the surface. The prothallus may spread throughout the thallus giving the specimen a lead grey background colour. Apothecia are common with crenulate margins. Spores, 10–18 x 5–6μm. Spot Tests: K–.

Nature Notes: Found in urban areas on calcareous materials such as cement and brick. Becoming very common in Ireland, particularly on the tops of walls.

Confusion: With *Candelariella vitellina*. Differs from *Caloplaca* species by reacting K–.

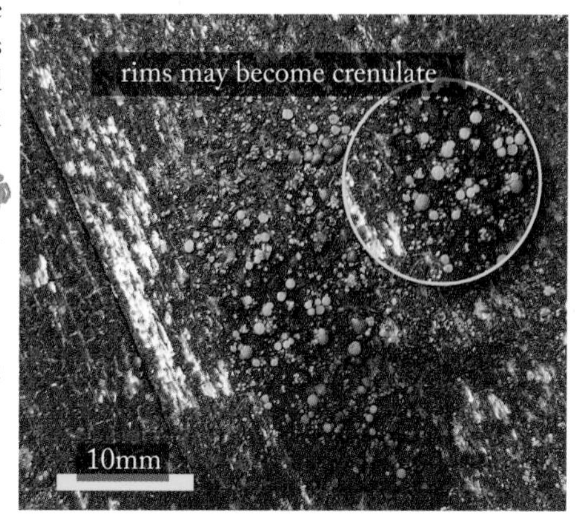

Candelariella coralliza – crustose

Description: Has a bright yellow granular thallus with deep cracks dividing it into many islands. The granular texture is due to tiny spherical sand sized grains less than 0.3mm in diameter. Apothecia are rare and usually only one or two are associated with a thallus. They range in size from 0.6–1.5mm in diameter with a granulate or crenulate rim. Spores, 9–15 x 3–7μm.

Spot Tests: None.

Nature Notes: Found on siliceous rocks in exposed habitats, such as erratics. It prefers nutrient rich bird perches and is associated with boulders from coastal areas to uplands. Considered an ecotype of *Candelariella vitellina*. Both have been found side by side. Rarely found in urban areas.

Candelariella medians – crustose, placodioid

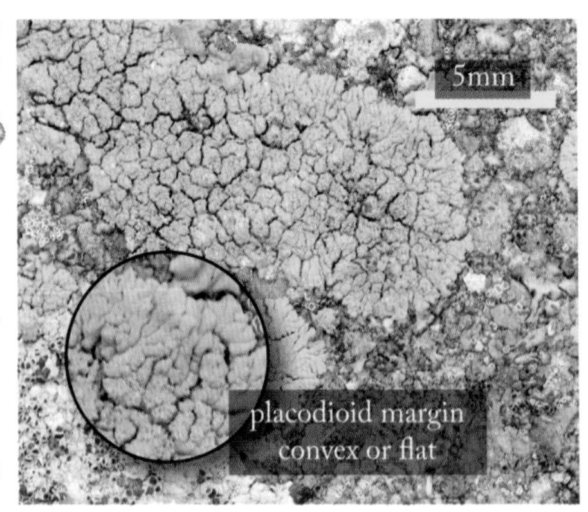

Description: Flat yellow placodioid thallus with radial marginal lobes forming patches up to 3cm in diameter. Turns green-grey in the shade. Lobes about 1mm wide, may be flat or convex with pruinose tips. Central area of thallus is areolate with isidia giving it a coral-like appearance. Apothecia are occasional. Discs are dull yellow and flat to convex with crenulate rims. Spores, 11–17 x 4–6μm.

Spot Tests: K–.

Nature Notes: Prefers calcareous substrates especially in graveyards and near bird perches.

Candelariella vitellina – crustose, squamulose

Description: Has a distinctive mustard yellow colour. Thallus areolate, consisting mainly of granules giving it a lumpy thick appearance, but equally can be thin and lightly granular. Apothecia and pycnidia are common. Apothecial discs are dirty yellow and generally flat. Thalline rims are smooth or crenulate. Spores, 9–15 x 3–7μm.

Spot Tests: None.

Nature Notes: Grows on both calcareous and silica-rich rocks. Likes nutrient rich areas such as bird perches. May occur on brick or even trees.

Catinaria – 1 species recorded in Ireland.

Catinaria atropurpurea – crustose

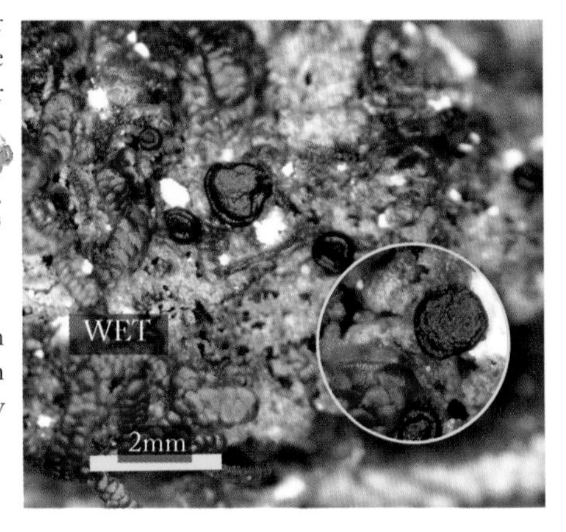

Description: Thallus is minutely granular and pale grey to green-brown in colour. The black apothecia are small, reaching a diameter typically of just 0.6mm. They take on a distinctive matt reddish wine-gum appearance when wet. Discs start convex and develop to concave. Asci are 8 spored. Spores, 10–15 x 5–7μm. Spot Tests: Negative.

Nature Notes: Occurs on bark (oak and ash mainly) in old woodlands and parklands, often as part of the Lobarion community. Frequently found growing on mossy branches.

Confusion: Similar to *Porina coralloidea*.

CETRARIA – 4 SPECIES RECORDED IN IRELAND.

These are erect foliose lichens (bordering on being fruticose) with a colour range from yellow to reddish brown to olive brown. They darken when exposed to direct sunlight. Branches are flattened to cylindrical with prominent pseudocyphellae. Sexual reproduction is through apothecia. Apothecial margins or rims are the same colour as the thallus. Spores are packed 8 per ascus, colourless and simple. Black pycnidia are common and found in side projections or stalks. The photobiont is a green *Trebouxia*.

Cetraria islandica – foliose, fruticose

DESCRIPTION: Chestnut brown and resin-like shrubby thallus ranging in height from 2–6cm. Lobes are long, narrow and deeply channelled with many small projections along the margins. They tend to curl back in towards the body of the thallus. The base is frequently reddish brown and pitted. Overall the appearance is of a tangled mass of lobes loosely attached to the substrate. Marginal projections vary in size from 0.1–1mm. Dark pycnidia occupy tips of projections. White pseudocyphellae populate the lower surface to the margins of the lobes. Apothecia are rare and discs vary from 2–20mm in diameter. Rims are distinct and crenulate.

SPOT TESTS: C–, K–, KC–, Pd+ orange. UV–.

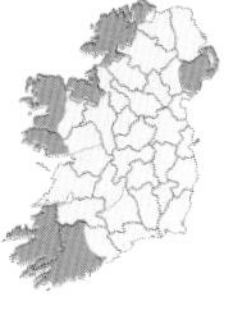

NATURE NOTES: Found on acidic soils in upland regions, especially among mosses and heather. Rare in Ireland, but locally abundant where it occurs. In Norway it is called breadmoss. Often eaten as bread or made into a soup by adding milk. Sometimes ground down and added to flour or potato.

CONFUSION: *Cetraria ericetorum* which is distinguished by being Pd–.

Cetrelia – 1 species recorded in Ireland.

Thalli are foliose. Superficially similar to *Parmelia* species. Pseudocyphellae are found on the upper surface. Apothecia similar to *Cetraria* species; lecanorine with 8 spores per ascus. Apothecia have never been found on Irish specimens.

Cetrelia olivetorum – foliose, almost fruticose

Description: Develops as large foliose patches up to 10cm in diameter. A *Parmelia* lookalike, it has a glaucous grey thallus often tinted with brown. Lobes may overlap, rounded at the tips and turned up a little. The upper surface is sprinkled with white pseudocyphellae. The lower surface is black. Edges lack cilia and rhizines, but rhizines occur throughout the rest of the underside. Soralia present on the upper margins. Apothecia are unknown in Irish specimens. Spores 12–15 x 7–10μm.

Spot Tests: K–, P–, C± red, KC± pink or red.

Nature Notes: Prefers an acid environment and occurs among mosses on broad leaved trees in well lit woodland (hazel and willow).

Confusion: With *Parmotrema perlatum*, but it has marginal cilia.

Chaenotheca – 7 species recorded in Ireland.

Thalli are crustose/granular and show a range of colours from gold to yellow to brown. Apothecia are stalked and look like pins, the head being an unprotected cluster of spores or mazaedium. Spores are globose and brown to light brown.

Chaenotheca furfuracea – crustose, granulose

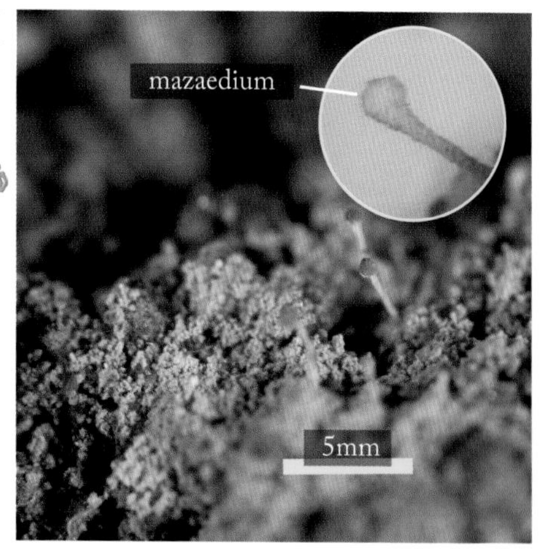

Description: The thallus has a lime green to sulphur-yellow colour. It is composed of fine granules giving it a leprose or powdery texture. Apothecia are rare. They are pinheaded in shape with stalks up to 3mm high. The black head (mazaedium) is covered in a frost-like pruina making it concolorous with the thallus.

Spot Tests: None. UV+ pink.

Nature Notes: Found on silica-rich rocks, especially in crevices or overhangs in damp shaded areas. Also found on old tree stumps. More common in upland areas than other habitats.

Confusion: Distinguished from *Psilolechia lucida* which glows orange under UV light.

Chrysothrix – 4 species recorded in Ireland.

A leprose form, the thallus being composed of powdery globose granules. They lack lobes, the edges often being diffuse. Soredia may be present. The group has a distinctive colour range, from bright lemon yellow to yellow-green. Generally found on trees, sawn wood and siliceous rocks.

Chrysothrix candelaris – leprose

occurs on rough bark on the shaded side

Description: Thallus is thin, diffuse and yellow-gold in colour. The powdery surface has a matt texture. Soredia are globose, common and very small, rarely over 0.3mm in diameter. Apothecia have not been found in Ireland but are recorded on French specimens. They are the same colour as the thallus and combined with their diminutive size (≤0.5mm) are almost impossible to see with a hand lens. Discs are flat to convex.

Spot Tests: Pd± orange, K± orange, C–. UV–.

Nature Notes: Occurs in crevices among the rough bark of mature trees such as oak, particularly on the shaded side where it is dry. Also found on shaded vertical rock faces. Known to occur on old stained glass.

Confusion: With *Psilolechia lucida.*

Chrysothrix chlorina – leprose

Description: Thallus is thick, powdery, granulated and often cracked. It has a bright citrus fruit yellow colour with a cotton-like texture. Granules are relatively large when compared to other leprose lichens. The prothallus is faint. Apothecia unrecorded.

Spot Tests: C–, K± watery orange or red, Pd–. UV+ orange.

Nature Notes: Found mainly on silica-rich rocks in dry sheltered areas such as overhangs or crevices. It is not found in upland regions. Rare on trees and especially rare on conifers.

Confusion: With *Psilolechia lucida* (not as powdery and less brightly coloured). Very similar to *Chrysothrix candelaris* which tends to be yellow-orange and *Caloplaca xantholyta*, which is K+.

CLADONIA – 48 species recorded in Ireland. Fruticose, squamulose, cup lichens.

This is an attractive group for beginners, but the diverse variation in body shape within a species makes them particularly difficult to identify with certainty. They are all composed of tiny scales or squamules. The body is created in two stages. A scaly thallus covers the substrate and its squamules are consequently termed primary squamules (also basal squamules). The primary squamules have a distinct upper and lower side. They lack a cortex and never produce rhizines, but may, however, produce soredia. A stalk-like structure called a podetium develops from the centre or edge of the primary squamules. Podetia may rise several centimetres, branched or unbranched. Podetia are hollow and their outer surface is either smooth or coated with secondary plate-like squamules or covered in small spherical granules. Tips of the podetia may be pointed like an obelisk, or develop into cups termed scyphi. If a tip is fertile, then brown or red apothecia develop there. Podetia may be sterile. Sometimes the primary squamules die away leaving just the podetia visible. Attention to the chemical spot tests is recommended, particularly the Pd and K tests.

Cladonia bellidiflora – fruticose, squamulose, cup lichen

DESCRIPTION: Primary squamules are variable in size ranging from 1–3mm in length. They are deeply lobed and lack soredia. Squamule colour tends to be greeny grey but they may have a tint of yellow also, especially towards the base. Primary squamules die away with age leaving just podetia. Podetia range from 3–5cm high and are covered with numerous yellow-green squamules that are inclined to peel off. Squamules near the base have an red-brown underside. Podetia are unbranched, but may develop new growths from the cup margins. Tips may have a narrow cylindrical cup or else lie blunt. Cups sometimes have apothecia that may become large, bright red in colour and spill out over the cup edges.
SPOT TESTS: C–, K–, KC+ yellow, Pd–. UV+ white (good identification aid).
NATURE NOTES: Found mainly on acid soils, in heathlands close to rocks and on rotting tree stumps covered with moss or heather. Widely distributed throughout the country, but not abundant.
CONFUSION: With *Cladonia squamosa* which has brown apothecia and is KC–.

adonia coccifera – fruticose, squamulose, cup lichen

:SCRIPTION: Apothecia and pycnidia abundant and bright red, sitting the top of the yellowish grey-green detia. Cups or scyphi open out wide. detia range in height from 1–2cm. detia are regular and well formed, eir surface being smooth and composed of coarse, en granules, forming the outer cortex. The base y be populated with rounded primary squamules ich sometimes have small indents; their under-face colour varies from yellow to orange-brown. OT TESTS: C–, K–, KC+ yellow, Pd–. UV–. ATURE NOTES: Occurs on acidic peaty or sandy ls. Rarely found on mossy soils, but may be seen the tops of old walls in coastal or upland areas.

ladonia coniocraea – fruticose, squamulose, cup lichen

ESCRIPTION: The primary or basal squamules are riable in shape, vibrant green when wet (dull when y) on the upper surface and pale be-w. They may also be lightly sorediate. detia are unbranched, narrow, quently curved this way and that, d usually pointed at the top, reach-g a height of 3cm. If cups or scyphi e present they are very small, never wider than the ameter of the podetia. SPOT TESTS: Pd+ red, K–. ATURE NOTES: Prefers acid substrate of recently ad trees and wood. Not so common on heathland. ery common throughout Ireland.

ladonia diversa – fruticose, squamulose, cup lichen

ESCRIPTION: Bright red apothecia often merge to l the scyphi. Podetia (≤2cm high) fall to the left d right like old headstones. They are coated in fine anules and sometimes with small scattered sec-ndary squamules that adds to their untidy appear-nce. Colouration varies from yellow-green to yel-w-grey. Pycnidia are also red and form the rim of the scyphi as a row of lit-e red dots. Primary squamules incised, llow-green with white undersides. POT TESTS: KC+ yellow, Pd–. UV–. IATURE NOTES: Common in upland eas on old rotting tree stumps and acid soils, par-cularly pockets of soil in rock crevices.

Cladonia diversa showing red apothecia merged and filling the scyphi.

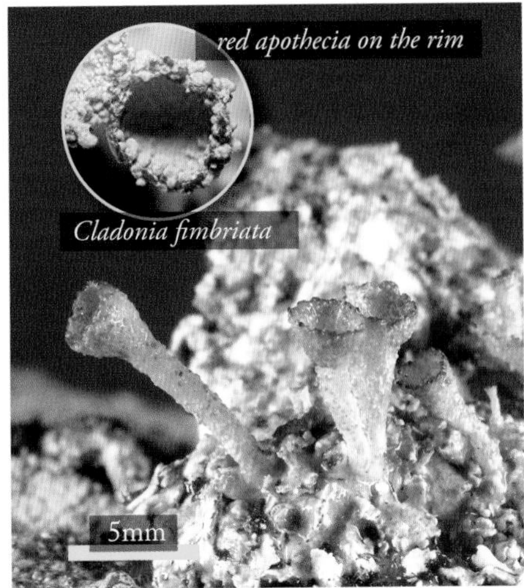

'adonia fimbriata – fruticose, squamulose, cup lichen

ESCRIPTION: Podetia rise like small tubes and abruptly open out trumpet-like. ·othecia reside along the rims of the scyphi or cups which range from 1–1.5cm in ight and are usually coated in a fine dust of soredia. Soredia may form large granules, t this is rare. Rims of the podetia are even, unless they are actively reproducing, in ich case apothecia make the rims lumpy or irregular. Primary squamules are greeny ·y to green in colour, with small indents. Squamules may be sorediate or dusty. ores are colourless, 1-celled, 8 per ascus. SPOT TESTS: K–, Pd+ rust red. UV–.
ATURE NOTES: *Cladonia fimbriata* is shade-loving, usually found on acidic soils and rotting ·od, typical of raised bogs in Ireland where it is shaded by the heathers *Erica* and *Calluna*. Found th in coastal areas and inland. Rare on old walls, trees and rocks.
ONFUSION: With *Cladonia chlorophaea* and *Cladonia foliacea*.

'adonia floerkeana – fruticose, squamulose, cup lichen

ESCRIPTION: Podetia range ·m 1–3cm high, with a diam. 1.5mm. They may be branched the tips, although branching is ore frequent at the base near e primary squamules (8mm ng). Coarse squamules cover podetia which e brown in exposed habitats. Apothecia and cnidia are red and form on the tips of podetia ot from the cups). Primary squamules are een on the upper surface and white with an ange tint underneath.
·OT TESTS: K+ yellow. UV+ blue.
ATURE NOTES: Occurs on rotting logs, fence ·sts or well drained soil with a high humus ·ntent. Also occurs in open heathland.
ONFUSION: With *Cladonia macilenta*.

Cladonia foliacea – fruticose, squamulose, cup lichen

Description: Basal squamules make up the bulk of the thallus. They are elongated and shield-like, forming compact upright clusters that have a yellow-green tint on one side while the other side is pale. Pycnidia are abundant, brown in colour and develop on the squamules. Apothecia are also brown.

Spot Tests: K–, Pd+ red, KC+ yellow. UV–.

Nature Notes: This is essentially a coastal species (very rare inland) enjoying windswept sunny areas. Frequently grows among moss, in rock crevices and on sand dunes.

Confusion: With *Cladonia fimbriata* and *C. firma,* with which it often occurs, but *C. firma* is K+ yellow with grey-violet squamules.

Cladonia furcata – fruticose, squamulose, cup lichen

Description: Podetia are hollow, narrow and vary from 2–8cm in height, dichotomously branched, they form irregular spiky tufts. Walls are white with green veins giving a marbled effect. They lack cups or scyphi. The ends are pointed and home to brown coloured pycnidia. Brown apothecia form on short side or lateral branches on the upper third of podetia. Primary or basal squamules frequently to die off leaving just a few which tend to be round with white under-surfaces.

Spot Tests: C–, K± yellow, KC–, Pd+ red. UV–.

Nature Notes: Occurs on both acid and non-acidic substrates in heathlands, dunes, grasslands and mossy rocks in uplands and heath areas .

Confusion: With *Cladonia rangiformis* which is more richly branched and with wider angles.

Cladonia gracilis – fruticose, squamulose, cup lichen

DESCRIPTION: Podetia range in size from 2–6cm in height with a typical diameter of 1.5mm giving rise to tall slender stalks rising to a point when scyphi are absent. Individually they are smooth (lack scales) and green through grey to brown in colour. The bottom of the stalks are often black. Tips may be branched by the formation of new cups. Scyphi are shallow with 10 to 25 'teeth'. The basal squamules (green above and white below) are indented and small, falling in the range of 2–5mm. Apothecia are rare and reach a width of 7mm, while pycnidia are common and reach just 0.2mm in diameter.

SPOT TESTS: C–, K–, KC–, Pd+ red-brown. UV–.

NATURE NOTES: Found on acidic soils that are sandy (well drained), decaying wood and sand dunes.

CONFUSION: With *Cladonia furcata* which lacks scyphi.

Cladonia macilenta – fruticose, squamulose, cup lichen

DESCRIPTION: Basal or primary squamules are small (≤2mm), rounded (rarely with indents) and relatively thick. Podetia are unbranched, grey to greenish grey in colour, slender and usually less than 30mm high. They lack scyphi. Apothecia are bright red. Podetial walls rarely display squamules, but are covered in soredia.
SPOT TESTS: C–, K+ yellow-orange, KC–, Pd+ orange. UV–.
NATURE NOTES: Typically found among mosses in acidic habitats such as heathlands. Also found on rotting wood and soil.
CONFUSION: With *C. polydactyla* which has apothecial cups and more incised squamules.

Cladonia pocillum – fruticose, squamulose, cup lichen

DESCRIPTION: Podetia have a tendency to take on a brown colour and may grow as tall as 1.5cm. The cups (scyphi) often reach 1cm in diameter. Rims are uneven, housing dark brown apothecia and pycnidia. Soredia are absent. Smooth granules line the cups. Basal or primary squamules tend to be small, round and lack indentations, however, old woodland specimens may show large primary squamules forming a carpet of rosettes around the podetia.
SPOT TESTS: C–, K–, KC–, Pd+ red. UV–.
NATURE NOTES: Occurs on calcareous grasslands and in pockets of soil on limestone ourcrops.
CONFUSION: With *Cladonia pyxidata* and distinguished from it by examination of the primary squamules in particular.

Cladonia polydactyla – fruticose, squamulose, cup lichen

Description: Podetia are greeny grey to white in colour and typically about 2cm tall, but may reach a height of 3cm. Initially rather pointed, the podetia may become branched and the cups open out abruptly from the stalks, reaching a diameter of 5mm. Apothecia and pycnidia begin brown but become bright red and form on the tips of the podetia, frequently in clusters. Basal or primary squamules are very small with an orange tint to the base and may be lightly sorediate and incised.

Spot Tests: Basal squamules: K+ purple. Thallus: K+ yellow, Pd+ orange. UV–.

Nature Notes: Found on decaying wood, especially tree trunks and old fences. Common in low lying heathland and among mosses.

Cladonia portentosa – fruticose, squamulose, cup lichen

DESCRIPTION: Forms open sponge-like clumps. Podetia are yellowish green to grey-white. They branch two or more, often three times and point in any direction. Colourless pycnidia develop on the tips of the richly branched podetia.

SPOT TESTS: C–, K–, Pd–, KC± yellow. UV+ white.

NATURE NOTES: Sometimes referred to as 'reindeer lichen', it is common in upland areas, heathlands, sand dunes and especially in pockets of soil where it grows in large tufts or mats. Soft when wet; brittle when dry.

Cladonia pyxidata – fruticose, squamulose, cup lichen

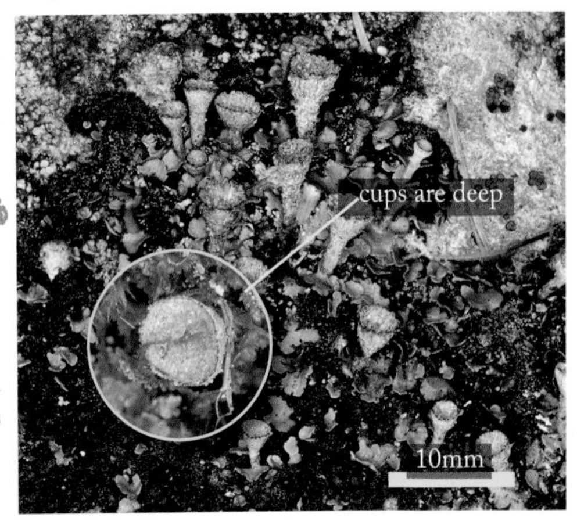

DESCRIPTION: Apothecia are rare. Podetia are pale greeny grey to white and range from 1–3cm tall, but some have been recorded with a height of 4cm. Cups are deep. Small squamules cover both the inside and outside of the podetia. The primary squamules are often 4mm long and vary in width from 2mm to 10mm.

SPOT TESTS: Thallus: Pd+ red.

NATURE NOTES: Occurs on fence posts, rotting logs and well drained soil with a high humus content. Also occurs on open heathland.

CONFUSION: With both *Cladonia chlorophaea* and *Cladonia pocillum*.

Cladonia ramulosa – fruticose, squamulose, cup lichen

DESCRIPTION: Apothecia are abundant, brown in colour, swollen and turning semi-translucent when wet. They sit at the tops of podetia which may reach a height of 3.5cm. Podetia lacking apothecia appear unbranched or poorly branched. Scyphi are weakly formed. Basal squamules have a yellow-grey-green colour, are small, brittle and incised.

SPOT TESTS: C–, K–, KC–, Pd+red. UV–.

NATURE NOTES: Found on rotting tree trunks, fence posts, the tops of walls and sandy heathlands. Occurs on dead Sea Pink.

Cladonia rangiferina – fruticose, squamulose, cup lichen

DESCRIPTION: Thallus forms a mat of highly branched podetia. Four equal branches (rarely three) are produced each time the podetial stems divide. Podetia are grey-white turning brown towards the top, sometimes with a tint of purple. Tips are fatter than the stems. Surface texture of the stems is fine, uniform and fibre-like. Apothecia are brown, small and extremely rare.

SPOT TESTS: C–, K+ yellow, KC–, Pd+ red. UV–.

NATURE NOTES: Inhabits exposed areas such as uplands, heather and open moorland. Found in coastal rocky areas where bog has become exposed by the sea. Also occurs in pockets of acidic soil in coniferous woodlands.

CONFUSON: the K+ yellow reaction separates it from *C. arbuscula*.

Cladonia rangiformis – fruticose, squamulose, cup lichen

DESCRIPTION: A highly branched and spiky sponge-like *Cladonia*. Podetia are 2 to 6cm high and are grey-white to mottled green in colour (best seen when wet), due to the green photobiont showing through the cortex. Branching is prolific, with new stems forming with wide angles between stems. This, and the mottled green colour are characteristic. Basal squamules are small and have white undersides. Squamules are rarely attached to the podetia. Scyphi are absent and brown apothecia are extremely rare. Brown pycnidia are abundant and found at the tips of podetia. Soredia are absent.

SPOT TESTS: C–, K+ pale yellow (characteristic). KC–, Pd± red. UV–.

NATURE NOTES: Found throughout Ireland on calcareous grasslands and along the coast, especially near dunes. Common in the Burren.

CONFUSION: With *C. furcata* which is more brown and K–.

Cladonia squamosa var. squamosa

Cladonia squamosa – fruticose, squamulose, cup lichen

Description: This is a variable species. Primary squamules form dense mats and range in size from 2–7mm long and 1mm wide. They are greenish to brown on the upper surface and white below. Finely divided and persistent. Podetia are characteristically tall, reaching heights of 9cm, although they can be small and squat reaching just 2–3cm. Frequently densely branched with each cluster rising to the same height (corymbose). Tips may be pointed (lacking fruiting structures) or with scyphi that develop holes. Podetia exhibit characteristic bald patches due to the loss of scales or squamules. These squamules are green in shaded areas and brown in sunny sites. Apothecia are brown and rare; pycnidia may be present and are also brown. Soredia are absent.

Spot Tests: Thallus: C–, K–, KC–, Pd–. UV+ (white).

Nature Notes: Prefers mossy rocks near streams, rotting tree stumps and heathlands.

Confusion: With *Cladonia crispata.*

Cladonia squamosa var. subsquamosa

Cladonia squamosa var.subsquamosa

Description: Similar to *C. squamosa* above, but much sturdier in appearance. Podetia are densely clothed with finely divided squamules and has fewer bald patches.

Spot Tests: C–, K+ yellow-orange, KC–, Pd+ orange. UV–.

Cladonia subcervicornis – fruticose, squamulose, cup lichen

Description: Podetia are short and stubby, sometimes irregular or deformed looking. Small dark brown apothecia are abundant and form along the rim of the scyphi, sometimes in clusters. Pycnidia are dark brown and also form on the rim. Basal squamules are large and elongated, developing up to 2cm in size and forming dense interlocking mats (as in the photograph). Their margins may be indented; the upper surface is grey and underneath white with blackened bases. When wet, squamules take on a characteristic green colour.

Spot Tests: C–, K+ yellow, KC–, Pd+ red. UV–.

Nature Notes: Occurs in pockets of humus among silica-rich rocks and boulders in upland heaths and moorland. Also occurs in woodlands and acidic soils close to the coast.

Cladonia uncialis subsp. biuncialis – fruticose, squamulose, cup lichen

Description: Primary squamules and soralia are absent. Podetia are yellow to greeny grey and often swollen. They branch dichotomously and end with two to four spikes. In section the podetia are hollow. Scyphi or cups are absent. Apothecia are very rare. Pycnidia are brown.

Spot Tests: C–, K–, KC+ yellow, Pd–. The medulla is UV+ white.

Nature Notes: Forms entangled mats that are spiky when dry. Grows in heathlands and peat bogs. Water saturated specimens have swollen podetia.

Confusion: Superficially like *Cladonia portentosa* in forming mats in bogs.

COLLEMA – 21 species recorded in Ireland. Known as 'jelly' lichens.

This group is known as 'jelly' lichens. When dry, they are crisp and brittle but when wet, they swell up and become jelly-like. *Collema* lichens do not have an algae as photobiont, but instead depend on *Nostoc* (cyanobacteria) for photosynthesis. Their internal structure is not layered as in the usual foliose lichens; cyanobacteria, for example, are dispersed throughout the fungal tissue. Nor do they have a cortex, a feature that distinguishes them from the genus *Leptogium* (which also has the photobiont *Nostoc*). *Collema* lichens are found in areas of high rainfall or humidity. In Ireland this places them mainly in the west. They are a difficult group for beginners to identify because of the variation in form and texture between wet and dry specimens. Where possible in the text, photographs of wet and dry forms have been included.

The body type of *Collema* species is variously described as foliose, crustose, jelly or gelatinous. Apothecia are lecanorine (rim the same colour as the thallus); asci contain 2 to 8 spores; spores are septate to muriform. Pycnidia occur. All chemical reactions or spot tests are negative.

Collema auriforme – foliose, crustose (jelly)

DESCRIPTION: *When dry*: thallus is black-brown and crisp looking. Lobes are typically 2–4cm in diameter, but may reach 10cm. They are generally smooth but may have small striations or wrinkles. Isidia are numerous and appear like tiny grapes, often in clusters or crowded over much of a lobe. Lobes margins are turned up and indented.

When wet: thallus is dark olive green and swollen. Lobes are fattened (looking like ear lobes). Isidia are spherical, swollen and have the appearance of little beads. Spores are ellipsoidal to oval, submuriform and 26–36 x 8–13μm in size.

Apothecia are rare and discs 2–3mm in diameter. SPOT TESTS: None for *Collema*.

NATURE NOTES: Found on calcareous rock and on mortar, often loose among mosses (which provides a damp humid environment). Particularly common in the Burren on limestone walls.

CONFUSION: With dry *Collema fuscovirens*. Moisten to help differentiate.

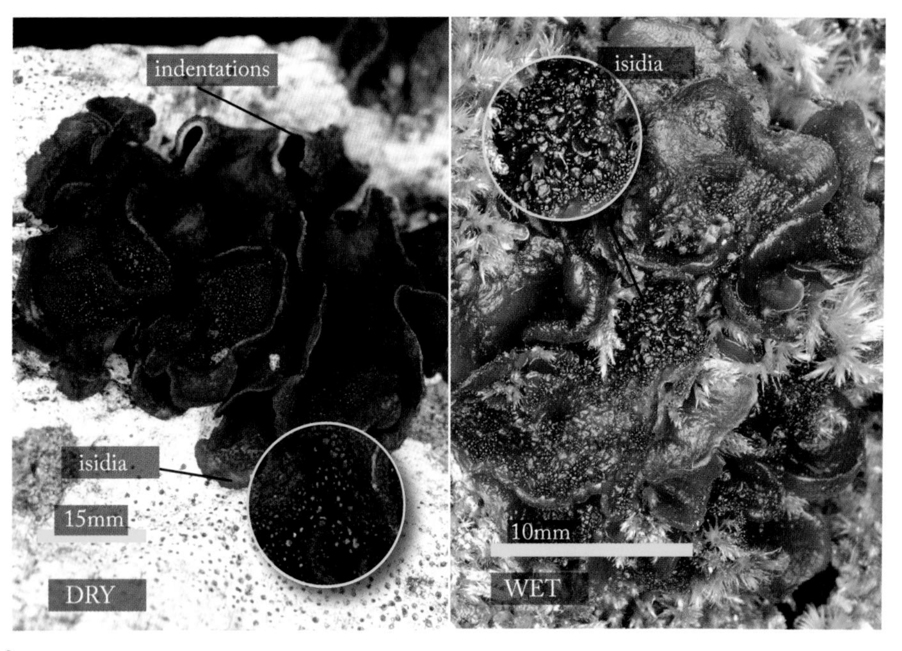

Collema crispum – foliose, crustose (jelly)

DESCRIPTION: *When dry*: thallus is black to dark brown. Forms small patches (≤5cm) which are thin and flattened on the substrate. Does not swell much when wet. Consists of numerous small lobes with margins turned up, (margins are often lacerate and wavy). Lobes have numerous isidia that are globular or characteristically ear-like (or squamule-like) that may cover the thalline lobes. Apothecia are rare; discs ≤2mm in diam. and the rims lumpy or slightly lobate. Underside may have small white rhizines. *When wet*: thallus is slightly swollen and the black colour is lightened by the emergence of olive green. Spores are 26–34 x 13–15μm 3–septate or submuriform.

SPOT TESTS: None for *Collema*.

NATURE NOTES: Found throughout Ireland on calcareous rocks (limestone) and old crumbling mortar. Prefers shaded locations. Occurs on monuments and gravestones.

CONFUSION: With *Collema cristatum* but has many apothecia and forms larger patches.

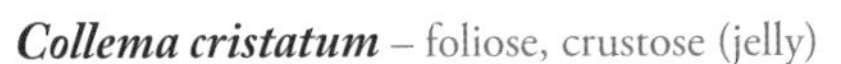

Collema cristatum – foliose, crustose (jelly)

DESCRIPTION: Not too much of a difference between the wet and dry forms. Grows in large patches up to 10cm diam. which often die away towards the centre. Colour tends to be black but turns dark olive green or reddish brown when wet. Lobes are thin and narrow (≤3mm) with irregular branching. Lobe edges are ascending and wavy. Apothecia are numerous and sometimes crowded together. Reddish brown discs may reach a diameter of 5mm. Thalline rims are smooth.
Spores, 18–32 x 8–13μm, ellipsoidal and submuriform.

SPOT TESTS: None for *Collema*.

NATURE NOTES: Prefers hard calcareous rocks and sometimes mortar.

CONFUSION: With *Collema crispum* which is smaller and has very fewer apothecia.

Collema fascicular growing over Loba virens on an ash tr (Killarney)

Collema fasciculare – foliose, crustose (jelly)
Description: It has a profusion of apothecia, often looking like suckers, crowded and frequently obliterating the thallus completely. Thalline margin is often wrinkled and prominent. Both thallus and apothecia are dark brown to olive green in colour. The whole lichen reaches a width of ≤1.5cm and a height of 1cm, making it almost hemispherical in shape. Spores are 50–90 x 4–5μm 9–17 septate, giving them a spiral worm-like appearance.
Spot Tests: None for *Collema*.
Nature Notes: It sits cushion-like among mosses, especially in old woodlands. Likes areas of high humidity so it is inclined to be found on the sheltered side of trees. Also found on hard limestone outcrops. Frequently occurs in hazel woods.

Collema flaccidum – foliose, crustose (jelly)

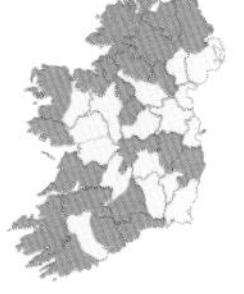

Description: This dark olive green thallus has lobes as wide as 1.5cm and often forms large patches. Membranous lobes are smooth, except where they are covered with extensive carpets of isidia to the edge of the lobes. Isidia may be small and finger-like when young or scale-like when older and the same colour as the thallus. Lobe margins turn upwards. Overall the thallus looks wavy and sometimes crumpled, especially when dry. Apothecia are rare but when present they occupy the central area of the lobes. Rims are either smooth or striated and the discs grow up to 25mm in diameter. Spores are 3–5 septate and 24–36 x 6–7μm in size. Spot Tests: None for *Collema*.
Nature Notes: Occurs on silica-rich rocks in damp areas such as near streams and lakes or in association with mosses in seepage cracks. Thrives in areas of high humidity and is considered an amphibious species. It has a papery texture when dry. Rarely found on trees or calcareous rocks. Colonies are often doughnut-shaped with a clear area of visible substrate at the centre.
Confusion: With *Leptogium cyanescens*, which differs in being blue-grey.

Collema furfuraceum – foliose, crustose (jelly)

Description: Referred to as 'bat wings', the thallus is a dark brown to black membranous structure with large lobes that have characteristically prominent ridges. Overlapping lobes reach 1cm in width and turn up at the tips. The thallus itself may reach 10cm in width but typically develops to 3–6cm. Isidia are abundant along the lobe ridges. Apothecia are rare. Spores, 40–80 x 3–7μm in size.
Spot Tests: None.
Nature Notes: Does not swell much when wet. Likes high humidity. Occurs on trees, typically among moss. Prefers coastal habitats exposed to sea mists and fog.

Collema fuscovirens – foliose, crustose (jelly)

Description: Leathery looking, the pale to dark olive green to black (when dry) thallus grows to 5cm in circumference. Often appearing untidy and scruffy due to the irregular position of lobes and branching. Lobe edges turned up and blister-like isidia on the thallus add to its dishevelled appearance. Isidia are numerous, globose, the same colour as the thallus and grow out to the lobe margins. Apothecia are common and small with the disc reaching a diameter of 1.5mm. Disc rims are usually thickened (but may be thin) and smooth. Spores become muriform, 15–25 x 6–12μm. Spot Tests: None for *Collema*. Nature Notes: Takes on a translucent pale to dark olive green colour when wet but does not swell much. Prefers hard limestone rocks and is common in the Burren. It is also found on asbestos. Confusion: With *Collema auriforme*, which is thinner and darker with more globose isidia.

Collema multipartitum – foliose, crustose (jelly)

Description: Thallus is dull green to black and highly branched. Loosely attached to the substrate, it regularly grows in rosettes often reaching a diameter of 10cm. Central regions have a tendency to grow up from the substrate in a mat of convex lobes, while the edge, where the branching is more obvious, is tidy and shows regular and repeated branching. Brittle lobes are narrow, just 1–2mm wide. It lacks isidia. Apothecia are common and grow in a scattered fashion across the thallus. Discs are flat to convex and develop to less than 2mm in diameter. Rims are thick, entire and sometimes crenulate. Spores are ellipsoid, 3–septate and 26–43 x 4.5–6.5μm. Spot Tests: None for *Collema*. 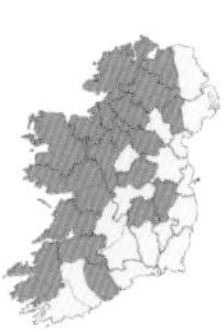
Nature Notes: Found on hard limestone in exposed sunny locations, often in association with *Collema polycarpon*. It is prolific in the Burren.

Collema nigrescens – foliose, crustose (jelly)

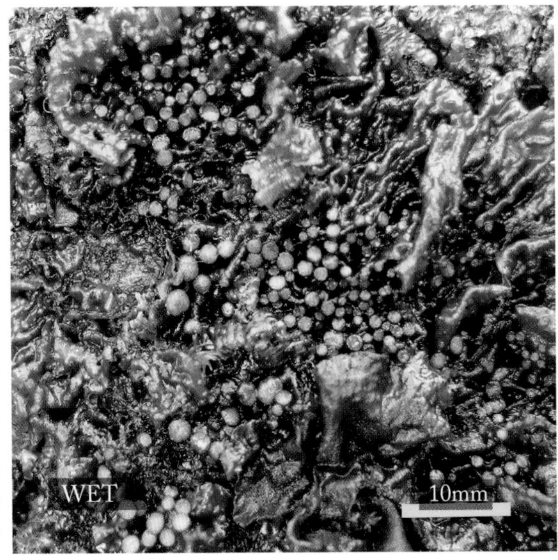

DESCRIPTION: Thallus is flat and develops in a circular form if left unrestricted, reaching a diameter of around 10cm. Brown when dry and dark olive green when wet. Lobes are typically 5–10mm in width and contain radiating ridges with many small blisters and isidia. Circular apothecia are common and reach a diameter of 1mm. Discs are flat to convex. Rim margins are thalline, narrow and on close examination may be isidiate. Spores are 4–12 septate and show a size range of 50–90 x 3–4.5μm.

SPOT TESTS: None for *Collema.*

NATURE NOTES: Tends to occur on nutrient rich bark, especially near the coast. The specimen here was photographed on a horizontal branch in a farming area of Killarney. It is considered a rare species in Ireland.

CONFUSION: With *Collema subnigrescens* which lacks isidia and with *Collema furfuraceum* which typically lacks apothecia and has numerous isidia.

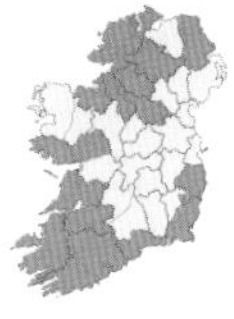

Collema polycarpon – foliose, crustose (jelly)

DESCRIPTION: The dark green to black thallus is crowded with apothecia. Lobes are narrow (1–2.3mm wide), relatively thick and grow in a compact crowded manner, radiating from the centre to produce circular rosettes between 2–6cm in diameter. The central area of the rosette bulges up above the rest of the thallus. There are no isidia. Apothecia sit on tiny stalks, long enough to make them stand proud of the thallus. These occur most frequently towards the edge of the thallus. Their narrow rims are smooth and are the same colour as the thallus. Discs are flat to convex and range from 0.5–1.5mm in diameter.

SPOT TESTS: None for *Collema.*

NATURE NOTES: Found on hard limestone in damp exposed and humid habitats. It is associated with *Collema multipartitum.*

CONFUSION: With *C. cristatum.*

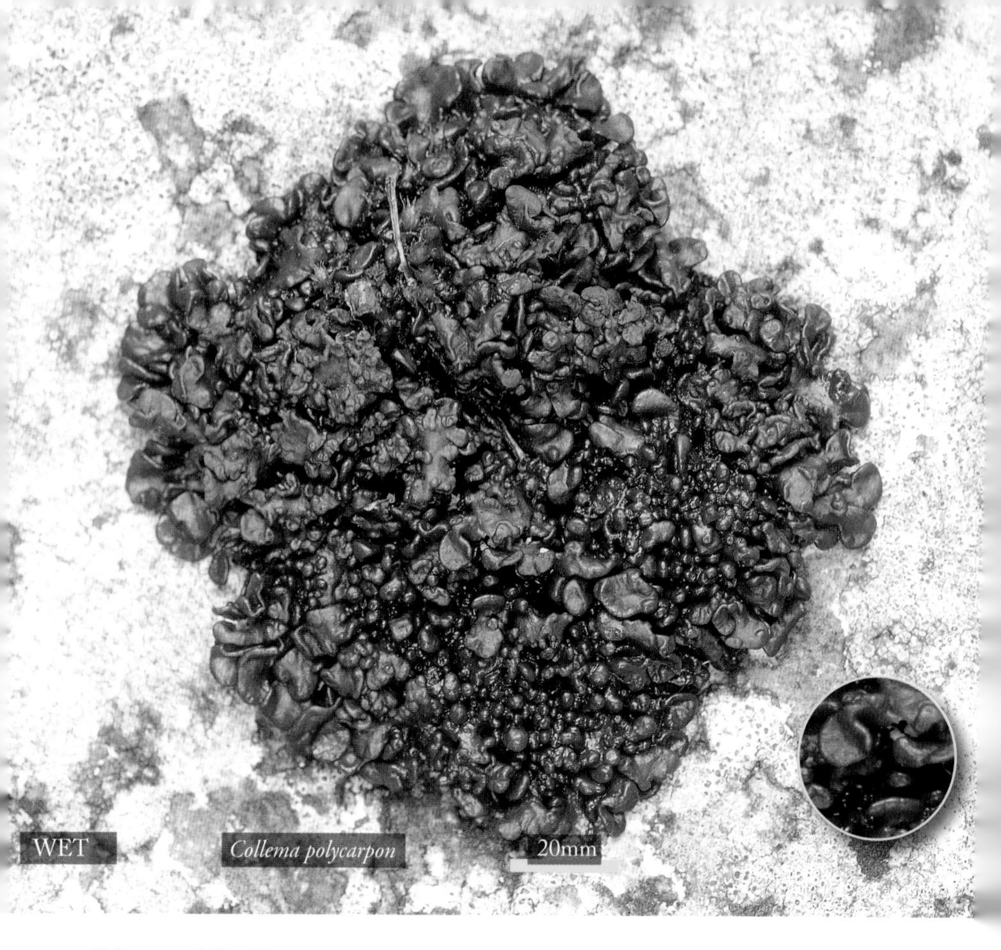

Collema subflaccidum – foliose, crustose (jelly)

DESCRIPTION: Almost black thallus looks unkempt due to a high density of isidia and folded crumpled lobes. Lobes are large (2–6mm) relative to the size of the whole thallus, which rarely develops above 6cm in diam. Lobes either lack or have few isidia, providing a smooth surface. Edges are generally rounded, but some appear tattered. Isidia are bead-like and have the same colour as the thallus. Apothecia are rare. Spores, 40–55 x 5–7μm 5–7 septate.

SPOT TESTS: None for *Collema.*

NATURE NOTES: Prefers basic barked trees in sheltered damp places, especially ash.

CONFUSION: With *Collema flaccidum*, which is larger.

Collema tenax – foliose, crustose (jelly)

Description: Thallus is black when dry. When wet it swells and takes on a brown to dark olive green colour. The edges are characteristically irregular and sometimes ascending. Frequently forms neat radiating rosettes where it has the space. The centre of the thallus is regularly folded over on itself increasing the height of the centre. Wide lobes (≤1cm) are isidiate and granular. Pycnidia are frequent. Apothecia are sometimes abundant often obscuring the thallus. They reach a diameter of 3mm, are often deeply convex and have a distinct and characteristic red-brown colour. Discs are smooth, as are the rims, although they may become warted. Spores are 15–25 x 6–10μm.

Spot Tests: None for *Collema.*

Nature Notes: Found on basic or calcareous soils and mortar often occurring on the north side of limestone walls around graveyards and churches. It is a common *Collema* and is very variable in form. Easiest to recognise with wet. Four different morphologies exist in Ireland. (i) var. *ceranoides* has many thin ascending lobes and rarely displays apothecia, (ii) var. *corallinum* has apothecia and more crustose than the others (rare in Ireland). (iv) var. *vulgare* has short plump convex lobes and many apothecia.

Degelia atlantica – foliose, squamulose

DESCRIPTION: The fan-shaped metallic grey-blue thallus is adpressed and thins towards its centre. Lobes are thick, smooth and shiny near the margins, with a dense black tomentose underside, often protruding around the thickened edges. Lobes grow radially from the centre and are round at the outer margins where they may turn upwards. Apothecia (≤0.5mm) are very rare. Discs are flat to convex and dark red in colour with paler rims. Isidia are numerous and nodular in appearance, giving an untidy and granular aspect. Longitudinal striae are rare.
SPOT TESTS: None. NATURE NOTES: A typical old woodland indicator species. It is happiest in humid shaded mossy woodlands, especially hazel. Found only in the west of Ireland.
CONFUSION: With *Degelia plumbea* and *Degelia cyanoloma.*

Degelia cyanoloma – foliose, squamulose

DESCRIPTION: Has a thick fan shaped thallus, pale to bluish grey and loosely attached to the substrate. It is rather smooth and shiny and lacks squamules in the central region. Grows larger than any other *Degelia* species. Isidia are absent. Lobes turn up at the margins and have longitudinal striae on over 70% of specimens, with curved transverse ridges. Apothecia are common and sometimes form in groups. Discs are plum red to black, but may turn bright red. Rims are black and smooth. Laminal pycnidia may occur.
SPOT TESTS: None. NATURE NOTES: Occurs in oceanic hazel woods on both bark and rock. Sometimes called the 'western plum' lichen. Distribution needs reevaluation.
CONFUSION: With *Degelia atlantica* and *Degelia plumbea.*

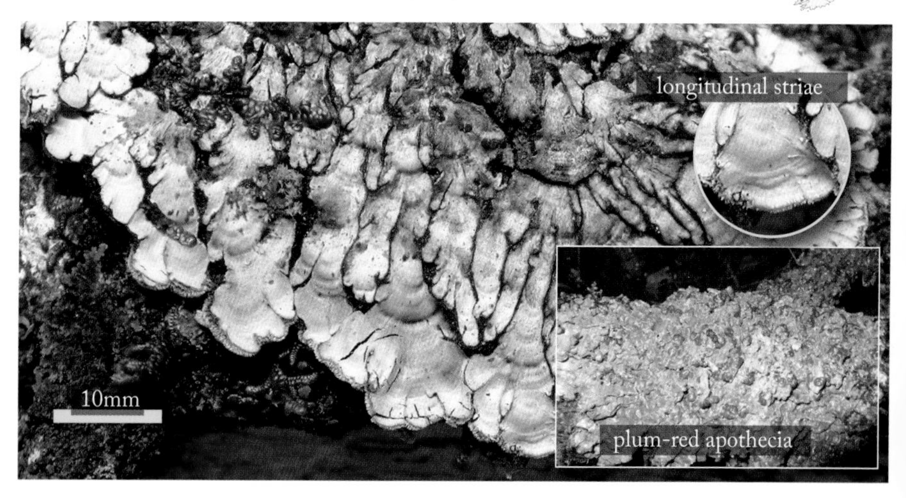

Degelia ligulata – foliose, squamulose

DESCRIPTION: Thallus is steel grey, large (≤10cm diam.) rigid and thick. Lobes are smooth, with distinct radial ridges. Colour may develop to dark grey due to an abundance of small (≤1mm) reproductive scales (schizidia). Apothecia are very rare and ≤0.5mm in diameter with brown to black discs and have a paler rim. Unlike *D. atlantica* it lacks isidia. SPOT TESTS: None.

NATURE NOTES: Rare in Ireland, confined to coastal areas that are exposed to sea mists. Grows on silica-rich rocks and young trees.

Degelia plumbea – foliose, squamulose

DESCRIPTION: Thallus is large (≤10cm diam.) and light grey to steel blue in colour. Marginal lobes have crescent shaped ridges that often develop to a reticulation pattern. The underside has a well developed hypothallus that appears 'furry' and protrudes just beyond the margin of the upper surface. There are no isidia, but has abundant brown-red apothecia. Rims become hidden or excluded as they mature. SPOT TESTS: None.

NATURE NOTES: Occurs on basic bark and silica-poor rocks in well lit woodlands (oceanic type) and scrub habitats. Distribution needs reevaluation.

CONFUSION: With *Degelia ligulata*.

DERMATOCARPON – 5 SPECIES RECORDED IN IRELAND.

Dermatocarpon miniatum – foliose

DESCRIPTION: Thallus is attached to the substrate by a single holdfast. Lobes vary in size, from 10–75mm, and readily grow in a circular pattern, often incised, giving a multi-lobed appearance. Surface has a whitish powdery or pruinose appearance. Thalline colour varies from reddish brown to grey to dark brown. Dark brown perithecia cover the surface. Lower surface lacks rhizines, but may show small blisters or ridges. Lobes are concave and incised. Spores are colourless and single celled, ellipsoidal and packed at 8 per ascus: 10–14 x 5–6μm. SPOT TESTS: Negative.

NATURE NOTES: Occurs on calcareous rocks on seashores and lakes, often in water run-off fissures.

CONFUSION: With *Dermatocarpon intestiniforme*, which is multi-lobed.

Dimerella – 2 species recorded in Ireland.

Dimerella lutea – crustose

Description: The thin and short lived thallus is rarely visible. When present, it has a light grey tint, sometimes going grey-green. Apothecia are very distinctive in both colour and texture; yellow-orange and shiny when wet and vivid yellow and matt when dry. They grow as large as 2mm in diameter. Discs are concave to flat and rarely convex. Rims are often wavy and paler in colour than the discs, which may have a translucent appearance, particularly when wet. Pale yellow pycnidia are also present. Spores, 9–15 x 2–4μm.

Spot Tests: Negative.

Nature Notes: Grows typically among mosses on the bark of trees in old woodlands that are damp and shaded. Occasionally it is found among moss on soil or siliceous rocks. Thallus often acts to bind the moss together, almost like a cobweb covering.

Diploicia – 1 species recorded in Ireland.

Diploicia canescens – crustose, placodioid

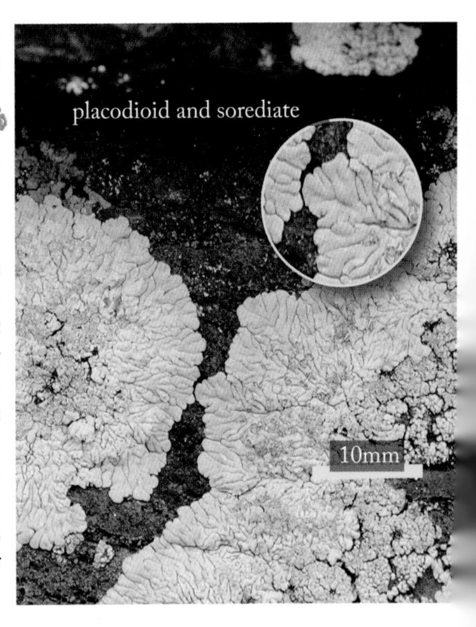

Description: Thallus is white to light grey-green throughout and frequently takes on a fan-like shape of 40–55mm diam. Central area is dusty or sorediate and often green due to the photobiont chlorococcid. Narrow radiating convex lobes are distinctive around the edge of the thallus (placodioid) and are often a bluish grey-green colour. Thallus may die away towards the centre. Apothecia are small and rare, but when present tend to be near the centre of the thallus. They lack rims and the discs themselves are black. Pycnidia usually immersed in the thallus. Spores are septate and dark in colour: 9–15 x 2–4μm.

Spot Tests: C–, Pd–, K+ yellow, KC+ yellow. UV± dull yellow.

Nature Notes: Found throughout Ireland, especially along the coast, near farms and other nutrient rich areas. Tolerant of pollution.

Diplotomma – 4 species recorded in Ireland.

Diplotomma alboatrum – crustose

Description: The thallus is chalky white to grey and rather lumpy. Apothecia are numerous and range from small (≤1mm diam.) immature ones to larger mature types. Discs are flat to convex and characteristically pruinose. Spores are colourless or brown and 3–septate. 15–20 x 8–12μm.

Spot Tests: Negative.

Nature Notes: Found throughout Ireland in coastal areas, particularly on limestone and schists. Has a preference for calcareous stonework (old walls, churches and monuments). Also found on coarse nutrient-rich basic bark of deciduous trees such as *Ulmus* and *Fraxinus*. It is sometimes found as a parasite on *Caloplaca* and *Xanthoria* species.

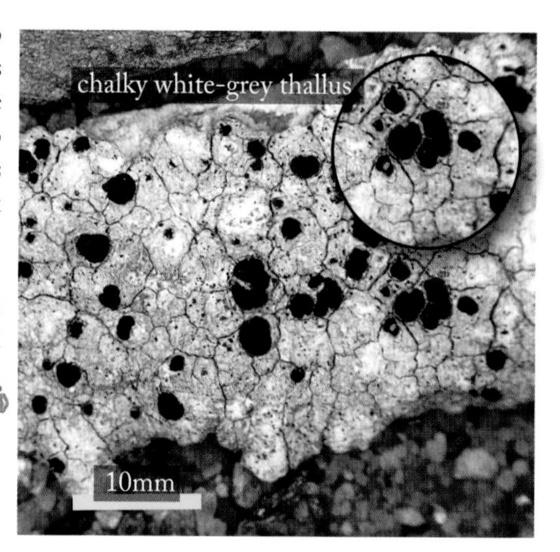

Enterographa – 5 species recorded in Ireland.

Enterographa crassa – crustose

Description: Thallus is very variable in colour and texture. Frequently olive green with creamy patches, it may also be grey to grey-brown. Texture varies from smooth to lumpy, with irregular cracking (rimose). Thallus may be thin or thick. Mosaics show a distinct brown (or sometimes black) prothallus, delimiting the various individuals. Apothecia are numerous, small and very variable in shape, ranging from circular to wavy and thread-like; they are rimless and immersed in the thallus. Pycnidia are common. Spores, 20–40 x 4–7μm.

Spot Tests: Thallus: C–, K–, Pd–. UV–.

Nature Notes: This is a very common mosaic forming lichen in Ireland, occurring on the lower part of the main bole of broadleaved trees and large shrubs in shaded woodlands. It is tolerant of low light conditions. Ireland's frequent cloud cover suits it very well. It is also tolerant of moderate levels of air pollution. May occur on siliceous rocks.

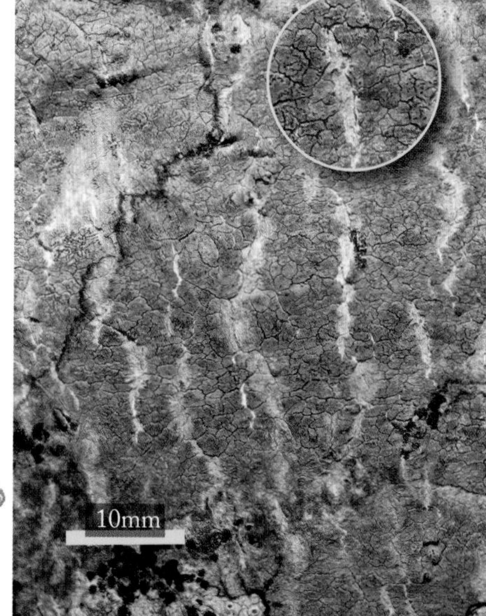

Ephebe – 2 species recorded in Ireland.

Ephebe lanata – fruticose, filamentous

Description: Thallus is composed of shiny hair-like filamentous strands that show very little branching. Its dark colour ranges from almost black to dark olive green. Thalli grow to 20–30mm wide. Apothecia are rare, but when present occur on the hairs as nodules concolorous with the thallus. Spores, 10–20 x 4–6μm.

Spot Tests: No lichen products detected.

Nature Notes: Likes damp humid areas such as stream banks and in ravines, particularly on flat seepage rocks or boulders. It commonly overgrows other lichens.

Confusion: With *Pseudephebe pubescens* (not treated in this book), which has softer textures and is found on siliceous rocks in upland areas.

Evernia – 1 species recorded in Ireland.

Evernia prunastri – foliose, appears fruticose

Description: Thallus is pendulous to semi-erect, feels soft and reaches a length of 10cm. Strap-like lobes grow to 6mm wide and 1mm thick. Colour varies from green-grey to yellow-grey on the upper surface; the lower surface is characteristically white. Sometimes green blotches may be seen near the ends of lobes. Pycnidia are common and lobes may be twisted and/or branched (antler-like) with the edges covered in soredia. Apothecia are stalked and very rare; dark red discs grow to 3mm in diam. Spores, 7–11 x 4–6μm.

Spot Tests: Cortex: K+ yellow. Medulla: C–, K–, KC–, Pd–. UV–.

Nature Notes: Thrives on acid to neutral tree trunks in sunny areas such as wayside trees, parklands and hedgerows. Found also on wooden fences, gates and sometimes on the stems of heather (*Calluna*).

Confusion: With *Ramalina farinacea*.

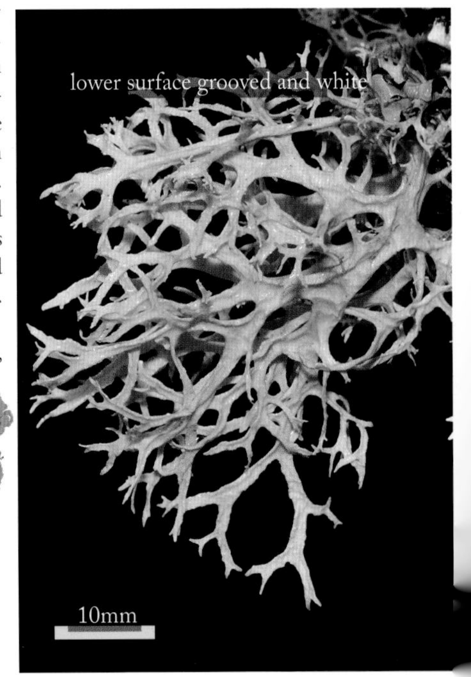

FLAVOPARMELIA – 2 species recorded in Ireland. Similar to *Parmotrema* species.

Flavoparmelia caperata – foliose

DESCRIPTION: Thallus is large, conspicuous and pale green, green yellow to green-grey in colour. It can reach a size of 20cm in diam., especially on siliceous rocks. Lobes range in size from 5–13mm and are round at the tips, sometimes with indents. It has a corrugated appearance. Apothecia are rare. They are relatively large, growing up to 8mm in diameter, with rust red discs and sorediate margins. Rims are the same colour as the thallus. Coarse granular soralia inhabit the central area of the thallus. The lower surface is black apart from the very edge. Rhizines are present, but absent from the edge. Spores are ellipsoid, 15–20 x 9–10μm.

SPOT TESTS: K–, C–, KC± red, Pd+ red. UV–.

NATURE NOTES: It is sensitive to SO_2 pollution and has a liking for acidic bark and silica-rich rocks. Found countrywide in towns on memorials, fences, trees, roofs, coastal turf and overgrowing mosses on trees. It turns grey in shaded areas.

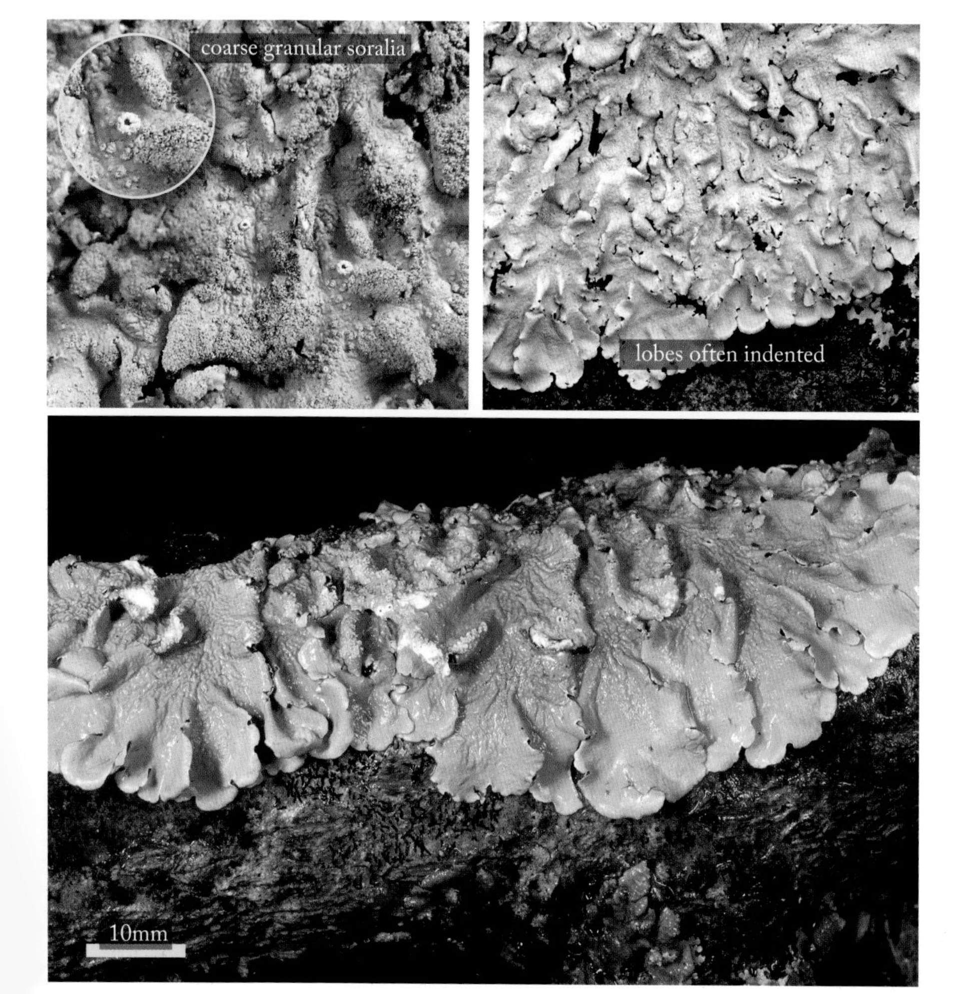

Flavoparmelia soredians – foliose

Description: Thallus is grey to yellow-green-grey and tightly adpressed. Typically grows to about 5cm in diameter, but may occasionally reach 10cm. Lobes are narrower than other *Flavoparmelia* species, reaching a width of 7mm. Apothecia are very rare. Fine powdery soredia often fuse to form large soredate patches.

Spot Tests: Cortex: K–. Medulla: C–, K+ yellow → red, KC+ red, Pd+ orange. UV–.

Nature Notes: Occurs on both basic and acidic bark on broad leaved trees, especially in parklands, wayside trees and near the coast. Also found on walls, fences and old monuments.

Fuscidea – 10 species recorded in Ireland.

Fuscidea cyathoides – crustose

Description: Often found forming large mosaics. The prothallus is dark brown to black. Thallus surface itself varies from grey to mouse brown and is cracked and areolate. Pycnidia are abundant, usually brown in colour, sometimes immersed. Apothecia are small and usually immersed. Narrow rims, paler than the dark, flat to convex discs. Spores, 9–12 x 4–6μm.

Spot Tests: K+ dirty yellow, Pd+ red. UV–.

Nature Notes: Occur on siliceous rocks often forming mosaics. The Pd+ red test will distinguish it from other *Fuscidea* in Ireland.

Fuscopannaria – 2 species recorded in Ireland.

Fuscopannaria sampaiana – squamulose

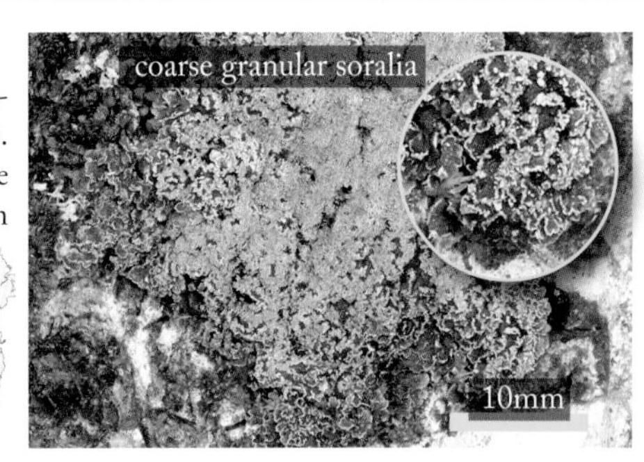

Description: Thallus is blue-black and composed of thick squamules, rounded at the ends. Hypothallus is blue-black and can be seen at the edges. Granular dirty yellow soralia may form extensive patches over the thallus.

Spot Test: None.

Nature Notes: Occurs on mossy, basic barked trees, especially ash or elm. An old woodland indicator.

Graphina – 3 species recorded in Ireland.

Graphina anguina – crustose

Description: Thallus is thin and often smooth, although may become a little cracked when mature. Colour ranges from grey-white to silver-white. Apothecia are flat with the surface, or just slightly raised above it. They may be rather long and serpentine, almost curling around each other in a dense grouping, or short and straight or slightly curved. Rims are black and not furrowed, while discs tend to be pruinose.
Spores, 25–50 x 12–15μm.
Spot Tests: None.
Nature Notes: A very dramatic lichen when a good serpentine specimen is discovered. Occurs on smooth bark in both shaded and well lit locations such as wayside trees and around the edge of woodlands.
Confusion: With *Graphis scripta* although *Graphis scripta* never reaches such serpentine lengths.

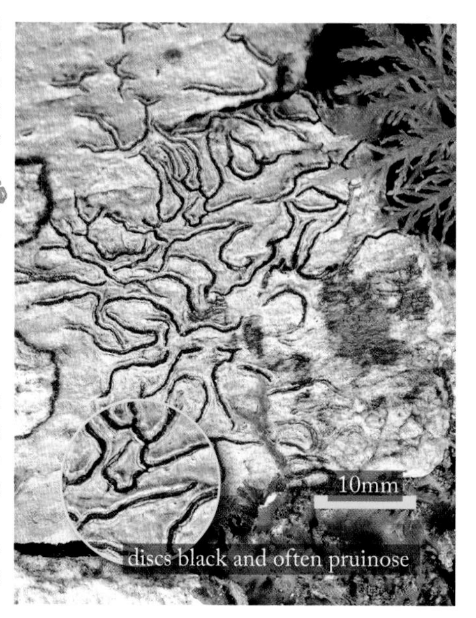

Graphis – 2 species recorded in Ireland. The 'script' or 'writing' lichens.

Graphis elegans – crustose

Description: Apothecia are elongated (lirellae) and rather variable, being either short or long and frequently curved and branched. Apothecial rims are black to lead grey, with between 1 to 6 furrows outside the slit-like disc. Discs are never pruinose. Despite the variation in size and shape of the apothecia, the furrows or ridges are characteristic features. Thallus is smooth, slightly cracked and often a little glossy. It takes on various tones of light grey. Young specimens may not have developed lirellae ridges. Spores are colourless 30–50 x 6–12μm.
Spot Tests: C–, K+ red (distinguishes it from *G. scripta)*, Pd+ yellow → orange. UV–.
Nature Notes: Occurs on a wide range of trees with smooth or moderately rough bark in shaded areas.

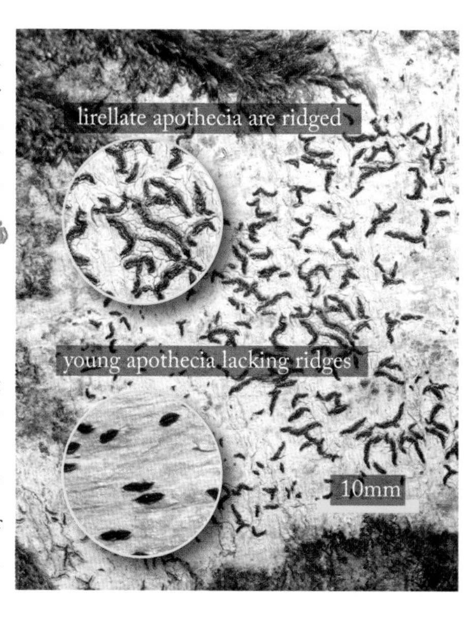

Graphis scripta – crustose

DESCRIPTION: Elongated black apothecia form the 'writing' (graphis) found on many trees. Lirellae are elongated, pointed at their ends, irregular and either simple or branched. They appear as if they erupted through the thallus (erumpent), leaving it pushed back out of place. Elongated discs are white pruinose. Pycnidia are rare. Thallus is smooth to slightly uneven and varies from white to grey, with some tinting of green. Spores, 25–70 x 6–10μm. SPOT TESTS: Pd–.
NATURE NOTES: It is an indicator of old woodlands. Prefers the shaded dry aspect of twigs, branches and tree trunks.
CONFUSION: With *Graphis elegans*.

GYALECTA – 4 species recorded in Ireland.

Gyalecta jenensis – crustose

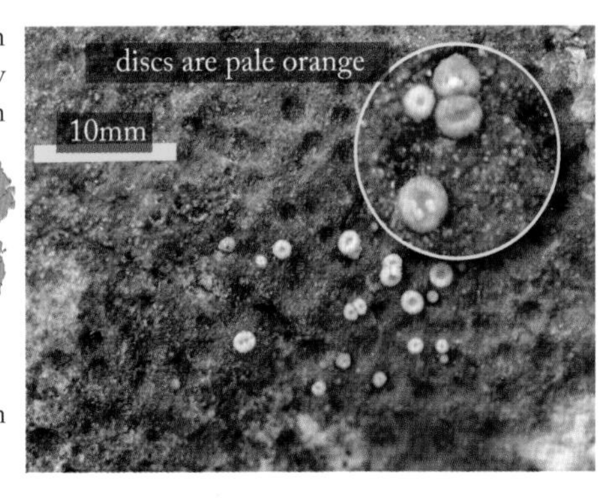

DESCRIPTION: Thallus tends to be thin with an orange-pink colour, becoming grey, possibly with age. The sessile apothecia are small (≤1mm diam.) and numerous, with a thin rim. Discs are pale orange with a translucent appearance. Apothecia have the colour and texture of a cooked shrimp. Spores, 12–25 x 6–10μm.
SPOT TESTS: Negative.
NATURE NOTES: Occurs on hard limestone in damp shaded areas, usually on slopes.

HERTELIANA – 1 species recorded in Ireland.

Herteliana gagei – crustose

DESCRIPTION: Thallus is thick and cream coloured, developing extensive patches up to 30cm diam. Texture is smooth to cracked. Prothallus may be present and if so, is black and well defined. Small apothecia (≤0.8mm) are ruby red and highly convex. Spores, 18–22 x 8–10μm.
SPOT TESTS: K+ yellow, KC+ yellow. UV–.
NATURE NOTES: Prefers damp silica-rich rocks and boulders in shaded oceanic woodlands.

Hypocenomyce – 2 species recorded in Ireland.

Hypocenomyce scalaris – squamulose

Description: Thallus is composed of grey-green squamules (1–2mm in length) sometimes turning olive brown and even dark brown in exposed areas. Squamules turn up at the edges, giving them a convex appearance. They do not merge together but remain separate. The turned up edges may be covered by soredia, giving them a white colour. This white sorediate colour may also be seen on the underside of the squamules. Apothecia are rare; they have a black disc and vary in size from 1.5 –2.5mm. Discs may be covered in white pruina.

Spot Tests: Thallus: C+ red, K–, KC+ red, Pd–.
Medulla and soralia: UV+ white.

Nature Notes: Found on the acid bark of coniferous trees, especially in pine woodlands. Also occurs on walls, in graveyards, on siliceous rocks, dead wood and boulders in woodlands.

Hypogymnia – 2 species recorded in Ireland.

Hypogymnia physodes – foliose

Description: Thallus is loosely attached, grey to yellowish green in colour and forms large irregular patches (<10cm). Hollow lobes are 2–3mm wide. The outer edge turns up and is frequently covered with white powdery soredia underneath. Lower surface is black, wrinkled and has some browning towards the lobe margins. Pycnidia are black and abundant. They create a pepper-like effect across the upper surface. Apothecia are rare. Discs are red-brown with narrow rims.

Spot Tests: Cortex: K+ yellow. Medulla and soralia: C–, K–, KC+ red, Pd+ orange to red. UV+ pale violet.

Nature Notes: Prefers acid substrates such as the bark of larch, *Salix* and *Calluna*. Also occurs on peaty soil, old wooden posts and silica-rich rocks. Sensitive to SO_2 levels.

Hypogymnia tubulosa – foliose

DESCRIPTION: Thallus consists of a network of matt overlapping concave branches, loosely attached to the substrate. It varies in colour from bluish grey through greeny grey to mineral grey. Individual branches are 2–4mm wide and specimens can grow to 80mm in length, with the thallus taking on a wrinkled or rough appearance towards the centre. Lobes around the perimeter are finger or tube shaped and rise upwards from the substrate, giving a semi-erect appearance. The tubular lobes also fan out at the tips and are covered with soralia. Apothecia rarely occur. Under-surface of the thallus is almost black in colour and lacks rhizines. Soredia are abundant and form blanket-like or ring-shaped soralia over the lobe tips.
SPOT TESTS: K+ yellow, KC+ red. UV+ purple.
NATURE NOTES: It tends to favour an acidic substrate such as siliceous rocks, trees and *Calluna* (heather) stems, showing a wide range of habitats from the sea shore to uplands. Sometimes grows with *Hypogymnia physodes*, which is less common. It is an indicator of old growth forests. Produces an anti-bacterial substance.
CONFUSION: *Hypogymnia* is superficially similar to *Parmelia* species.

HYPOTRACHYNA – 6 SPECIES RECORDED IN IRELAND.

Hypotrachyna laevigata – foliose

DESCRIPTION: Loosely attached to the substrate, the lobes are rather angular and usually dichotomously branched; irregular branching may occur. Lobe surface is smooth and shiny, coloured blue-green with blackened granular laminal soralia. Pycnidia are also scattered across the lobes. Apothecia are stalked with dark brown discs and very rare. Under-surface is black, turning brown near the margins and highly branched rhizines. When scratched, the medulla shows white. Spores, 18–21 x 9–13μm.
SPOT TESTS: Cortex: K+ yellow. Medulla: C+ orange, K–, KC+ orange, Pd–. UV± blush grey.
NATURE NOTES: Found in high rainfall areas on acidic barked trees such as holly, alder, oak and birch. Grows over moss on both trees and rocks.
CONFUSION: With *H. revoluta* which is C+ pink, and *H. sinuosa*.

Hypotrachyna revoluta – foliose

Description: Thallus is extensively lobed with a smooth to matt texture that ranges in colour from light-grey to green-grey. It can form extensive patches and may be loosely or tightly adpressed. Lobes look slightly burned or singed around the edges. The term 'revoluta' refers to the downturned edges of the lobes. Lobes are also indented, often slightly overlapping and lack any network of fine lines. Soredia form across the upper surface and develop particularly well near the lobe edges, where they may take on a black tint. The under-surface is black with simple or branched rhizines (rare). Some large rhizines near the lobe edges may appear as cilia. Apothecia are very rare with discs developing to about 6mm; the rims may be sorediate.

Spot Tests: Cortex: K+ yellow. Medulla: C+ pink, K–, KC+ red, Pd–. UV–.

Nature Notes: Found on moderately acidic trees in open woodlands and on wayside trees. Also found on rocks. Sensitive to SO_2 pollution.

Confusion: With *Parmelia saxatilis* (which has square-cut lobes) and *Parmotrema perlatum* (which has few or no rhizines).

Hypotrachyna sinuosa – foliose

Description: A leafy angular lichen, the thallus grows to about 6cm in diameter. Lobes reach a width of 3mm and branch dichotomously. The upper surface is smooth with a yellow-grey-green colour. Each lobe is distinct, although frequently overlapping neighbouring lobes. They widen towards the apices, which often turn up to display powdery soralia. The underside is black with many rhizines that show dichotomous branching. Rhizines frequently protrude around the rim of the lobes. Apothecia and pycnidia have not been recorded in Ireland.

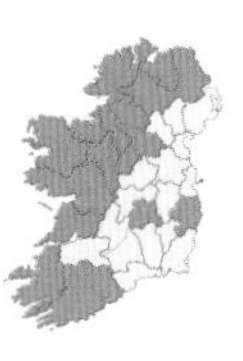

Spot Tests: Cortex: K–. Medulla: C–, K+ yellow → red, KC+ red, Pd+ orange. UV–.

Nature Notes: Likes a damp, well lit habitat such as around woodlands. Substrate includes silica-rich rocks and acidic bark, especially twigs and small smooth branches. Often associated with willow and hazel. Found mainly in the west and north of Ireland.

Confusion: With *Hypotrachyna laevigata*.

Icmadophila – 1 species recorded in Ireland.

Icmadophila ericetorum – crustose

Description: Thallus has a distinct vibrant green colour when wet and is blue-grey when dry. It is composed of many small soft granules crowded together, forming continuous patches. Sometimes seen growing over other lichens. Apothecia are large and distinctive; yellow discs are smooth and shiny when wet. They tend to grow out over the rim, hiding it completely. Discs may be slightly pruinose and reacts with K → orange. Rims, when visible, are lighter in colour than the yellow discs (although they may be the same colour). Spores, 13–27 x 4–6μm.

Spot Tests: Thallus: K+ orange, KC+ orange, Pd+ orange, C–. UV+glaucous. Apothecia: K+ orange and UV–.

Nature Notes: Thrives in damp areas (*Icmadophila* = 'damp loving') such as moorlands, undisturbed peat bogs and rotting tree stumps.

Confusion: Superficially similar to *Dibaeis baeomyces*, which has apothecia on stalks.

Ionaspis – 1 species recorded in Ireland.

Ionaspis lacustris – crustose

Description: Thallus is thin and buttery yellow to reddish brown in colour. Generally smooth, rimose (cracked) near apothecia. Prothallus is lighter in colour than the thallus and turns dark red-brown in mosaics. Apothecia are immersed and very small, ranging from 0.15–0.4mm in diam. Rims are raised slightly and lighter in colour than the orange discs.

Spot Tests: None.

Nature Notes: Occurs along the banks of fast flowing streams on silica-rich rocks, especially in uplands where they are regularly submerged. An amphibious species, frequently associated with *Rhizocarpon lavatum* which has larger apothecia.

Japewiella – 1 species recorded in Ireland.

Japewiella tavaresiana – crustose

Description: Thallus is powdery white and frequently indistinct due to being immersed in bark. Prothallus is dark brown to black. It does not form mosaics. Apothecia are abundant, deep red to purple to black in colour and <0.5mm in diam. Discs are flat. Spores, 13–18 x 8–10μm.
Spot Tests: K± yellow.
Nature Notes: Found on smooth bark of young trees and twigs, especially happy growing on willow around lakes. Frequently accompanied by *Lecanora jamesii.*

Lecania – 17 species recorded in Ireland. All are crustose or placodioid.

Lecania aipospila – crustose

Description: Forms distinct light purple-grey patches that sometimes merge. Thallus composed of many lumpy papillae and is lobed at the margins, with a pale prothallus turning dark if in contact with a different species. Apothecia are common, with dark discs. Spores, 9–15 x 4–6μm.
Spot tests: Negative.
Nature Notes: Found on silica-rich coastal rocks, particularly near bird perches.

Lecanora – 57 species recorded in Ireland.

Lecanora albescens – crustose

Description: Pearly white fragmented swollen areolate thallus with pink-brown apothecial discs, often pruinose. Thallus may form continuous patches up to about 1cm in size. Frequently appears broken or scattered with a grey tint. Apothecia are common and display a distinct white crenulate rim. Discs vary in colour from pearly pale grey to pearly pink. Spores, 8–15 x 4–6μm.
Spot Tests: K–, C–, KC–, Pd–. UV–.
Nature Notes: Occurs on mortar walls, concrete, old monuments, headstones and hard calcareous rocks in well lit situations.

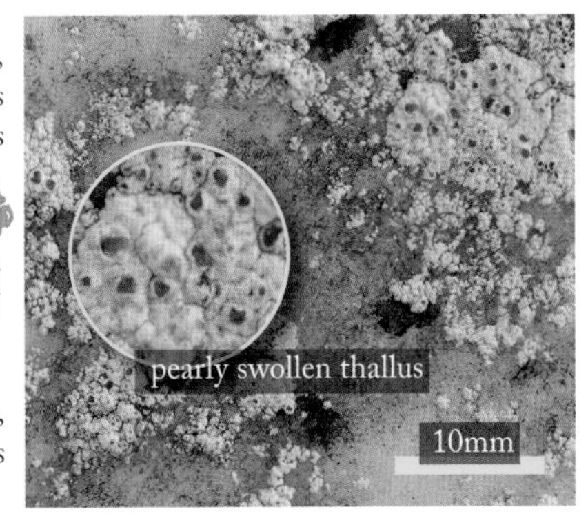

Lecanora carpinea – crustose

Description: Thallus is white to grey and rather smooth, developing cracks towards the centre as it ages. Prothallus is white. Small pruinose apothecia tend to be crowded into groups. Discs are convex and vary in colour from cream to creamy purple to reddish brown. Spores, 10 x 6μm.

Spot Tests: Thallus: K+ (yellow), C–, Pd–. Apothecia: C+ yellow-orange.

Nature Notes: Typically found on smooth bark such as that of twigs and small branches of deciduous trees. Rarely occurs on rocks. Frequently parasitized by the lichenicolous fungus *Sphaerellothecium propinquellum*.

Lecanora chlarotera – crustose

Description: Apothecial discs are brown to reddish brown in colour, with conspicuous grey rims. They are abundant and frequently crowded together, often blocking out the thallus. Thallus is creamy grey in colour and sometimes cracked or areolate. There is no prothallus.

Spot Tests: Thallus: Pd–, K+ yellow. UV+ dull orange. The disc rim is Pd–.

Nature Notes: One of the most common lichens on trees in Ireland. Also occurs on sawn wood. Sometimes grows in lines, following the expansion of bark as a tree expands. It is a background species.

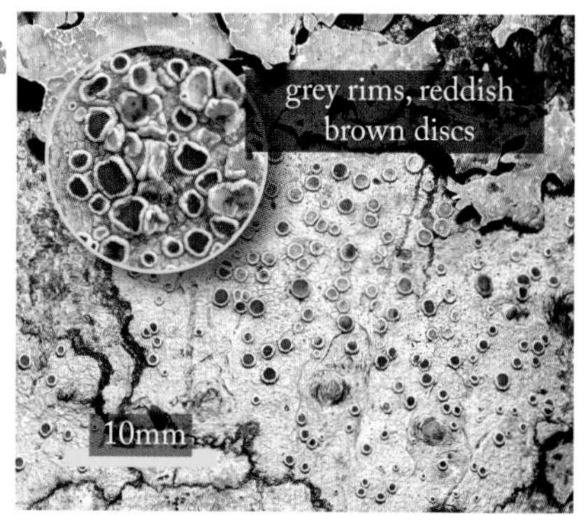

Lecanora gangaleoides – crustose

Description: This is a variable lichen. Thallus is composed of lumpy convex areoles, grey in colour, often with a tint of green. Prothallus is white. Apothecia are common and have characteristic charcoal black discs with thick grey thalline rims or exciples. Exciple may be crenulate or smooth. Spores, 12–15 x 6–8μm.

Spot Test: K+ yellow, Pd+ orange. UV–.

Nature Notes: Occurs on hard silica-rich rocks mainly in coastal areas, but also found locally inland.

Confusion: With *Tephromela atra* which has a whiter thallus and lacks any hint of green.

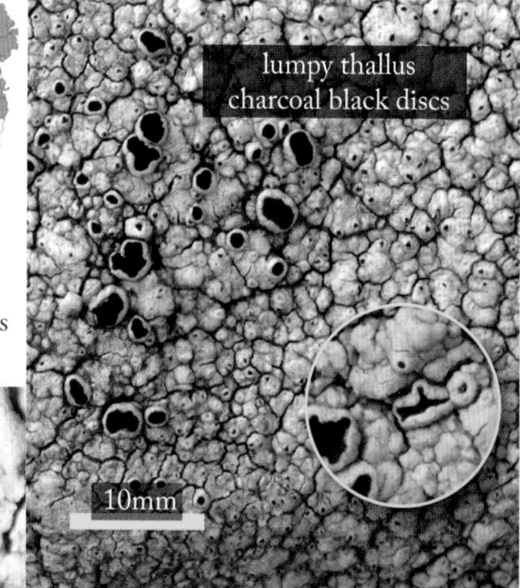

Lecanora muralis – crustose

Description: Thallus tends to be circular, reaching 10cm in diameter. Frequently 'bald' in the central area where the mature areoles die off. Thalline colours are greenish yellow to greenish brown, with a well defined placodioid tightly adpressed prothallus. It may be slightly shiny or pruinose. Apothecia are clustered towards the centre of the thallus and are typically 0.5–1.5mm in diam. Thalline rims are well developed and vary from being complete to crenulate to wavy (flexuose). Discs are yellow to yellow-brown and vary from flat to convex. They are never pruinose.
Spores, 10–15 x 4.5μm.
Spot Tests: Pd+ yellow, K–, KC+ yellowish, C–.
Nature Notes: Occurs on concrete, paving slabs, tarmac and on nutrient rich calcareous rocks.

Lecanora poliophaea – crustose

Description: Thallus is granular, grainy and areolate with a white-green colour. Edges are poorly defined and have a white prothallus. Areoles are variable in size. Apothecia may be abundant, but some lack apothecia altogether. Generally <0.8mm they are variable in appearance, some have a clear thalline rim with a pink-brown to black disc; in others the rim is occluded. Discs are convex and often slightly pruinose. Spores are ellipsoidal, 9–13 x 5–7μm.
Spot Tests: C–, K–, Pd–. UV–.
Nature Notes: Found near large lakes and by the coast, especially on silica-rich rocks in nitrogen-rich areas such as near bird colonies.

Lecanora pulicaris – crustose

Description: Apothecial discs are flat, range in size from 0.3 to 1.5mm. and are reddish brown to black in colour. Apothecial rims are smooth or at times a little lumpy. Thallus takes up a circular growth pattern if unimpeded, reaching 4cm in diam. Central area of the thallus is lumpy or areolate with a crazy-paving appearance. Prothallus ranges from white to dark blue. Spores are ellipsoidal, 11–15 x 7–10μm. Spot Tests: Pd+ orange (most useful test), K+ yellow, KC–, C+. UV+ blue.
Nature Notes: Occurs on bark and sawn wood especially in the nodes between branches.

Lecanora stenotropa – crustose

Description: Thallus is granular to areolate varying from dark brown to green-grey. White prothallus may exist. Apothecia <0.8mm and can be dispersed or in clusters where they push up against each other. Apothecia rims frequently excluded. Discs pale (flat to convex). Spores, 8–12 x 3–4μm. Spot Tests: KC– light yellow. Nature Notes: Likes sandstone (rare on wood) under run-off from mortar. Confusion: With *Lecanora polytropa* which is more common.

Lecanora sulphurea – crustose

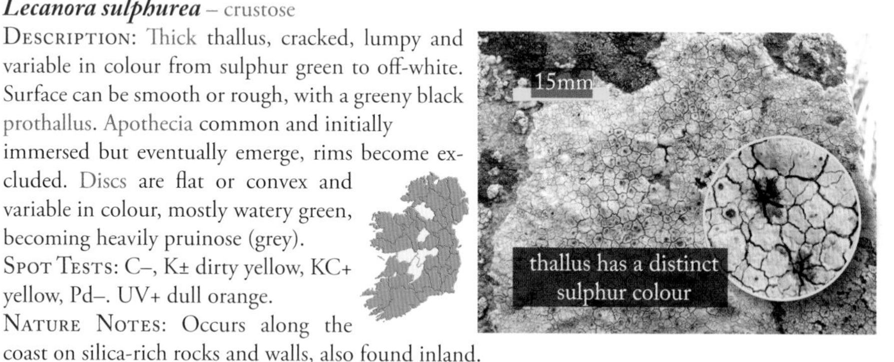

Description: Thick thallus, cracked, lumpy and variable in colour from sulphur green to off-white. Surface can be smooth or rough, with a greeny black prothallus. Apothecia common and initially immersed but eventually emerge, rims become excluded. Discs are flat or convex and variable in colour, mostly watery green, becoming heavily pruinose (grey). Spot Tests: C–, K± dirty yellow, KC+ yellow, Pd–. UV+ dull orange. Nature Notes: Occurs along the coast on silica-rich rocks and walls, also found inland.

Lecanora varia – crustose

Description: Shiny granular creamy white thallus with a green or yellow tinge. Cracked or areolate form when mature. No soralia. Apothecia are circular, cup-shaped with tan discs and smooth or crenulate rims. Spores, 9–16 x 5–8μm. Spot Tests: K–, Pd+ yellow. Nature Notes: Occurs on fences and posts, particularly on well lit horizontal surfaces.

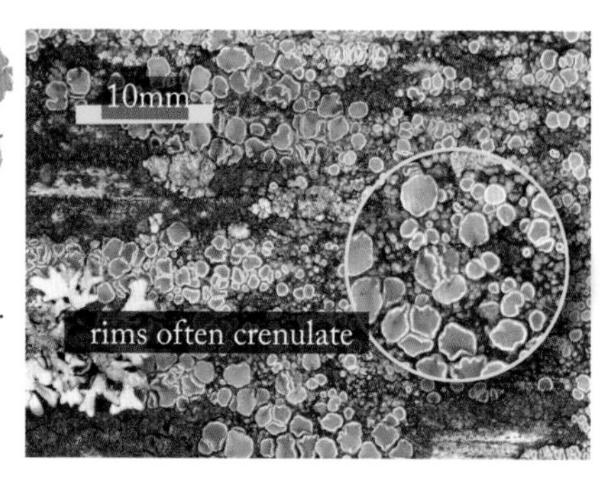

Lecanora zosterae – crustose

Description: Thallus is immersed in the substrate, which is typically dead drift wood or dead sea thrift. Apothecia are ≤3.5mm in diameter and develop in clusters with thin and flattened light grey discs (becoming concave) and thin pale thalline margins. Spores are ellipsoid and colourless: 9–13 x 4–6μm. Spot Tests: Negative. Nature Notes: Occurs on the coast, being found on dead sea thrift stems on exposed shores. It is also found on drift wood and soil.

LECIDELLA – 8 species recorded in Ireland. They are similar to the genus Lecidea.

Lecidella asema – crustose

DESCRIPTION: Thick areolate lumpy thallus is off-white to yellow. Black to brown convex discs on small apothecia, (≤1mm) often exclude a black rim. Prothallus is black.
Spores, 10–13 x 6–9μm.
SPOT TESTS: K+ yellow, C+ orange.
NATURE NOTES: A seashore species occurring on silica-rich rocks. Found occasionally on wood.

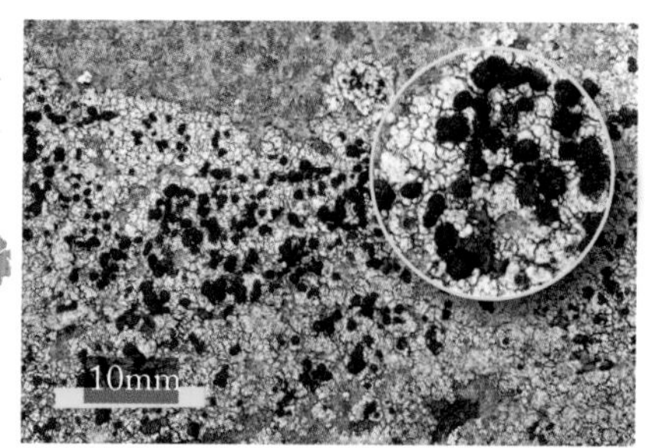

Lecidella elaeochroma – crustose

DESCRIPTION: Thallus is creamy yellow to grey and smooth in texture, turning green when shaded. Prothallus is darker than the thallus, often forming mosaics. Apothecia are small and immersed but later emerge. Discs are flat to convex and become black in well lit areas. Spores, 12 x 8μm.
SPOT TESTS: KC+ yellow, C+ orange. UV+ orange.
NATURE NOTES: Occurs on shrubs, fences, twigs and small branches with smooth bark.

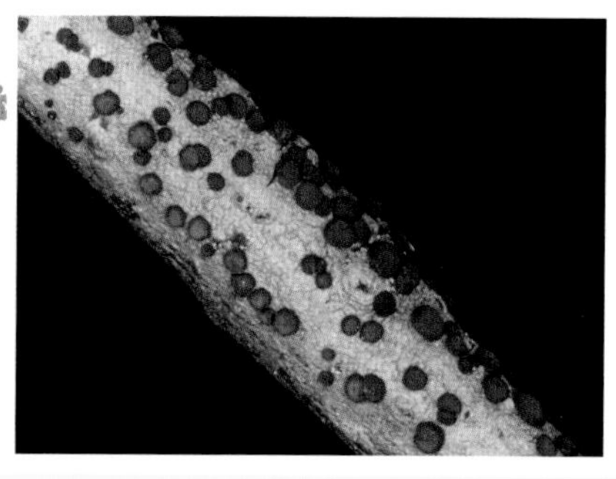

LEPRARIA – 18 species recorded in Ireland. Loose hyphae rather unstructured.

Lepraria incana – leprose

DESCRIPTION: Thallus generally luminescent green to grey-green in colour. Powdery looking, as it is composed of tiny fluffy granules, smaller than *L. lobificans* below. It lacks both a medulla (does not scratch white), and apothecia.
SPOT TESTS: Negative. UV+ white.
NATURE NOTES: Likes shaded damp areas and can be found growing on silica-rich rocks and trees.

Lepraria lobificans – leprose

DESCRIPTION: Green granular 'mouldy' looking thallus. When scratched, reveals a white medulla. Granules are variable in size with an abundance of large ones (relative to *L. incana* above). Apothecia unknown. SPOT TESTS: K– but may show light yellow. C–, Pd+ orange.
NATURE NOTES: Prefers a more calcareous substrate than *Lepraria incana*. Grows on damp shaded cliff overhangs, old buildings, trees, soil and moss.

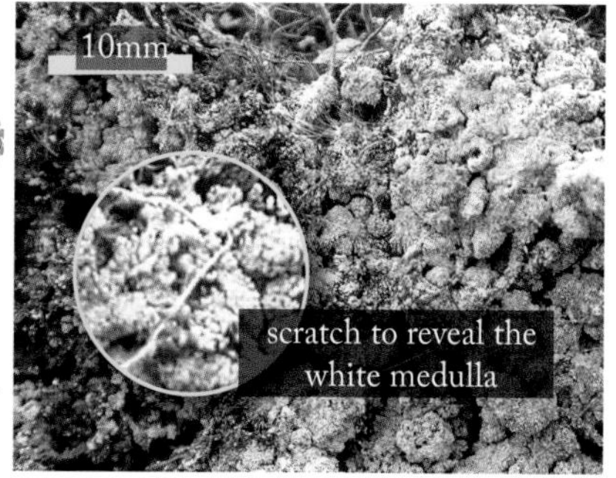

LEPROCAULON – 1 RECORDED IN IRELAND. SIMILAR TO LEPRARIA.

Leprocaulon microscopicum – leprose

DESCRIPTION: The primary thallus has a watery green colour and powdery or leprose texture. The secondary thallus grows out of the primary one. This consists of tiny (1–2mm tall) white finger-like structures called pseudopodia. They are covered with minute white granules.

SPOT TESTS: UV–.

NATURE NOTES: Occurs in coastal habitats, especially on silica-rich rocks. Separated from the *Lepraria* group by tiny white pseudopodia.

LEPTOGIUM – 20 RECORDED IN IRELAND. 'JELLY LICHENS' LACK A CORTEX.

Leptogium brebissonii – crustose to foliose

DESCRIPTION: A gelatinous lichen with distinct brain-like wavy ridges (whether wet or dry), covered in coarse brown granulose isidia. Thalline colour varies from grey-black when dry to green when wet and jelly-like. The lower surface is similar to the upper, but paler. It lacks a tomentum. Apothecia have not been recorded in Irish specimens.

SPOT TESTS: No spot tests.

NATURE NOTES: This is a rare species, found in wet woodlands on deciduous trees. It has a preference for basic bark. It also occurs on calcareous rocks. Mainly confined to the southwest of Ireland.

Leptogium cochleatum – crustose to foliose

DESCRIPTION: Shiny thallus (when wet) is dark grey to greenish blue in colour. Texture is matt when dry, with gentle elongated ridges. Apothecia are common, with red-brown discs and wrinkled rims. Thalline lobes are tightly packed, overlapping, wavy and may develop to 10cm or more. Spores, 20–30 x 12–16μm.

SPOT TESTS: Negative.

NATURE NOTES: Found in damp, shaded woodlands and on mossy rocks. Occurs on hazel, ash and other basic trees. A rare lichen in Ireland that requires protection.

Leptogium diffractum – crustose foliose

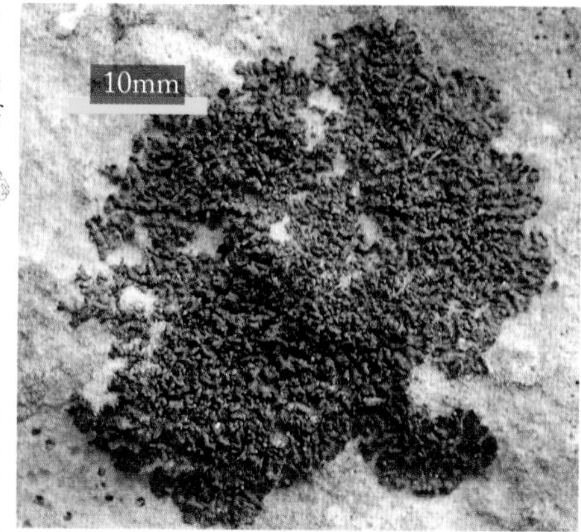

Description: A delicate and discrete thallus, brown in colour, it often forms radiating patterns of 1cm or so on limestone. Lobes are convex to flat, finely divided and tend to be of equal length. Edges are placodioid and tightly adpressed to the substrate, while the centre of the thallus may die away. Apothecia are rarely present.
Spores, 15–30 x 8–12μm.
Spot Test: None.
Natures Notes: Found on hard limestone and is a common species in the Burren. Tends to occur where limestone is damp, such as around the base of outcrops or near shallow depressions.

Leptogium gelatinosum – crustose to foliose

Description: Thallus is made of many paper-thin overlapping lobes. When wet it looks like a gelatinous film. Variable in colour from blue-grey in the shade to red-brown in direct light. Lobes are 1–3mm wide and either ascending or adpressed, with the edges entire, divided or wrinkled. Apothecia are common, with discs flat to convex. Lacks isidia.

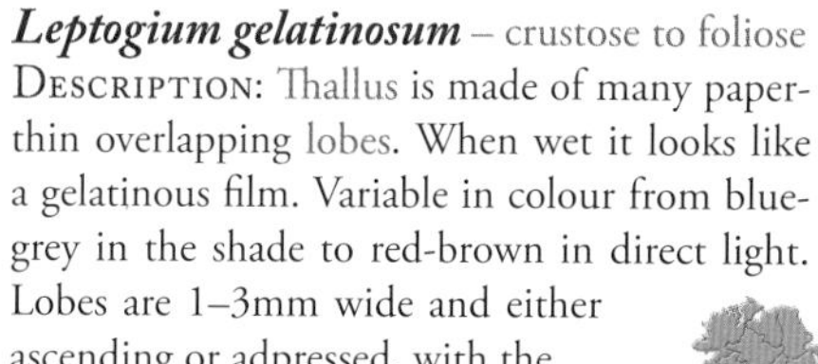

Spores, 25–35 x 12–14μm.
Spot Tests: None.
Nature Notes: Rare on trees, but tends to occur on mosses and calcareous soils or rocks.
Confusion: With *Leptogium lichenoides*.

Leptogium hibernicum – crustose to foliose

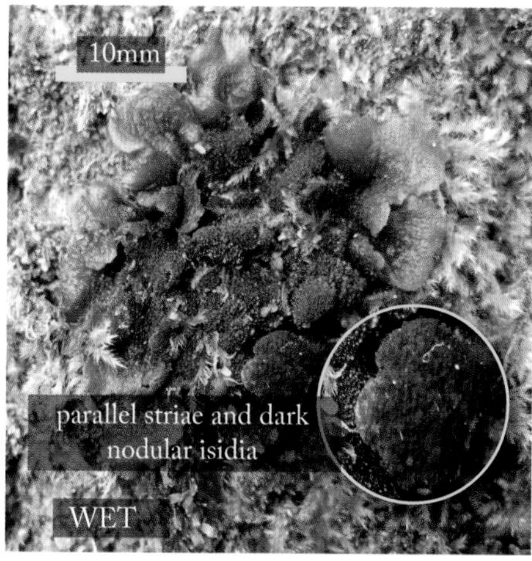

Description: Distinctly swollen when wet, with lobes up to 1cm wide. Looks fleshy with a green to grey colour. Lobes have characteristic parallel striae and overlap a little, turning up from the substrate. Centre of thallus is heavily populated with dark nodular isidia. Lower surface pale with tomentose hairs. Apothecia unrecorded in Irish specimens.
Spot Tests: None.
Nature Notes: Occurs in old woodlands in sheltered and moist locations on the bole of trees, especially ash, oak, hazel and sycamore. An Oceanic species and rare in Ireland.

Leptogium lichenoides – crustose to foliose

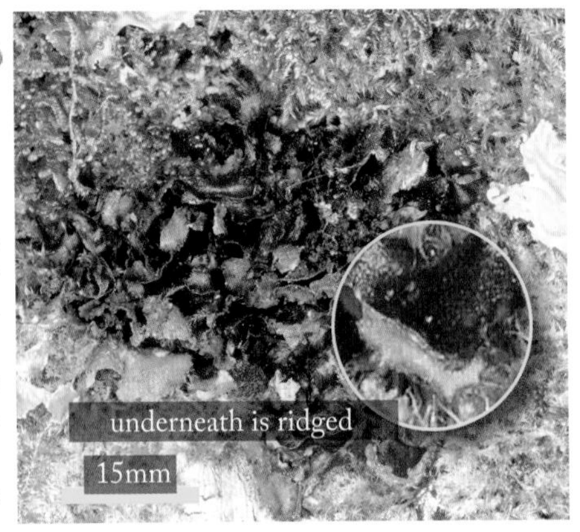

DESCRIPTION: Dark brown to grey lobed thallus has a distinctive ragged appearance, due to margins of lobes having many tiny characteristic finger-like isidia. Apothecia (<1mm) are rare, but if present they also have isidia growing from the rim, giving an eyelash appearance. The thallus itself has a shiny and wrinkled upper surface and is ridged underneath. SPOT TESTS: None.
NATURE NOTES: Occurs among mosses on the bole of mature trees such as ash, in damp woodlands. Also occurs on mossy silica-rich rocks.
CONFUSION: With *Leptogium gelatinosum* which lacks apothecial isidia.

Leptogium schraderi – crustose to foliose

DESCRIPTION: Dark red-black to greeny brown and glossy when wet; it forms small patches generally less than 18mm in diameter and 5mm thick. When dry, it has a very shrivelled appearance. The thallus consists of many udder-like ascending structures about 1mm wide and 25mm long; often branched at the base. Apothecia (<1.5mm diam.) are rare. Discs are concave to flat.
SPOT TESTS: None.
NATURE NOTES: Found associated with calcareous grasslands and on mortar-rich walls, especially around undisturbed graveyards.
CONFUSION: When dry and shrivelled it looks similar to *Leptogium teretiusculum*.

Leptogium teretiusculum – crustose to foliose

DESCRIPTION: Brown to grey thallus, smooth when wet. It forms small patches, generally less than 5mm in diam. When dry, it has a very shrivelled ragged spiky appearance. Thallus consists of many coral-like ascending structures, forming dense mats. Apothecia are very rare. Discs are concave to flat. Isidia are common. SPOT TESTS: None.
NATURE NOTES: Occurs in old woodlands (ash) and on calcareous rocks and mortar.
CONFUSION: With *Leptogium schraderi*.

Lichina – 2 recorded in Ireland, both seashore species.

Lichina confinis – fruticose

Description: Thallus is dark olive brown and grows as small compact tufts among seaweeds of the middle to upper shore. The tufts are rarely longer than 5mm, while the area covered can reach 20cm x 8cm. The medulla and cortex are not easily distinguishable, both being a gelatinous mass of hyphae, algal cells and cyanobacterial photobionts. Spherical apothecia are found at the ends of the branches, up to 0.5mm diam. Spores, 12–18 × 10–15μm.

Spot Tests: None.

Nature Notes: Most abundant where the shore is sheltered and exposed to direct sunlight.

Confusion: With *Lichina pygmaea*.

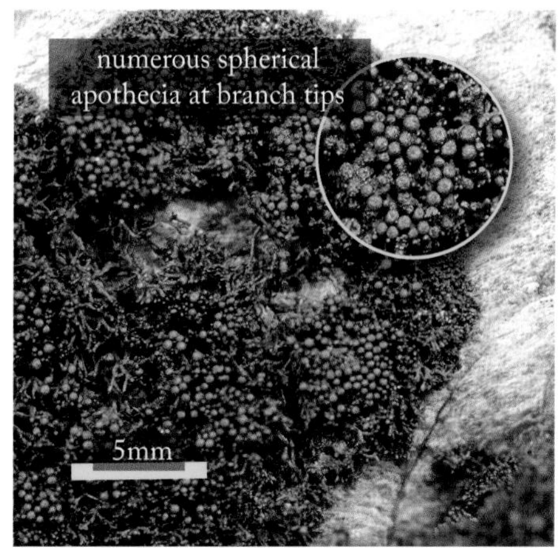

Lobaria – 4 recorded in Ireland, 'old' woodland indicators and 'lungwort' lichens.

Lobaria amplissima – foliose

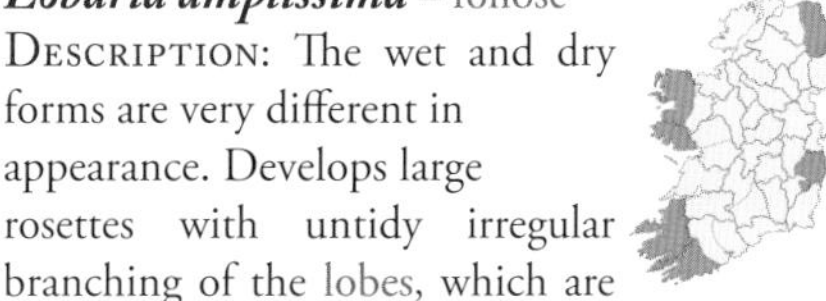

Description: The wet and dry forms are very different in appearance. Develops large rosettes with untidy irregular branching of the lobes, which are notched at the margins. Lobes overlap towards the centre. When dry, the thallus is grey-white and brittle looking. When wet, it is green-grey and fleshy. Pycnidia are wart-like, large and common. Apothecia are not so common and have brownish red coloured discs. Large, well developed cephalodia (≤2cm) may look like tiny shrubs.

Spores, 40–60 x 6–7μm.

Spot Tests: Medulla: K+ yellow (possibly K–), KC+ pink/red (possibly KC–).

Nature Notes: A rare species in Ireland. It occurs in old woodlands as do the other *Lobaria* species, but seems less tolerant of low light. Occurs on the boles of mature oak, ash, sycamore and elm. Known as the 'parchment' lichen.

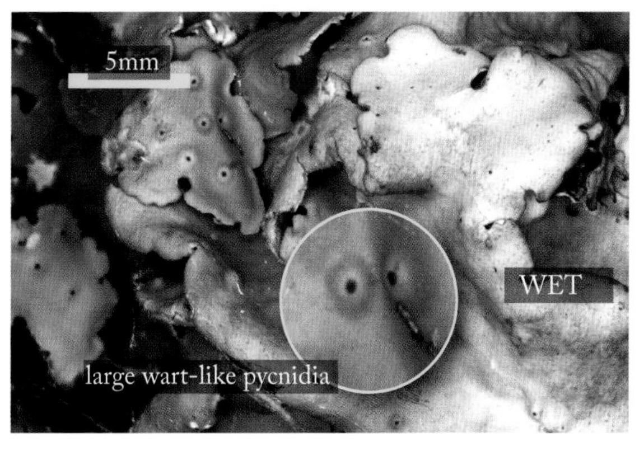

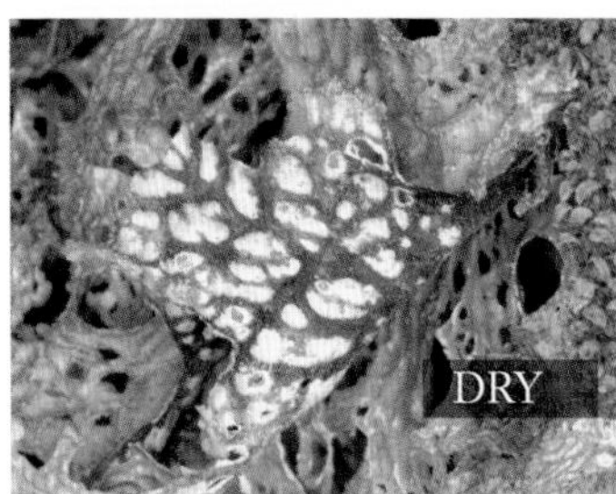

Lobaria pulmonaria – foliose, erect, tomentose

Description: Has large grey-green lobes when dry and bright green when wet. Thallus extends up to 60cm and is loosely attached. Lobes are up to 3cm wide, often incised at the ends and show a tendency for dichotomous branching. Superficially looks like lung tissue with its wrinkled ridged lobes. The lower surface is tan coloured with white concave regions. Soralia and isidia line both the lobe ridges and edges. Apothecia may also occur on the ridges. Red-brown discs have a thin thalline rim that may be occluded. Spores, 18–30 x 5–9μm.

Spot Tests: Medulla: K+ yellow → orange, Pd+ orange.

Nature Notes: This is an old woodland indicator lichen. Occurs on deciduous trees and mossy rocks in wet unpolluted areas. Produces apothecia in Atlantic woodlands with a long history of undisturbed continuity. Very sensitive to SO_2 pollution.

Lobaria scrobiculata – foliose, erect, tomentose

DESCRIPTION: Compared to other *Lobaria* species, it can look rather unclean and scruffy. Thallus grows up to 10cm wide. The upper surface is greeny yellow when dry and a distinctive dark blue-grey when wet. Lobes (10–20mm wide) are sculpted with ridges and depressions and are often turned up around the rim. Lobe margins may be entire or crenulate and are lined with a display of large blue-grey soralia and isidia. Under-surface is tomentose, black near its centre, developing to light grey at the margins. White regions are concave and not tomentose. Apothecia are rare. Discs are red-brown. Spores, 18–23 x 4–7μm.

SPOT TESTS: Medulla: K+ yellow. Pd+ orange.

NATURE NOTES: Typical of the *Lobaria* group, this is a species characteristic of old woodlands. It is found mainly in the west of Ireland, but some specimens have been recorded in woodlands along the rivers Suir and Blackwater. Prefers the edges of woodlands where it gains more light. It is also more tolerant of dry areas than other *Lobaria* species.

CONFUSION: White patches underneath may be mistaken for cyphellae leading to confusion with *Sticta* species.

Lobaria virens – foliose, erect, tomentose

Description: This has a large (10cm or more in diam.) leafy thallus with a distinct upper and lower side. The upper side is bright green when wet and dull greeny brown when dry. Lobes are wide, rounded and wavy, with a tendency to be concave; sometimes with a shiny oily appearance. A mature thallus will also display ridges. Apothecia are large (1–3mm) and frequent. When mature they have a reddish brown disc with a thalline margin. Immature apothecia look like tiny emerging volcanoes. Pycnidia with brown openings or ostioles are frequent. The lower surface is creamy white, with a thin, light brown, evenly spread tomentum. Cephalodia are present internally in the medulla and contain cyanobacteria, otherwise the primary photobiont is green algae. Spores are colourless turning brown when mature and 1–3 septate, 25–45 x 8–11μm.

Spot Tests: C–, K+ pale yellow or else K–, Pd–, KC± watery pink.

Nature Notes: It is an old woodland indicator, being mostly confined to ancient woodlands on both basic and acidic bark of oak, ash and elm. Sometimes found on beech and rocks in shaded areas. Prefers higher humidity than other *Lobaria* species. Found in Oceanic/Atlantic woodlands in the west of Ireland, especially near the coast. Common in Killarney National Park.

Loxospora – 1 species in Ireland.

Loxospora elatina – crustose

Description: Recognized by the little blisters of blue-green soralia that have a greenish to blue-yellow colour. The thallus is indistinct and difficult to see, it is dark grey and warty in appearance. Apothecia are very rare, but the discs are reddish brown. Spores, 35–50 x 4–5μm.

Spot Tests: K+ yellow.

Nature Notes: Occurs on rough bark, particularly oak trees and other old woodland trees.

Melanelixia – 2 species recorded in Ireland.

Melanelixia subaurifera – foliose

Description: Develops as a brown olive green closely adpressed thallus on larger twigs. It has a dull matt appearance and is speckled with tiny peg-like isidia and minute specks or soredia. Parts of the thallus may show whitish spots where the soralia have fallen off.

Spot Tests: Medulla: C+ red. UV–.

Nature Notes: Develops as rosettes if space allows, otherwise it wraps itself around twigs.

Melanohalea – 4 species recorded in Ireland.

Melanohalea exasperata – foliose

Description: Thallus is shiny, olive green and does not change colour when wet. Ranges in size from 2–10cm. Thallus divides into small lobes with a warty surface. The warts look like tiny volcanoes under a hand lens; each has a conical shape with a 'mouth'. Warts extend to the apothecial rims. Discs are concave or flat. Underneath is dark brown, with simple rhizines. Spores, 9–12 x 5–6μm.

Spot Tests: None.

Nature Notes: Occurs on coniferous trees and also on birch, willow, alder and oak. It is rare on rock substrates.

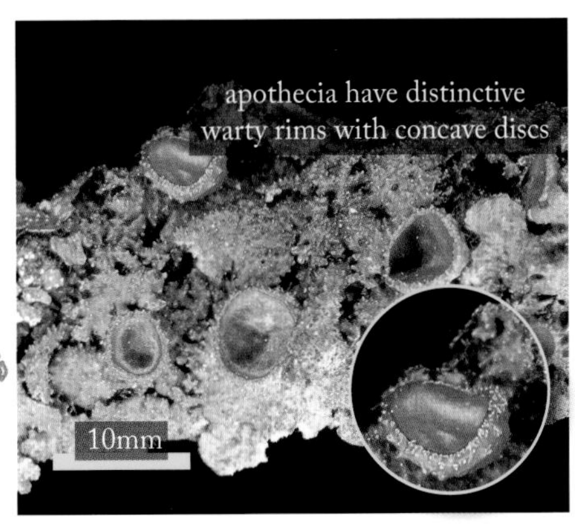

Menegazzia – 2 species recorded in Ireland.

Menegazzia terebrata – foliose

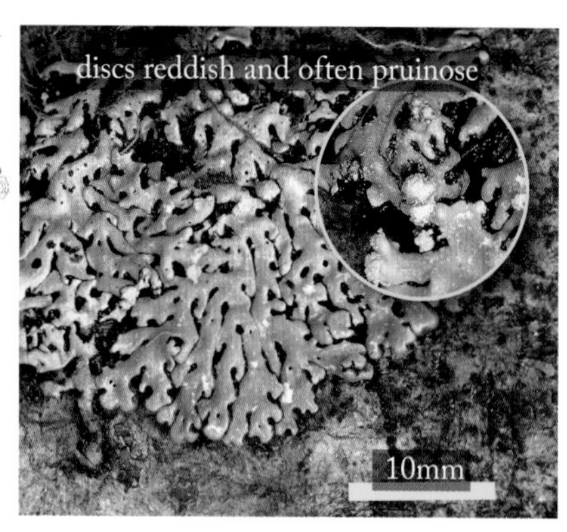

Description: Thallus forms neat, closely adpressed, regular hand-like forms on the substrate. Lobes are green to grey-green, convex, smooth, shiny and rounded at the tips. Lower surface is black, wrinkled and lacking rhizines. Both apothecia (red-brown discs) and pycnidia are rare. Lobe surfaces and tips may be covered with soralia. Spores, 50–68 x 30–36μm.
Spot Tests: Cortex: K+ yellow.
Medulla: K+ yellow, Pd+ orange-yellow.
Nature Notes: Occurs on acidic bark in damp humid woodlands (oak, birch, alder). Also on mossy silica-rich rocks.
Confusion: Closely resembles *H. physodes*.

Mycobilimbia – 2 species recorded in Ireland. Easy to confuse with Biatora.

Mycobilimbia pilularis – crustose

Description: Finely granular thallus is green to grey-green in colour. Granules superficially resemble soralia. No pycnidia are present. Apothecial discs are convex to globular in shape and beige to pink to orange in colour.
Spot Tests: None.
Nature Notes: Found in old woodlands and mountain gullies, especially on oak, typically near the base of the main trunk. Rarely found on moss covered stones.

Mycoblastus – 3 species recorded in Ireland.

Mycoblastus sanguinarius – crustose

Description: Thallus lumpy, uneven, thick, pale grey to white with small scattered papillae. Prothallus either dark or white. Apothecia common, black and convex to almost spherical. Sections through apothecia expose a bright blood red colour (termed a red heart). Large thick walled Spores, 70–100 x 35–45μm.
Spot Tests: Cortex: C–, K+ yellow, Pd+ yellow. Medulla: K+ red. UV–.
Nature Notes: Occurs on birch and siliceous rocks. Grows assertively over lichens and mosses.

Nephroma – 2 species in Ireland. 'Kidney' lichens after the shape of apothecia.

Nephroma laevigatum – foliose

Description: Thallus is loose and paper thin, up to 8cm in diameter. Wavy lobes 2–10mm wide, grey to deep red-brown in colour. Underside is smooth but may have striae. Lacks soredia and a tomentum. Apothecia with thalline rims develop at the lobe edges. Medulla is yellow. Spores, 17–20 x 5–7μm.
Spot Tests: Medulla: K+ purple.
Nature Notes: Occurs in humid oceanic woodlands on bark and moss. Photobiont is *Nostoc*. A defining species of hazel woodlands.

Nephroma parile – foliose

Description: Reddish chocolate-brown lobes with grey granular soredia along the margins. The under-surface is smooth and pale brown, but may be a little tomentose. Generally the underside lacks any other features. Apothecia are very rare. Distinguished from similar species by the white medulla. Spores, 18–20 x 6–7μm.
Spot Tests: Medulla: K+ purple.
Nature Notes: Found on mossy trees and walls in damp areas.
Confusion: With *Nephroma laevigatum*. Similar to *Peltigera collina* but lacks veining and rhizines on the under-surface.

Normandina – 2 species recorded in Ireland.

Normandina pulchella – squamulose

Description: Tiny grey or green-grey plate-like squamules (1–2mm) make up the thallus, the edges of which are pale. The 'plate' of the squamules often shows concentric ridges. Soredia may be sprinkled across squamules, giving a pruinose texture. Squamules are also pale underneath.
Spot Tests: Negative.
Nature Notes: Common, growing among mosses in areas with a moderate amount of light.

Ochrolechia androgyna – crustose

DESCRIPTION: Thallus texture variable from fine white powdery to yellow-white and granular. Soredia may be in clusters or develop evenly across the whole thallus. Thallus grows assertively, covering extensive patches and growing over other lichens and mosses. Apothecia are common (2–4mm diam.) with a thalline rim and pink disc. Spores, 30–45 x 13–22μm.

SPOT TESTS: C+ scarlet red, K–, KC+ red-orange, Pd–. UV–.

NATURE NOTES: Occurs on acidic bark (hawthorn in the photo), sawn wood and upland silica-rich rocks.

CONFUSION: With *O. tartarea*.

Ochrolechia parella – crustose

DESCRIPTION: White or buff lumpy thallus, develops as large circular or oblong growths. Smoother on trees than rocks. Prothallus is white. Apothecia are abundant and have a white tyre look due to the thick rims and pruinose concave discs. Spores, 45–75 x 25–45μm.

SPOT TESTS: Cortex: C–. UV–. Discs: C+ red, KC+ red. UV+ white.

NATURE NOTES: Likes direct sunlight and silica-rich rocks such as granite, schist and Old Red Sandstone (ORS). Common on the seashore. Discs may be infected with *Dactylospora parellaria*.

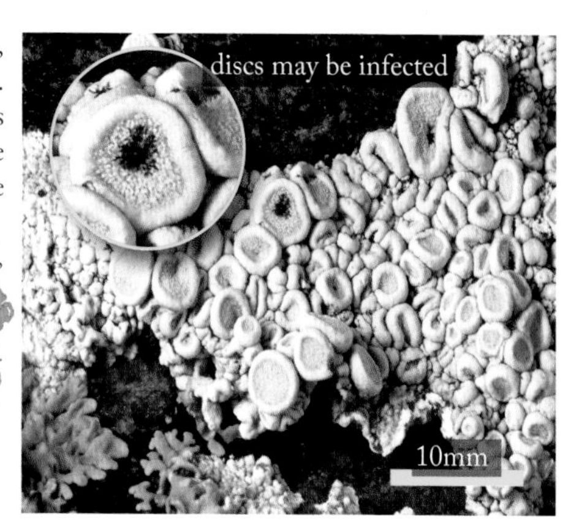

Ochrolechia tartarea – crustose

DESCRIPTION: Thick, lumpy cracked thallus, white to off-white in colour, with an even paler prothallus. Apothecia are common and have characteristic wavy thalline rims, with a dull orange disc that may be pruinose. Spores, 40–70 x 20–40μm.

SPOT TESTS: Thallus: C+ orange, K+ pale yellow, KC+ red. Medulla: Pd–. UV–. Discs: C+ red, K–, KC+ red, Pd–.

NATURE NOTES: Occurs in oceanic areas on silica-rich boulders and on acidic bark.

CONFUSION: With *O. androgyna* (K–).

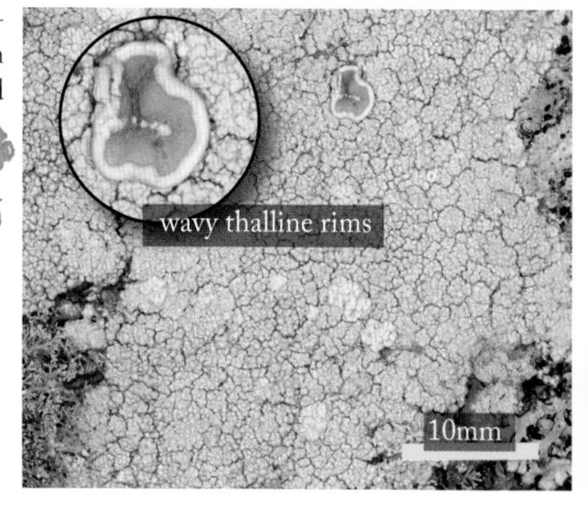

Opegrapha – 34 species in Ireland. Photobiont Trentepohlia.

Opegrapha atra – crustose

Description: Thallus silvery-white to light grey. Prothallus is darker and may form mosaics. Lirellae are long, numerous, crowded and sit high on the thallus, often forming regular elliptical or circular patches which may be branched or stellate. Spores, 14–20 x 3–5μm. Spot Tests: None.
Nature Notes: Shade loving, it occurs on smooth barked trees.
Confusion: With *Graphis scripta* (smaller lirellae).

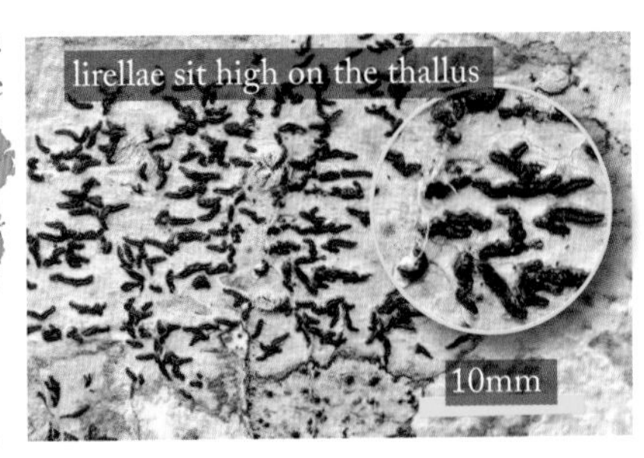

Opegrapha calcarea – crustose

Description: Pinkish immersed thallus. Lirellae are short and rarely branched. They are piled on top of each other, forming little heaps (a good identifying feature to note). Slit-like discs are visible with a hand lens.
Spores, 15–20 x 4–6μm. Spot Tests: None.
Nature Notes: Occurs on damp limestone and mortar. Also found in regions under the influence of the sea. Often seen on old mortar sea walls.

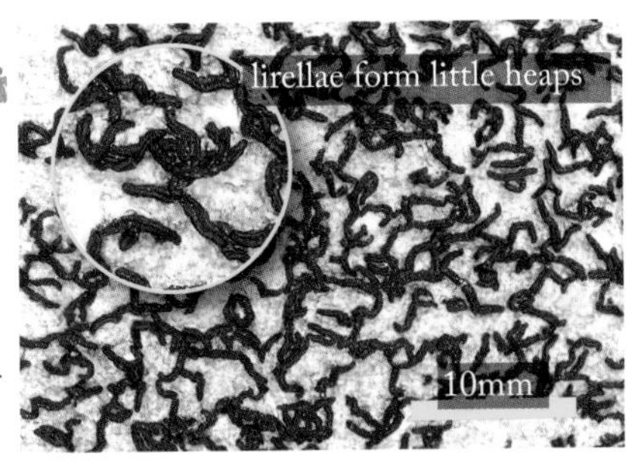

Opegrapha gyrocarpa – crustose

Description: Thallus is rusty red to brown to light tan, with a cracked crust. Prothallus may be visible, especially when the lichen forms mosaics. Surface scattered with tan coloured soralia. Apothecia infrequent, dispersed, and with a gyrose rim. Discs are only visible as tiny slits. Spores, 17–25 x 4–6μm. Spot Tests: Soralia: C+ red.
Nature Notes: Occurs on vertical shaded siliceous or neutral rocks in humid areas.
Confusion: With *Belonia nidarosiensis*.

Opegrapha vermicellifera – crustose

Description: Has a paper thin pale grey to buff green, unbroken thallus. Matt in texture. Apothecia very rare and very small. Discs are long and thin (slit like). Rims are furrowed. Pycnidia white to pale grey and very common.
Conidia 4–7 x 1–1.5μm. Spot Tests: Negative.
Nature Notes: Occurs on neutral to basic barked trees, often on the dry side or near the base (especially on ash and elm.

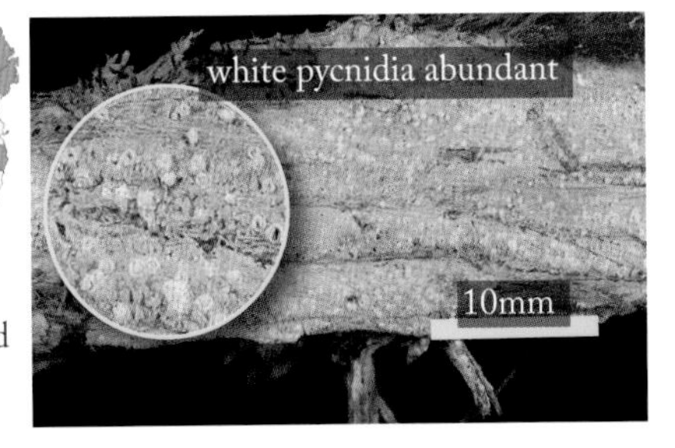

OPHIOPARMA – 1 SPECIES RECORDED IN IRELAND.

Ophioparma ventosa – crustose

DESCRIPTION: Thallus is thick, cracked or areolate forming large creamy or grey patches. Prothallus is light pinkish in colour. Apothecia common, round or irregular with a thalline rim, discs are flat to slightly convex, matt and blood or ruby red. Pycnidia common. Spores, 40–50 x 4.5–5μm.

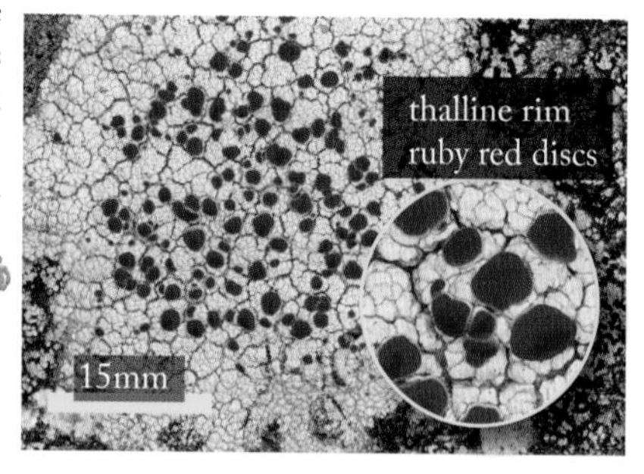

SPOT TESTS: Medulla: C–, K+ yellow, Pd+ orange.

NATURE NOTES: Occurs on coarse grained silica-rich rocks in upland regions.

PANNARIA – 3 SPECIES IN IRELAND. CALLED 'SHINGLE LICHENS'.

Pannaria conoplea – foliose, crustose, squamulose

DESCRIPTION: Grey thallus that often develops as neat rosettes or irregular clusters. Grey lobes are deeply incised and may be overlapping, slightly concave and turned up at the edges. Colour turns considerably paler towards the margins of the lobes. Granular isidia populate lobe margins and may spread over the surface, producing a granular effect. Underside is tomentose. Apothecia are very rare and range in size from 0.5–1.5mm with chestnut-red discs and often an isidiate rim. Spores, 15–19 x 9–10μm.

SPOT TESTS: Pd+ orange-red.

NATURE NOTES: Prefers basic bark, especially in well sheltered and humid moss covered areas. Occurs on hazel and willow in the west of Ireland.

Pannaria rubiginosa – foliose, crustose, squamulose

DESCRIPTION: Thallus is bluish grey with a scalloped appearance, due to the imbricate squamules forming large lobes. Lobe margins turn up. Brown orange apothecia are numerous and so crowded as to hide the thallus. Under-surface is covered in a thick blackish tomentose hypothallus. Lacks both isidia and soredia. Spores, 15–19 x 9–10μm.

SPOT TESTS: Pd+ orange-red.

NATURE NOTES: Occurs on moss and the bark of deciduous trees in sheltered humid areas. This specimen was photographed on hawthorn in the Burren.

Parmelia – 4 species recorded in Ireland.

Parmelia omphalodes – foliose

Description: Large brown thallus with a network of white veins and an overall metallic appearance. Soredia and isidia are absent. Apothecia are reddish brown and few in number, but frequently present. They may be small and difficult to find among the rough thallus. The underside is almost black with simple rhizines.
Spot Tests: Medulla: K+ orange-red, Pd+ orange.
Nature Notes: Associated with silica-rich rocks in exposed areas, from uplands to sea level. Rare on trees.

Parmelia saxatilis – foliose

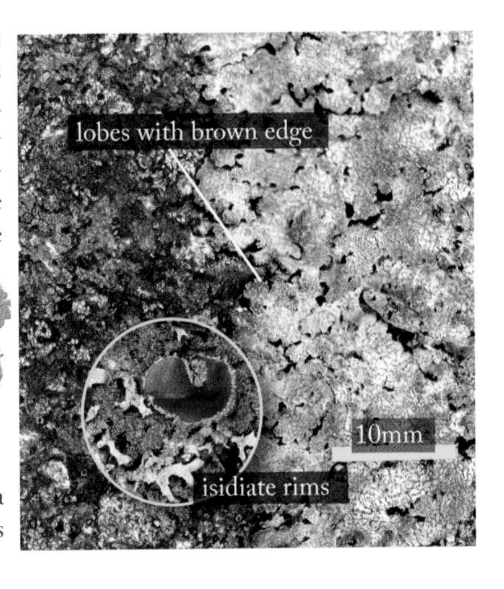

Description: Thallus forms neat circular shapes on trees and rocks. Lobes overlap and widen towards ends which have a squared appearance. Edges have a brown tint. A distinctive network of veins (pseudocyphellae) cross the upper surface. Isidia are abundant, giving the thallus a coarse appearance. The lower surface is black becoming lighter towards the margins. Apothecia are uncommon. Discs are red-brown and the thin rims are often isidiate or crenulate. Spores, 16–18 x 9–11μm.
Spot Tests: K+ orange → red, Pd+ orange. UV–.
Nature Notes: Found on trees, rocks and walls throughout Ireland. Frequently displays a reddish colour due to infection by a coral red fungus *Marchandiomyces corallinus*.

Parmelia sulcata – foliose

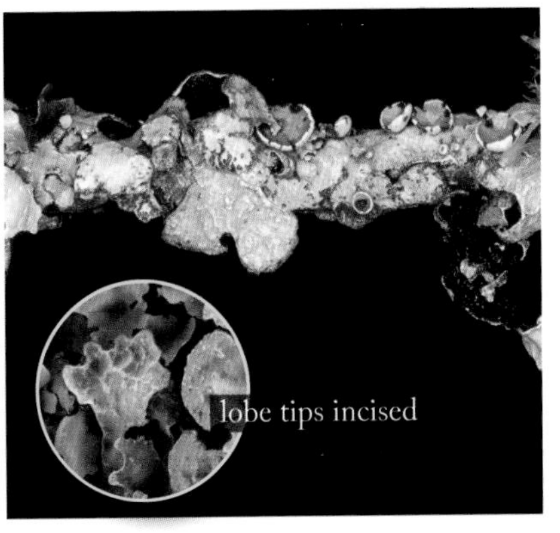

Description: Thallus is grey to white with brownish tips. Often develops as large rosettes, or wraps itself around twigs. Lobe tips incised. The network of veins is distinctive, being ridged and white. Soralia develop toward the centre. Underside is black with simple rhizines near margins. Apothecia are rare.
Tests: Medulla/soredia: K+ orange-red, Pd+ orange. UV–.
Nature Notes: Mainly a lowland species. Occurs on silica-rich rocks and trees, and sand dunes.

PARMELIELLA – 3 SPECIES RECORDED IN IRELAND.

Parmeliella parvula – foliose, squamulose

DESCRIPTION: Thallus consists of elongated and indented squamules 1–2mm long, giving them a frilly appearance. Flat to slightly convex in shape, their colour varies from watery blue-green to greeny grey to red-brown. Squamules may show large granular isidia on the margins or over the surface, giving the thallus a sugary appearance. Rare, apothecia are small (<0.5mm) with red-brown to blackish discs (flat to convex). Spores, 15–18 x 10–12μm.

SPOT TESTS: None.

NATURE NOTES: Prefers moist sheltered mossy woodlands of broad leaved trees, often near streams. Sometimes occurs on coniferous trees, but rarely on rocks or timber. When found in exposed sites, the squamules are brown red.

PARMELINA – 2 SPECIES RECORDED IN IRELAND.

Parmelina pastillifera – foliose

DESCRIPTION: Mineral grey thallus (4–15cm wide), with lobes (3–10mm wide) that overlap a little and are adpressed closely to the substrate, with rounded margins which have small irregular indents. Margins are frequently pruinose. Underneath is black, turning brown towards the margins where simple rhizines develop. Black to navy blue isidia are common and characteristic. Apothecia and pycnidia have not been found on Irish specimens.

SPOT TESTS: Cortex: K+ yellow, Medulla: C+ carmine red; K–, KC+ red, Pd–. UV–.

NATURE NOTES: Occurs on acidic barked trees such as ash and particularly in nutrient rich areas, such as near farms. Also likes silica-rich rocks and well lit areas such as roofs and town monuments.

CONFUSION: With *Parmelina tiliacea*.

Parmotrema – 6 species recorded in Ireland.

Parmotrema crinitum – foliose

Description: A light grey thallus with large incised lobes and coral-like isidia scattered across the surface, particularly towards the lobe edges. Large black eyelash-like cilia grow from the under-surface around the edges and sometimes through breaks in the thallus. These area distinguishing feature. Under-surface is black towards the centre and brown towards the edges, with simple rhizines. Apothecia rare, but when present have distinctive red-brown discs and crenulate or isidiate rims. Spores, 21–31 x 11–15μm.

Spot Tests: K+ yellow-orange, Pd+ yellow-orange, K+ orange. UV–.

Nature Notes: This is an old woodland species, occuring on well lit mossy trees and rocks. Found scattered throughout Ireland, but with the highest population west of the River Shannon.

Parmotrema perlatum – foliose

Description: A leafy or foliose lichen, with a grey-green thallus that is loosely attached to branches or rocks. A single specimen can grow up to about 15cm in size. Lobes may be 15mm wide, with wavy edges raised up from the substrate and heavily populated with soralia. Underside is black towards the centre and tan brown towards the margins. Margins themselves are characteristically black, giving rise to the popular name 'black-edged leaf lichen'. Apothecia are rare.

Spot Tests: K+ yellow, Pd+ orange, KC+ orange. UV–.

Nature Notes: Widespread in Ireland and particularly abundant in the south and west. It prefers acidic bark or silica-rich rocks in well lit areas. It is sensitive to SO_2. Frequently abundant on hawthorn.

Peltigera britannica – foliose

DESCRIPTION: Develops as a rosette of bright green lobes that are flat or concave. Button shaped laminal cephalodia are found on the upper surface only and never reach the lobe margins. They fall off leaving a white scar. Apothecia have not been recorded in Irish specimens. The underside is white and without veins (or poorly defined). Few rhizines. SPOT TEST: None.

NATURE NOTES: Occurs on both mossy rocks and trees in damp non-calcareous areas. Primary photobiont is a green algae, while *Nostoc* resides in the cephalodia which grow to maturity, fall off and develop into lichens based only on *Nostoc*, the thalline colour then being red-brown. Eventually it captures a green photobiont and produces green lobes.

Peltigera collina – foliose

DESCRIPTION: Lobes radiate out from a central point to a distance of 10cm. Upper surface colours are grey through blue-grey to brown, with a smooth texture. Underside is pale brown with simple non-branched rhizines. Lobes adpressed, except at the edges where the margins are raised and wavy or undulating; frequently it is pruinose with marginal soralia. Apothecia are rare and very small. Spores, are 39–7 x 4–5μm. SPOT TESTS: Negative.

NATURE NOTES: The only *Peltigera* with marginal soralia. Occurs on mossy rocks and trees.

CONFUSION: With *Sticta limbata* or *Nephroma parile*.

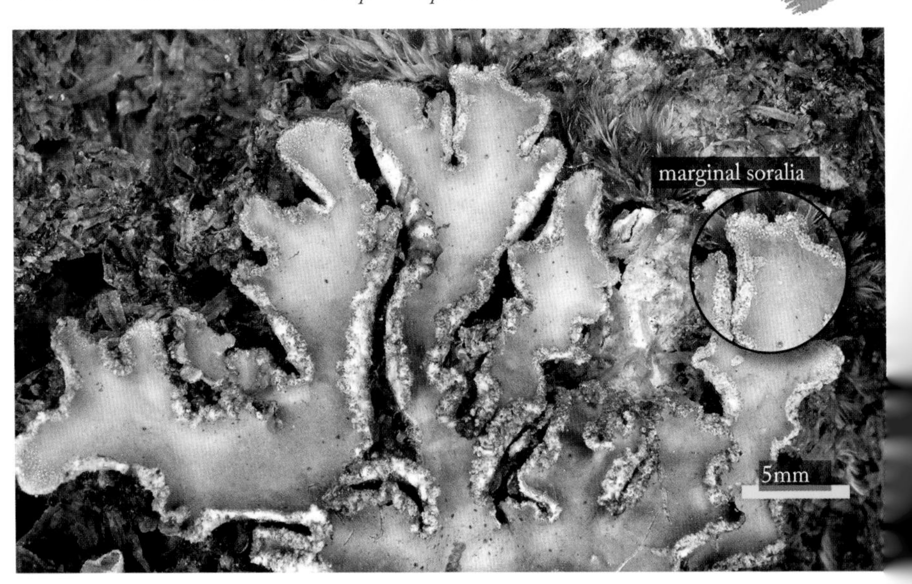

Peltigera horizontalis – foliose

Description: Thallus large, reaching 20cm in diameter, grey to red-brown and shiny, turning up at the lobe edges. Upper surface undulating with depressions corresponding to dark rhizines on the lower surface. It varies in texture from matt to shiny. Apothecia develop at the lobe edges and are characteristically round to oblong, with red apothecial discs held horizontally to the lobe surface. Underneath has neat rows of black rhizines and light coloured regions, but overall the underside is dark becoming white near lobe margins. Spores, 30–46 x 6–7μm.

Spot Tests: None.

Nature Notes: Occurs in woodlands on mossy rocks, trees and rotting logs. It is an indicator of old woodland continuity.

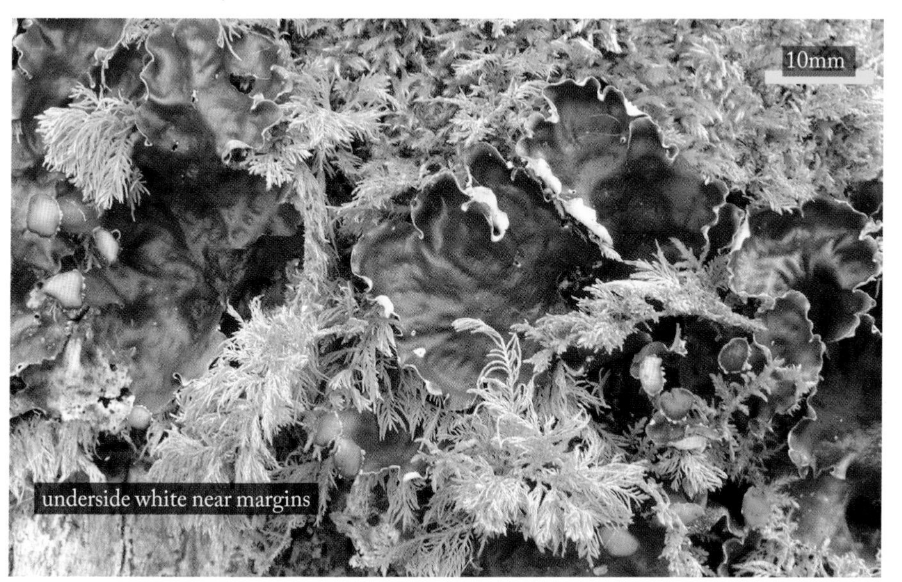

Peltigera hymenina – foliose

Description: An irregular spreading thallus up to 20cm in diam. Papery thin lobes develop to 2cm in width and 6cm in length. Colour variable; when dry becomes dark olive green to light grey, when wet it turns reddish brown with blue-grey margins. Upturned margins may be notched or unnotched. Felted white to buff underside with flattened ochre veins and thin hair-like rhizines that vary in colour from buff to brown. Apothecia rare, but when present are distinct, with dark red discs on marginal curled lobes. Spores, 65–80 x 4–5μm.

Spot Tests: None.

Nature Notes: Occurs in damp areas on mosses, acid soils, peat, at the base of mature trees and in sheltered dunes and grasslands.

Peltigera membranacea – foliose

Description: A thin thallus that is loosely attached and rather large, reaching up to 40cm in length (generally about 10cm.). Lobes range from 1–3cm wide, turn down at the margins and are typically brown when moist, turning silvery-grey when dry; often shiny, especially towards the centre, with a veined or undulating texture. Upper surface is finely tomentose (white frost appearance) and ridged. Underside is whitish to light brown with long pointed rhizines (some may be bottle brush shaped) and a network of prominent white veins. Apothecia are common, produced at the ends of the lobes, round in shape with reddish brown discs. Spores, 60–70 x 4–5μm.

Spot Tests: None.

Nature Notes: Grows among mosses on walls, rocks, on the ground (soil), old logs and on trees in damp areas. Moss is an essential ingredient of its ecology.

Confusion: With *Peltigera canina* which has thicker lobes and shorter tuft-like rhizines.

Peltigera membranacea

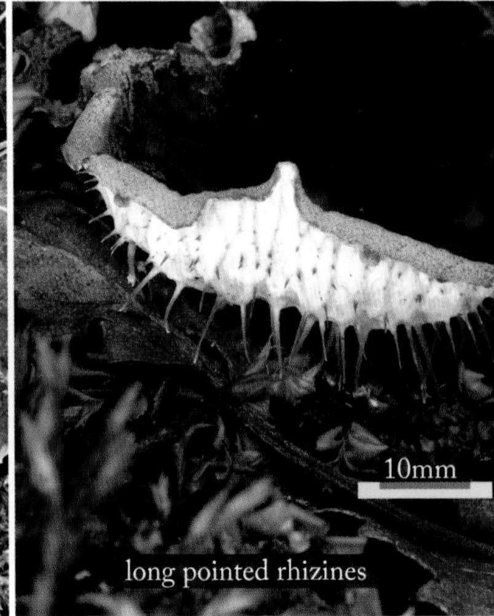

long pointed rhizines

Peltigera praetextata – foliose

Description: Apothecia are rare. Large thallus, round or irregular, up to 30cm long. Lobes are about 1cm wide (max. 1.5cm) with margins upturned, wavy or notched, but can be flat in some specimens. Upper surface may or may not be tomentose and sometimes has schizidia (scales). Colour varies from slate grey to reddish brown (when wet), particularly at the margins. Attached to the substrate centrally, it has white or brown veins. Rhizines are 4–6mm long. Spores, 35–58 x 2.5–5μm.

Spot Tests: None.

Nature Notes: Occurs on mossy rocks, trees, soil, rotting logs, walls, etc.

Confusion: With *Peltigera membranacea*, which lacks schizidia.

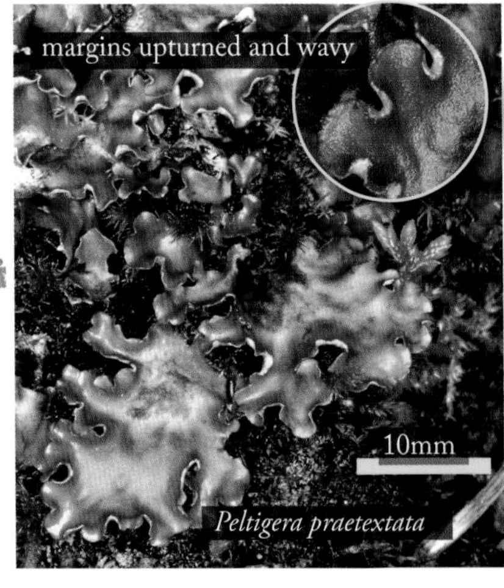

Peltigera praetextata

Pertusaria – 25 species recorded in Ireland. Apothecia look like perithecia.

Pertusaria albescens – crustose

Description: Thallus is light grey to green-grey, thick to thin. Numerous neat circular soralia are scattered throughout the thallus, except near the edges which have a distinct clear zone. Soralia more white than grey. Apothecia very rare. Spores, 170–300 x 50–115μm.

Spot Test: Negative.

Nature Notes: Grows on acid bark in woodlands, parks, on wayside trees and sometimes on silica-poor rocks.

Confusion: Distinguished from *P. amara* by not tasting bitter, or *P. albescens var. corallina* which is thicker and lumpy towards the centre.

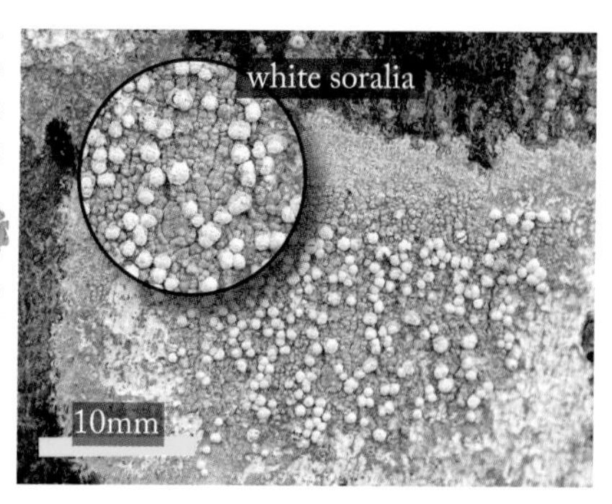

Pertusaria amara – crustose

Description: Thallus is light grey, sprinkled rather evenly with little clusters of white soralia. This species can be identified by its bitter taste. Try rubbing the soralia with a moistened finger and taste. The bitter (quinine like) taste is that of oxalic acid and takes a while to go. Apothecia are rare.

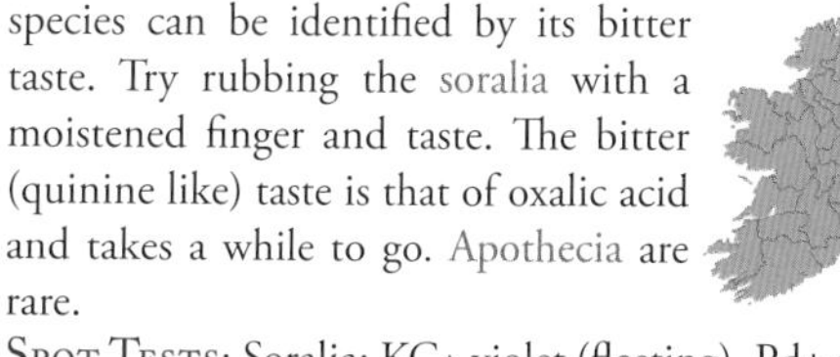

Spot Tests: Soralia: KC+ violet (fleeting), Pd± red.

Nature Notes: Common on trees, particularly beech and oak. Rarely grows on rocks, but may be found on those high in silica.

Confusion: With *P. albescens* which does not have a bitter taste.

Pertusaria aspergilla – crustose

Description: White to buff areolate and cracked thallus with a pale prothallus which forms a black boundary in mosaics. Soralia scattered and up to 1mm diam. Apothecia not known to occur.

Spot Tests: C–, K+ yellow-brown, KC+ yellow-red, Pd+ rust red to orange. UV–.

Nature Notes: Occurs on silica-rich rocks, especially outcrops or large boulders that wet and dry quickly. Also occurs on walls between fields. Common in upland areas.

Confusion: Distinguished from *P. amara* by the KC test, and taste.

Pertusaria hymenea – crustose

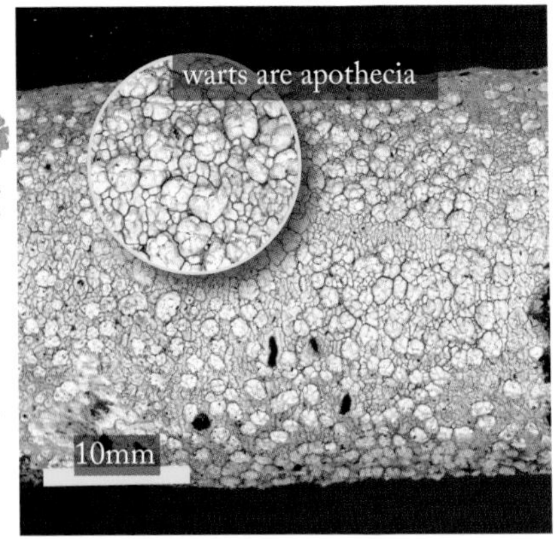

DESCRIPTION: Thallus is light grey to dark grey with tints of yellow and green. It varies from thin to thick with deep cracks and is rarely zoned around the edges. The warts are apothecia that look badly formed and crowded, often obscuring the thallus.
SPOT TESTS: C+ yellow, K–, KC+ orange, Pd–. UV± orange.
NATURE NOTES: Found on smooth bark, especially of young trees and twigs and on rough bark in the shaded parts of woodlands, wayside trees and parklands.

Pertusaria multipuncta – crustose

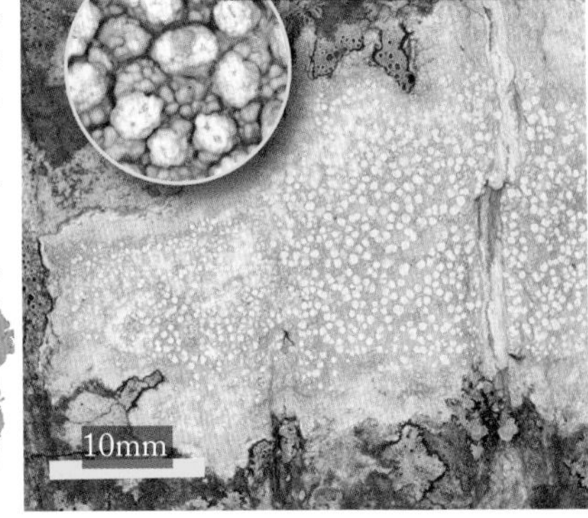

DESCRIPTION: Thallus is white-grey and generally thin, but may become a little thickened and often lightly cracked. Prothallus is usually present. Apothecia are raised and lighter in colour than the thallus, due to a sprinkling of soralia covering their discs. Spores, 90–170 x 30–70μm.
SPOT TESTS: C–, K+ yellow, KC+ yellow, Pd+ orange-red. UV–.
NATURE NOTES: Occurs on acidic barked trees, especially twigs.
CONFUSION: With *Phlyctis agelaea*. Check K reaction to distinguish.

Pertusaria pertusa – crustose

DESCRIPTION: Thallus is light grey to green-grey, rather lumpy with deep cracks between the warts. Each wart is home to between two to seven apothecia (up to 15 have been recorded), which are distinguished as tiny pinprick holes. Discs are black. Prothallus is sometimes ringed (growth pattern). Spores, 145–230 x 40–80μm.
SPOT TESTS: KC–, Medulla: K+ yellow, KC+ yellow, Pd+ deep orange. UV± orange.
NATURE NOTES: Common on trees but rarely found on rock.

Pertusaria pseudocorallina – crustose

Description: Thallus is thick or thin with a creamy white colour and grey tint, generally wrinkled or uneven. Isidia look like miniature golf tees with reddish brown tops, giving them a semblance of coral. They may fall out leaving tiny craters. Warts on the thallus contain several apothecia, the tiny discs giving them a perithecia-like appearance. Spores, 120–200 x 50–80μm.

Spot Tests: K+ blood red, C–, KC+ yellow-red, Pd+ yellow-red. UV–.

Nature Notes: Found on silica-rich rocks in both coastal and upland areas. Likes well lit locations.

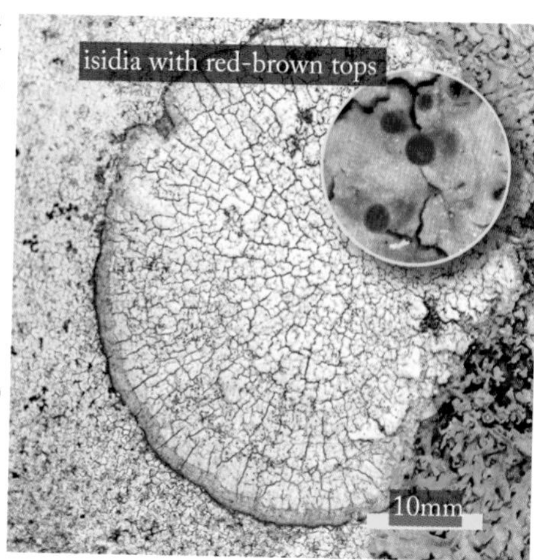

Phaeographis – 4 species recorded in Ireland.

Phaeographis dendritica – crustose

Description: Light grey to white thallus, with chalk-like texture, often cracked or areolate. Apothecia (lirellae) are immersed, wide, frequently branched and sometimes stellate with a pruinose appearance. Spores, 30–40 x 6–9μm, 7–9 septate.

Spot Tests: K+ red, Pd+ yellow-orange. UV–.

Nature Notes: Likes smooth acidic bark. Common throughout Ireland. In other countries it is considered indicative of old woodlands. Wide apothecia distinguish it from *Graphis* species.

Confusion: With *P. smithii,* below, (which has a smoother thallus). Apothecial sections of both species needed for certain identification.

Phaeographis smithii – crustose

Description: The thallus is very smooth and rarely cracked. Lirellae are less branched than *P. dendritica*, above. Spores, 25–40 x 7–9.5μm, 5–9 septate.

Spot Tests: K+ red, Pd+ yellow-orange. UV–.

Nature Notes: Found on smooth barked trees and shrubs. Scattered throughout Ireland.

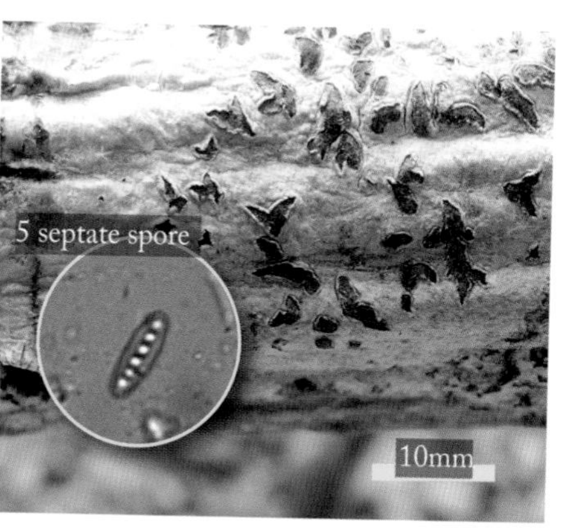

Physcia adscendens – foliose

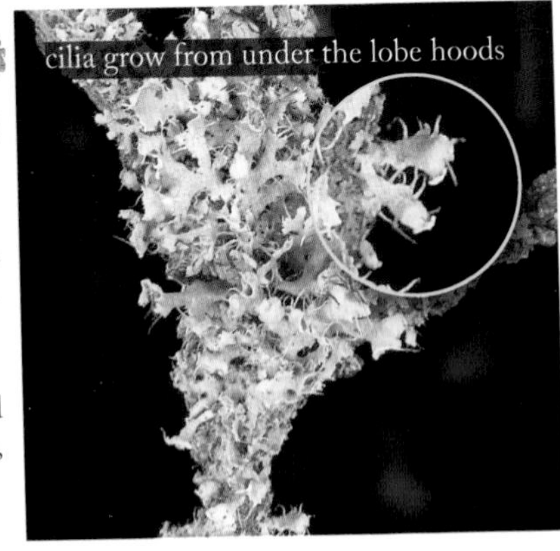

DESCRIPTION: Grey to greeny grey thallus, with narrow hood shaped lobes turned up at the ends. Long dark tipped cilia grow from under the hoods. Pseudocyphellae cover the upper surface. Soralia form at the edges of hoods to open out revealing soredia. Apothecia appear on short stalks with black pruinose discs. Spores, 16–23 x 7–10μm.

SPOT TESTS: Cortex: K+ yellow. Medulla: K–.

NATURE NOTES: Grows on both calcareous and siliceous rocks. Common on limestone monuments, twigs and tree trunks.

CONFUSION: With *Physcia tenella*.

Physcia aipolia – foliose

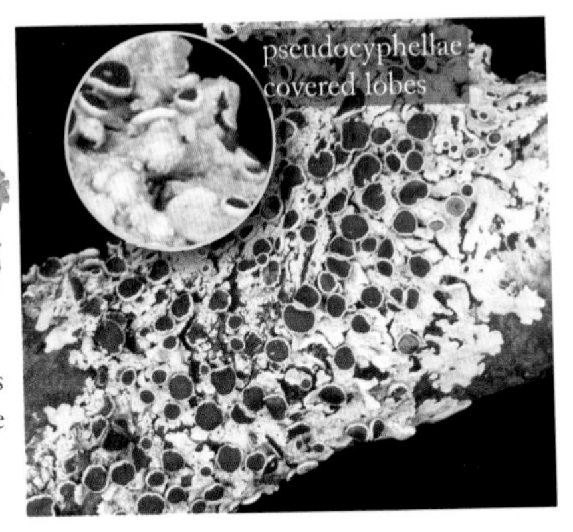

DESCRIPTION: Grey to blue-grey thallus, with flat creeping lobes covered in pseudocyphellae. The central region is normally covered with an abundance of apothecia, with dark brown discs that are heavily pruinose. Dark rhizines grow along the underside. Spores, 18–25 x 7–10μm.

SPOT TESTS: Cortex: K+ yellow. Medulla: K+ yellow.

NATURE NOTES: Tolerant of nutrient rich trees and shrubs in well lit situations. Often found in the nodes of new branches.

Physcia leptalea – foliose

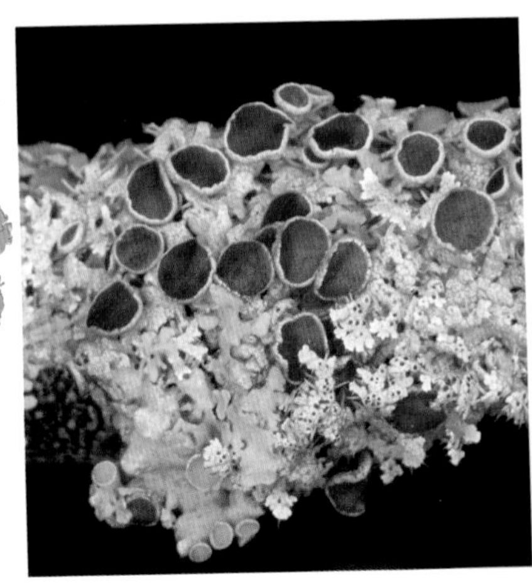

DESCRIPTION: Thallus is grey with distinct white flecks and lacking soralia. Pale to white cilia are found at lobe ends. Apothecia are large, very common and often lightly pruinose. Spores, 15–22 x 6–9μm.

SPOT TESTS: Cortex: K+ yellow. Medulla: K–.

NATURES NOTES: Rare on rocks, it tends to occur on the branches of trees and shrubs. More common near the coast than inland. Shows a sensitivity to sulphur dioxide and nitrogen enrichment.

Physcia tenella – foliose

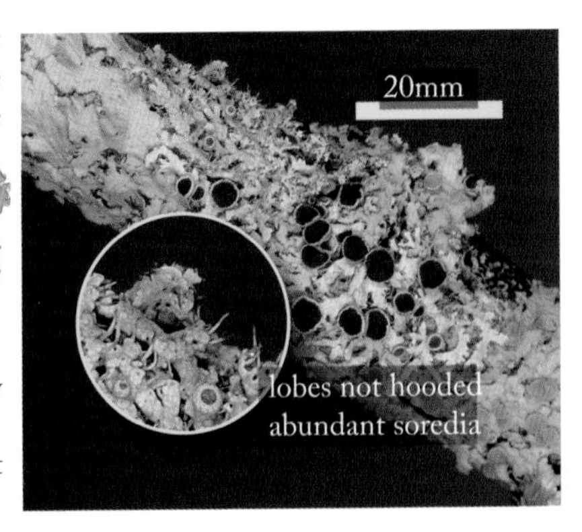

DESCRIPTION: Grey thallus with narrow lobes that are not hooded like *P. adscendens*, but instead are divided and open back to expose abundant white soredia. Long cilia grow along the lobe margins. Apothecia are common with discs that are almost black.
Spores, 16–23 x 7–10μm.
SPOT TESTS: Cortex: K+ yellow, Medulla: K–.
NATURE NOTES: Tends to occur more frequently on trees and twigs than on rock.
CONFUSION: So similar to *Physcia adscendens* that some consider them to be the same species.

***Physcia tribacioides* –** foliose

DESCRIPTION: Thallus is coral-like with short stout lobes. Colour varies from creamy white to light or watery green. Rarely develops a radiating pattern but tends to grow in an elongated manner. Concave, almost hemispherical laminal soralia which are large (<1.2mm) and abundant. Apothecia are rare, with reddish brown discs and thalline margins. No pycnidia. The underside is off-white to pale brown, with simple brown rhizines. Spores, 17–22 x 7–10μm.
SPOT TESTS: Cortex and medulla: K+ yellow.
NATURE NOTES: Occurs on nutrient rich bark of sycamore, ash, oak and elm, in well lit open parkland and on walls near the sea.

PHYSCONIA – 4 SPECIES RECORDED IN IRELAND. RELATED TO PHYSCIA, BUT LOBES LARGER.

Physconia distorta – foliose

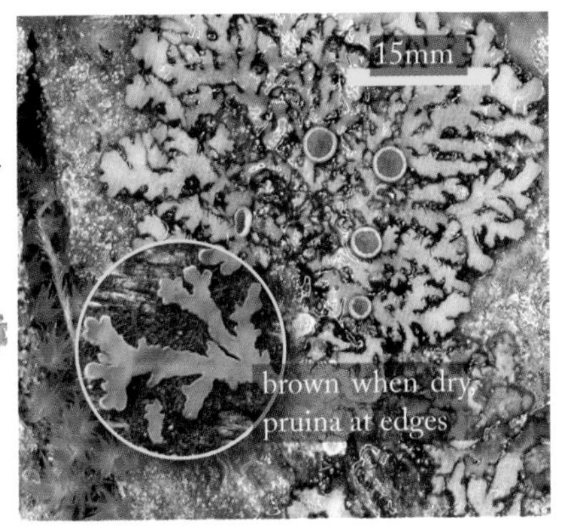

DESCRIPTION: The thallus is grey to brown when dry and green when wet. Large lobes with finger-like extensions at the growing edge, where they are covered in white pruina. Apothecia are common, with dark brown discs and a heavy coating of pruina. Under-surface is black to light brown, with rhizines. Spores, 25–40 x 12–20μm.
SPOT TESTS: K–.
NATURE NOTES: Occurs in well lit areas on basic bark in nutrient rich (nitrogen) areas.

Physconia grisea – foliose

Description: Thallus varies in colour from white to grey to brown when dry and green when wet. Lobes are short, slightly turned up at the ends and overlapping. Soredia develop along the lobe edges, but are also sprinkled across the thallus. Pruina cover the whole thallus. Underside is white with light coloured rhizines. Apothecia rare. Spores, 22–34 x 12–17μm.

Spot Tests: Medulla: K+ yellow.

Nature Notes: Likes basic barked trees, particularly on well lit wayside trees and trees in parks.

Pilophorus – 1 species recorded in Ireland.

Pilophorus strumaticus – crustose, squamulose

Description: Grainy, grey speckled thallus composed of minute squamules. Surface scattered with small brown nodules, the cephalodia, which contain the cyanobacteria *Stigonema*. Apothecia are black spheres on stalks (pin-headed). Spot Tests: Thallus: K+ yellow.

Nature Notes: Occurs in upland areas on silica-rich rocks (including boulders) in damp areas.

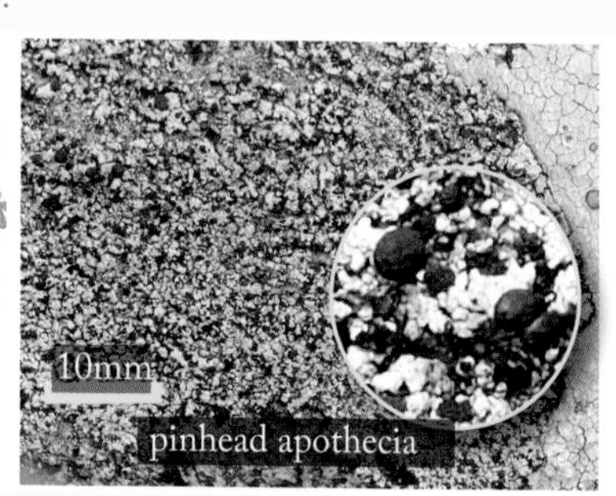

Placidium – 4 species recorded in Ireland.

Placidium squamulosum – squamulose

Description: Thallus consists of flattened squamules, brown to dark red on the upper side (paler underneath). Squamules often in side to side alignment or scattered and may turn up at the edges. Underside has colourless rhizines. Perithecia, with black openings, are common but immersed. Spot Tests: None.

Nature Notes: Found on calcareous soils and rocks, often in crevices with humus.

Placynthium – 7 species recorded in Ireland.

Placynthium nigrum – crustose, squamulose

Description: Thallus is blue-black, made of tiny squamules which may grow to 12cm and be lightly pruinose. The surface is areolate, with a distinctive smooth inky blue felt-like prothallus. Apothecia are rare, with black rims and black to brown discs. Spores, 9–18 x 3.5–5.5μm. Spot Tests: None.

Nature Notes: Occurs on calcareous rocks and mortar, especially on slow drying substrates.

wide inky blue prothallus

10mm

Platismatia – 1 species recorded in Ireland.

Platismatia glauca – foliose

Description: Green-grey thallus with large raised wavy lobes edged with isidia and/or soralia. Under-surface is black at the centre, turning white near lobe edges. May or may not have rhizines. Apothecia very rare. Discs tan with irregular rims. Spores, 4–10 x 3–5μm. Spot Tests: Cortex: K+ yellow.

Nature Notes: Occurs mainly on the upper side of horizontal branches. Also on silica-rich rocks in uplands.

Porpidia – 14 species recorded in Ireland.

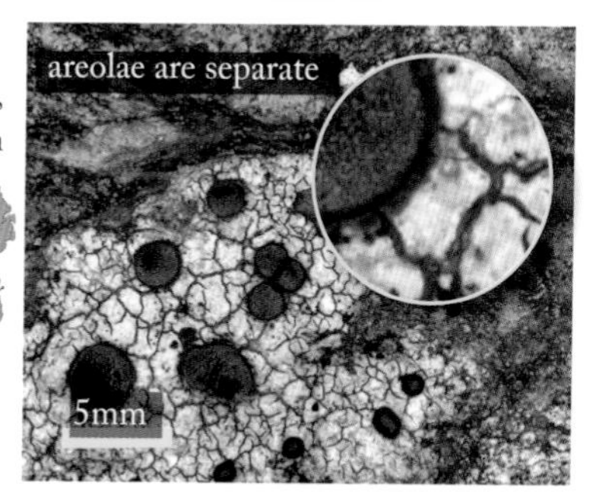

Porpidia cinereoatra – crustose

Description: Thallus is cracked, grey to grey-white, with a distinct black prothallus that is visible through the areoles. Apothecia, common and innate, mature to produce black convex pruinose discs with narrow black rims. Spores, 12–18 x 6–10μm. Spot Tests: Negative.

Nature Notes: Likes exposed siliceous rocks in upland or coastal areas.

Porpidia crustulata – crustose

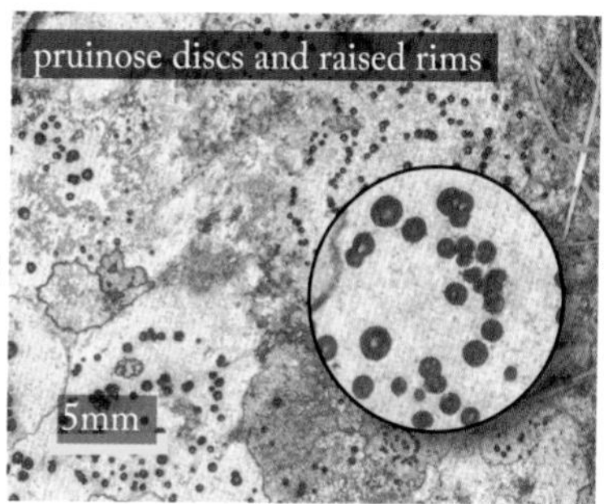

Description: Very thin, pale orange-grey thallus, sometimes tinted green. Prothallus brown. Apothecia common and often grow in concentric patterns, with black pruinose discs and raised rims. A red tint indicates that the thallus is oxidizing. Spores, 10–17 x 5–9μm. Spot Tests: Negative or not reliable. Medulla: C–, K± yellow, Pd± orange.

Nature Notes: Found on siliceous rocks and small stones, but also occurs on sawn wood. Regularly forms mosaics.

Confusion: Can resemble *P. macrocarpa*, which has larger apothecia. Confirm by measuring spores.

Porpidia flavocruenta – crustose

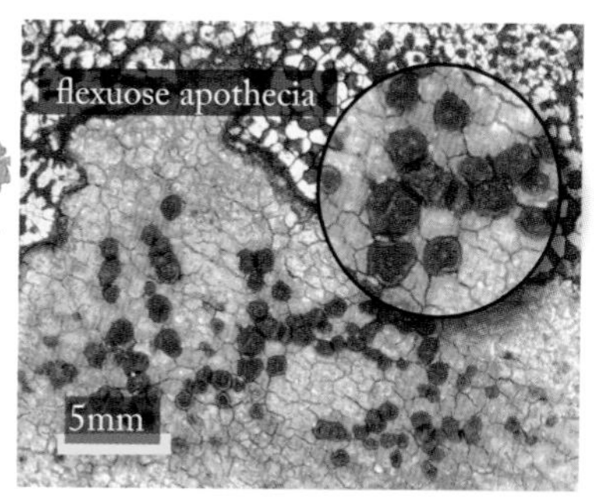

Description: Thallus is yellow-orange but often rust red due to iron uptake. Apothecia are circular to flexuose and develop on small warts. Black prothallus, forms mosaics. Discs are black and flat to convex. Spores, 15–19 x 8–10μm. Spot Tests: Negative.

Nature Notes: Occurs on damp siliceous rocks in shaded areas such as overhangs, especially in uplands.

Porpidia hydrophila – crustose

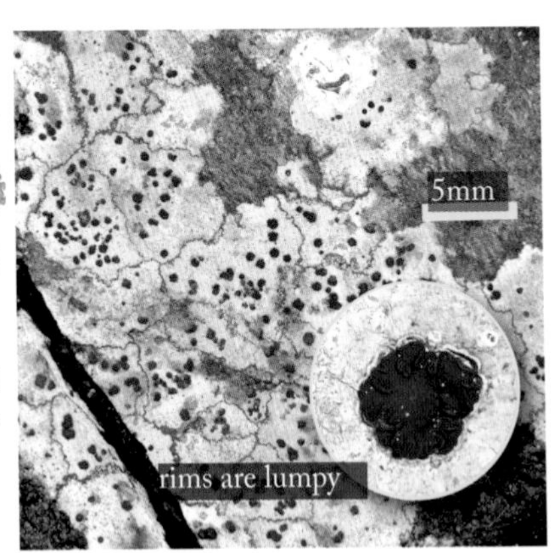

Description: Paper thin thallus, slightly cracked to areolate and creamy white to yellow or even orange. Prothallus is weak, unless mosaics are formed. Apothecia are matt to shiny and have distinctive thick rims that vary from round to crenulate or lumpy. Discs are flat to convex and may be pruinose. Spores, 18–23 x 7–8μm.
Spot Tests: Negative.
Nature Notes: Occurs on siliceous rocks and boulders along upland streams where it is regularly submerged by rushing water.

Porpidia tuberculosa – crustose

Description: Very variable in colour and texture. Thallus generally cracked or areolate and may be smooth or as rough as coarse sand paper due to the presence of many tiny papillae. Colour varies from blue-grey to oxidized copper-green (it may also be oxidized red, like *P. flavocruenta*). Flecked appearance is due to blue-grey soredia scattered across the thallus. Apothecia are rare. Discs flat and matt. Rims thick and glossy.
Spot Tests: Negative.
Nature Notes: Occurs on siliceous outcrops, boulders and even monuments.

Protoblastenia – 3 species recorded in Ireland. Related to Caloplaca.

Protoblastenia rupestris – crustose

Description: Thallus is green to brown in colour and has a cracked appearance, but is often immersed in the substrate making it invisible. Apothecial discs are dull orange and gently convex, but irregularly shaped and characteristically sit raised on the thallus. Spores, 8–17 x 5–8μm.
Spot Tests: Apothecia: K+ crimson.
Nature Notes: Very common in Ireland on mortar, limestone and other calcareous substrates. Often abundant on the tops of walls around graveyards and churches.
Confusion: With *Caloplaca holocarpa*.

PROTOPANNARIA – 1 SPECIES RECORDED IN IRELAND.

Protopannaria pezizoides – squamulose, crustose

DESCRIPTION: Apothecia are numerous and conspicuous, reaching a diam. of 2mm. Discs are bright orange (when dry) to browny orange or chestnut brown (when damp). Rims are distinctive, being scalloped and or granular. Both soredia and isidia are absent. Thallus is composed of small grey (when dry) to brown (when wet) squamules, often overlapping and sometimes displaying a reddish tint.

SPOT TESTS: Negative.

NATURE NOTES: Typically found in damp undisturbed areas such as among mosses and decaying wood. Also occurs on old walls and mature trees.

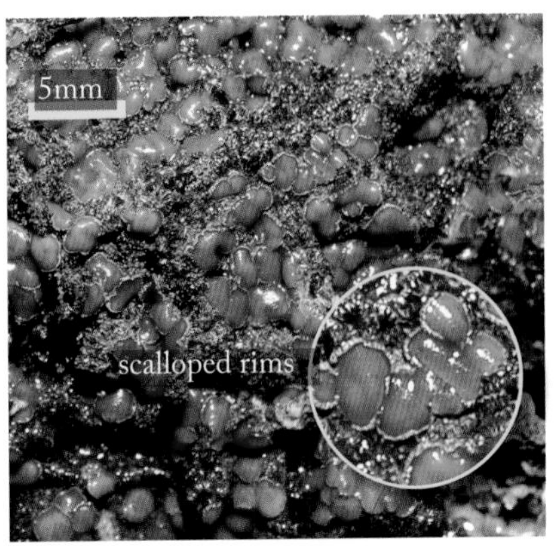

PUNCTELIA – 4 SPECIES RECORDED IN IRELAND.

Punctelia borreri – foliose

DESCRIPTION: Thallus has a green-grey colour with hints of yellow and brown at the ends of some lobes. Lobes vary considerably in size and are undulating with ascending margins. White pseudocyphellae are usually abundant, often merging. Apothecia are rare. Discs are red-brown. Pycnidia present on lobe surfaces. Underside is black but pale near margins. Rhizines are pale tipped.

SPOT TESTS: Cortex: K+ yellow. Medulla: K+ pink, K–, KC+ pink. Pd–. UV–.

NATURE NOTES: Likes deciduous trees in open, well lit, nutrient rich areas, such as near farms. Also occurs on wayside trees and in small towns.

Punctelia jeckeri – foliose

DESCRIPTION: Thallus is foliose and tightly adpressed. Central region is wrinkled. Lobe margins turn up a little and are pruinose. Plenty of white laminal soralia and pseudocyphellae give it a white spotty effect. Underneath is pale brown.

SPOT TESTS: Medulla and soredia: C+ red, KC+ red. UV–.

NATURE NOTES: Occurs on wayside trees and on trees in towns and villages.

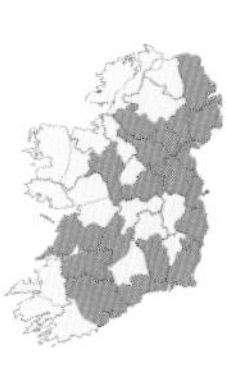

Punctelia subrudecta – foliose

Description: Green-grey thallus becomes bright green when wet. Covered with white powdery soredia. Underside is white to pale brown. Marginal soralia sometimes becomes labriform. Apothecia rare. Discs are concave and red-brown. Spores, 14–17 x 12–15μm. Spot Tests: K+ yellow. Medulla: C+ red, K–, KC+ red, Pd–. UV–.
Nature Notes: Occurs on siliceous rocks, moss and broadleaved trees in well lit areas.

Pyrenula – 8 species recorded in Ireland.

Pyrenula dermatodes – crustose

Description: Thallus is cracked or areolate, shiny and generally rusty red-brown, turning yellowish green. Perithecia are abundant and sunken into the thallus, with just the grey tips or ostioles showing. Spot Tests: C–, K+ orange-red, KC–, Pd–. UV+ yellow-orange.
Nature Notes: Found in old oceanic woodlands. Occurs on holly, beech, hawthorn and rowan.

Pyrenula macrospora – crustose

Description: Thallus is shiny textured and creamy yellow to green-brown in colour. Prothallus is black. It forms mosaics. Perithecia are volcano-like, with a centred ostiole at the tip. Pycnidia and pseudocyphallae occur near the edges. Spores, 25–35 x 8–12μm.
Spot Tests: C–, K+ yellow, Pd+ slight hint of yellow. UV± yellow to orange.
Nature Notes: Found on smooth bark in shaded areas.

Pyrrhospora – 1 species recorded in Ireland.

Pyrrhospora quernea **–** crustose

Description: Thick ochre thallus, composed of granular soredia. Apothecia common and prominent, with concave chocolate coloured discs. Prothallus black when present. Spores, 8–12 x 5–7μm.
Spot Tests: KC+ orange, C+ orange. UV+ orange.
Nature Notes: Occurs on rough barked trees, especially oak, in well lit, nutrient rich habitats.

Ramalina calicaris – fruticose

DESCRIPTION: Thallus is coarse to touch and brittle when dry. It has a grey-green colour, with the lobes or straps deeply grooved, particularly near the base. Apothecia are common on both the tips and edges of lobes. Spores, 10–16 x 5–7μm.

SPOT TESTS: Negative.

NATURE NOTES: Prefers basic bark in nutrient rich areas and is more frequent near the coast. Tends to occur on twigs and small branches rather than the bole of trees.

CONFUSION: Frequently with *Ramalina fraxinea* and sometimes with *Ramalina fastigiata*.

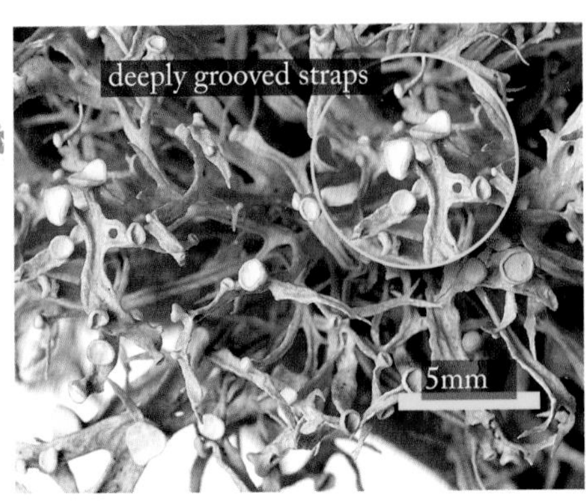

Ramalina cuspidata – fruticose

DESCRIPTION: The tufted, semi-erect, strap-like thallus has a shiny creamy grey colour. Main lobes or straps are almost circular in cross section. The bases of tufts are black, as are the openings of the pycnidia along the thalline straps.

SPOT TESTS: Three chemotypes known, hence, many combinations of the spot tests are positive.

NATURE NOTES: A rocky seashore (siliceous rocks) species found either with *Ramalina siliquosa* or a little lower down the shore.

CONFUSION: With *Ramalina siliquosa* which is more erect than *Ramalina cuspidata*.

Ramalina farinacea – fruticose

DESCRIPTION: Pendulous, tufted, shrubby and brittle to touch, arising from a single holdfast. Green-grey to yellow-green in colour, with a narrow matt, strap-like thallus with channels on one side. Oval or disc-like white soralia occur on the edges of the thalline straps. Apothecia are rare.

SPOT TESTS: K± yellow.

NATURE NOTES: Found in woodlands, even in shaded areas. Rare on rocks. Resistant to air pollution (SO_2) and high levels of nitrogen.

CONFUSION: With *Evernia prunastri*.

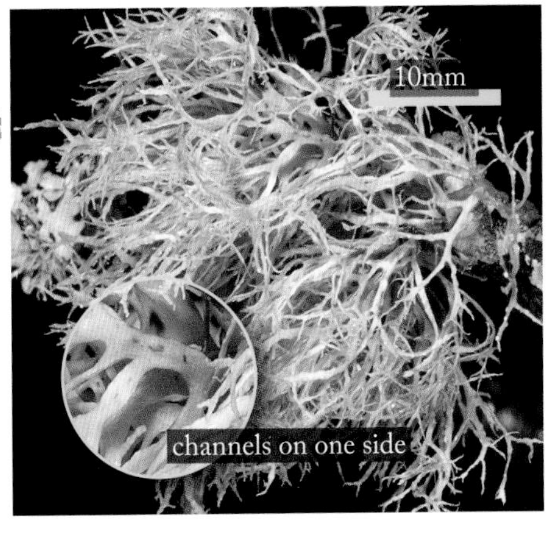

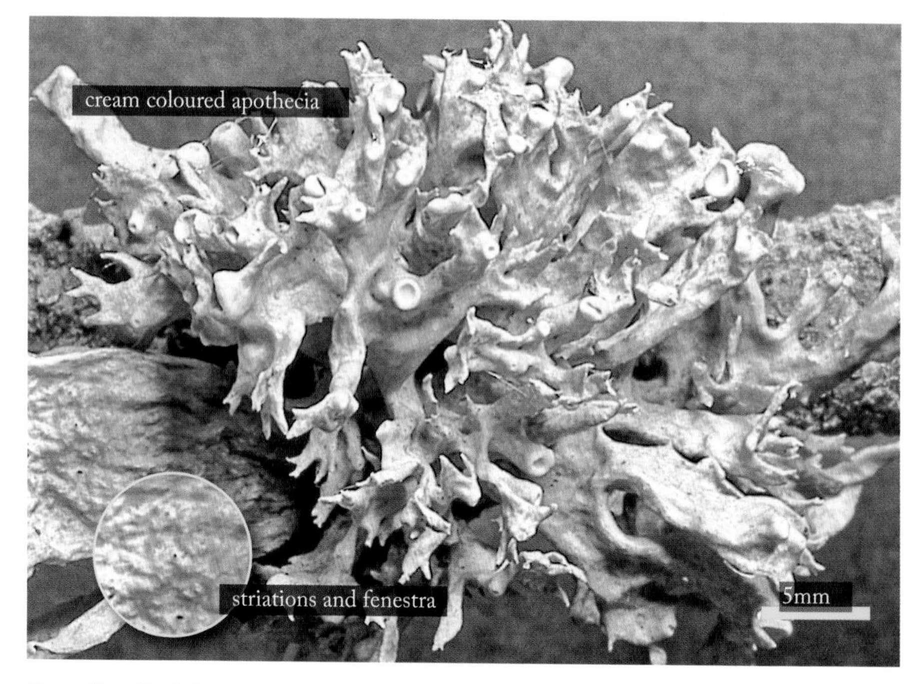

Ramalina fastigiata – fruticose

Description: Thallus is dense, highly branched and typically erect, reaching a height of 2–3cm. Thalline straps (lobes) are green-grey to grey, with cream apothecia that are concave when young and flat to convex when mature. Lobes are flat, swollen or inflated with many tiny openings (fenestra) and striations. Spores, 10–17 x 5–7μm.

Spot Tests: Medulla: K–, C–, P–. UV–.

Nature Notes: Very sensitive to air pollution (SO_2). Grows in tufts on tree trunks and twigs, usually on the side of the tree exposed to strong sunlight. Nitrogen tolerant.

Ramalina fraxinea – fruticose

Description: Lobes are widest towards the middle (as much as 4.5cm in some specimens) and tapering at both the point of attachment and toward lobe tip. Thallus is green-grey in colour, pendant and may be as long as 10cm. Individual lobes have a channelled, wrinkled appearance. Stalked, cup-like apothecia are common, with convex discs that run along both edges and laminae. Spores, 10–12 x 5–7μm.

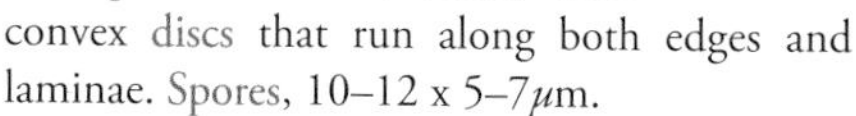

Spot Tests: Negative.

Nature Notes: Occurs on basic bark in windy, exposed and well lit sites. Found mainly on trees (ash, poplar, sycamore).

Confusion: With *Ramalina fastigiata*.

Ramalina lacera – fruticose

DESCRIPTION: Variable species. May have just one lobe or several rather ragged ones. Colour ranges from white to dirty yellow-green with a pale underside. Lobe edges may be indented with soredia. Soredia also occur on the lobe surfaces. Apothecia are unknown in Irish specimens. Lobe edges often develop a ragged growth.

SPOT TESTS: Negative.

NATURE NOTES: Occurs in well lit situations on wayside trees, parklands and hedgerows, especially near the coast. May occur on dry, sheltered, siliceous rocks. Prefers coastal areas.

CONFUSION: With *Ramalina canariensis.*

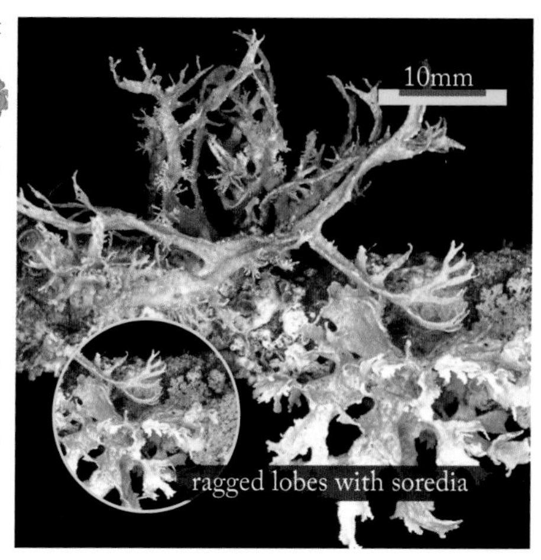

ragged lobes with soredia

Ramalina siliquosa – fruticose

DESCRIPTION: Thallus is erect (3–5cm high), brittle, pale greeny grey and sometimes rises from a crustose base. Apothecia are common, appearing more frequently on lobe ends rather than sides. Lobes are strap-like and 2–9mm wide, with little ridges and white spots towards the tips.

SPOT TESTS: Several chemotypes recognized.

NATURE NOTES: Occurs on silica-rich rocks in coastal areas. Rare inland, but it has been found 40km from the coast. Typical on the upper dry part of rocky sea shores.

rarely branched above the base

RHIZOCARPON – 19 SPECIES RECORDED IN IRELAND.

Rhizocarpon geographicum – crustose

DESCRIPTION: Thallus areolate, cracked, yellow to yellow-green and shiny. Black apothecia forming in the margins of the areoles are irregular in shape and grow to about 1.5mm in diam. Prothallus is distinctly black. Frequently forms mosaics.

SPOT TESTS: Medulla: Pd± yellow-orange, C± red. UV–.

NATURE NOTES: Common on hard siliceous rocks. Grows slowly. Some specimens have been dated at 1,000 years old in the Rocky Mountains (US) and specimens over 4,500 years old have been reported in Sweden.

apothecia form in the cracks

Rhizocarpon lavatum – crustose

Description: Develops as large (<10cm) pale grey patches on rocks near streams. Often tinted brown or rust red. Specimens in the shade take on a greenish colour. Prothallus is ill-defined. Apothecia (< 1.5mm) are rather flat, ranging from slightly concave to slightly convex. Rims are wide and discs may have a small mound of sterile tissue (umbo) at their centres. Spot Tests: Negative. Nature Notes: Found in upland regions on silica-rich or neutral rocks at the edge of small streams or around lakes. They like to be washed by water regularly. Red is due to iron uptake.

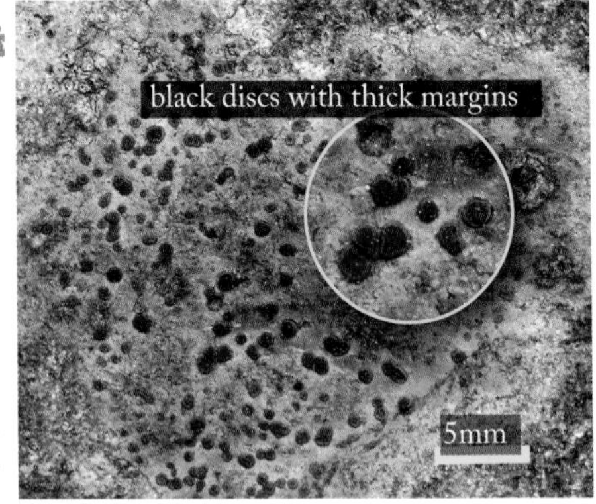

Rhizocarpon petraeum – crustose

Description: Thallus forms neat, circular, chalk white patches that show irregular cracking. Surface is very flat with matt, angular areoles. Apothecia have distinctive jet black discs, with thick pruinose rims. Invariably, the apothecia develop in concentric lines. Prothallus is dark and may be poorly developed. Spores, 20–30 x 13–25μm. Spot Tests: Medulla: K+ yellow, Pd+ orange. Nature Notes: Occurs on silica-rich rocks close to mortar or other sources of calcium. More frequent in coastal areas.

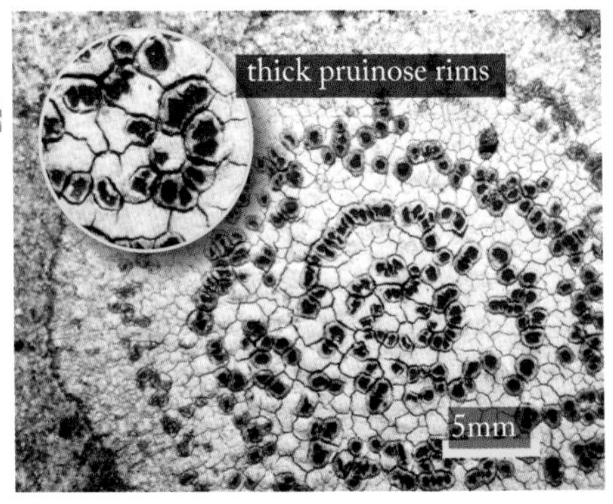

Rhizocarpon reductum – crustose

Description: Thallus is light to dark grey, areolate and forms distinct patches. The prothallus is thin and black. Black apothecia are innate and sessile with a thick rim, often slightly raised with a lighter tone on the inside. Discs are black, with flat to pronounced convex surfaces. Spores, 20–35 x 10–15μm.
Spot Tests: K+ yellow, Pd+ orange.
Nature Notes: Common on smooth silica-rich, newly exposed rocks (pioneer species).
Confusion: With *Rhizocarpon lavatum*.

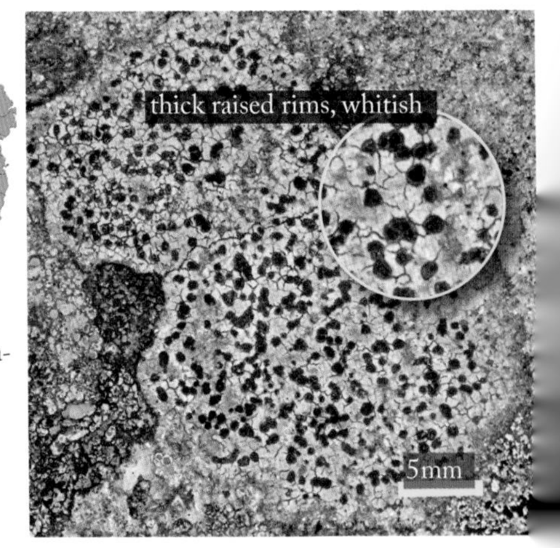

SOLENOSPORA – 3 SPECIES RECORDED IN IRELAND.

Solenospora holophaea – squamulose

DESCRIPTION: Thallus is composed of smooth, rounded squamules in an irregular mass. Squamules are olive green when wet and red-brown when dry. Apothecia have thin, well defined rims when young, but later are obscured as the discs grow out over them. Discs are reddish brown to black, often matching the rim colour. Spores, 12–18 x 4–5μm. SPOT TESTS: Negative.

NATURE NOTES: Occurs on rocks and soil on sheltered cliffs in maritime areas. Sometimes found on mortar and vertical shaded walls.

Solenospora vulturiensis – squamulose

DESCRIPTION: Squamulose thallus, lobes either crowded tightly or scattered loosely. Colour varies from blue-grey-white when dry, to olive green when wet. Apothecia are globular with a thalline margin. Discs are light brown with a pink tint. Thalline margin may become excluded. Squamule tips develop a white powder (soralia). SPOT TESTS: KC+ yellow, Pd–, K+ yellow.

NATURE NOTES: Occurs in well lit, nutrient rich, calcareous situations, especially on coastal rocks in tiny cracks where run-off water travels.

SPHAEROPHORUS – 2 SPECIES RECORDED IN IRELAND.

Sphaerophorus globosus – fruticose

DESCRIPTION: White-grey to brown thallus, sometimes with a tint of orange. Forms extensive cushions 1–5cm high. Branching is prolific and irregular. Side branches are narrower than main branches. Overall it has a coral-like appearance. Branch tips are blunt. Apothecia rare. Spores, 8–12 x 7–11μm.

SPOT TESTS: Medulla: C–, K± yellow, Pd± yellow. UV+ blue-white.

NATURE NOTES: Occurs on acidic bark, decaying tree stumps and rarely on siliceous rocks.

Stereocaulon – 8 species recorded in Ireland.

Stereocaulon vesuvianum – squamulose

Description: Primary thallus rarely seen. Secondary thallus composed of erect pseudopodetia, typically up to 4cm high. Coloured grey-white, globose soralia are frequently found at the tips. Tiny disc shaped phyllocladia with dark centres cover the pseudopodetia. Apothecia are rare. Cephalodia may be present (containing *Stigonema*) Discs are brown. Spores, 26–46 x 3–4μm.

Spot Tests: K+ yellow, Pd+ orange.

Nature Notes: Occurs as dense mats on siliceous rocks, particularly those rich in metals. Found in Ireland from upland areas to sea level.

Sticta – 4 species recorded in Ireland. Called 'stinky sticta' Contains two morphs.

Sticta canariensis – foliose (algal)

Description: Grows to produce extensive foliose patches. Lobes tend to overlap. Bright green when wet and often a little shiny. Lower surface white to brown, tomentose, with circular white cyphellae. Apothecia are rare. Photobiont is a green algae.

Spot Tests: None.

Nature Notes: Occurs in damp, shaded woodland among mosses. Its cyanobacterial morph is *Sticta deflourii* (below).

Sticta deflourii – foliose (cyanobacterial)

Description: Produces large foliose patches, similar to *Sticta canariensis*. Paper thin lobes, wrinkled and often incised. Branched isidia may cover the lobes. Pycnidia and apothecia are unknown in Irish specimens. Spot Tests: None.

Nature Notes: This is the cyanobacterial morph of *Sticta canariensis*. They occur in the same areas, hence the same distribution maps.

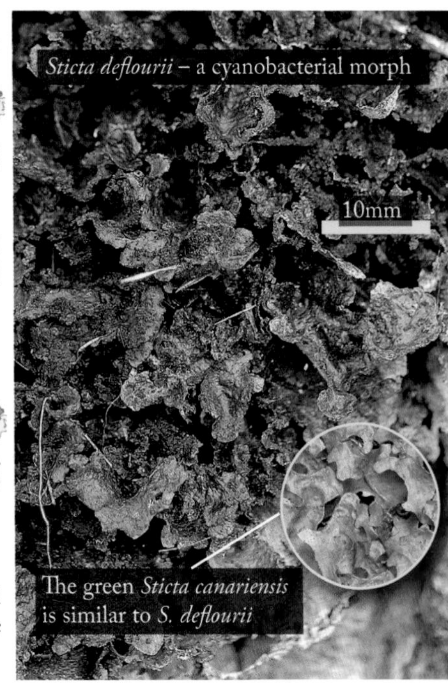

Sticta fuliginosa – foliose

Description: Often composed of just a single lobe, or very few. Lobes may or may not turn up at the margins. Colour is dark grey to brown and often covered with coralloid clusters of isidia, which further darken the lobes. Lower surface is brown, tomentose and scattered with true cyphellae of various shapes. Apothecia are rare. Discs up to 4mm diam. and red-brown in colour with paler rims. Spores, 30–33 x 5.5–8.5μm.
Spot Tests: None.
Nature Notes: Occurs in oceanic woodlands among mosses on both bark and rocks. Prefers the shaded damp aspect of these ancient woodlands. Smells fishy when wet.
Confusion: With *Sticta sylvatica*.

Sticta limbata – foliose

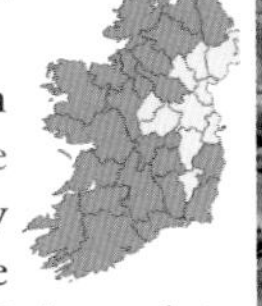

Description: Thallus is large and composed of just a few loosely attached lobes. Colour varies from brown to dark grey, with lobe margins upturned and rimmed by grey granular soredia. Soredia are also scattered across the thallus. Underneath is pale tan with true cyphellae and a tomentum. Apothecia are very rare. Spot Tests: None.
Nature Notes: Found among moss on old woodland trees (particularly hazel and ash) in the west of Ireland. It is also found on mossy rocks. It is the only *Sticta* species that is sorediate.
Confusion: With *Peltigera collina*.

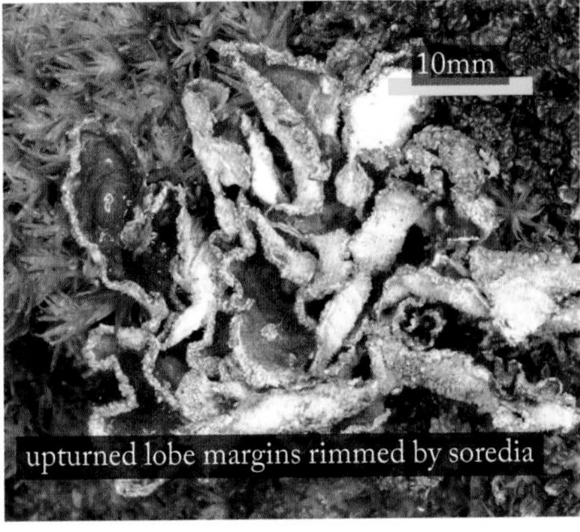

upturned lobe margins rimmed by soredia

Sticta sylvatica – foliose

Description: A large multilobed thallus reaching 8–10cm in diam. Its dark brown colour may have blotches of grey-brown areas, covered with a network of raised veins. Lobes are incised with ascending margins. Isidia are granular and scattered across the thallus, but more concentrated near raised lobe margins. Underneath is dark brown with light coloured cyphellae. Spot Tests: None.
Nature Notes: Found among mosses on rocks and trees in damp areas. It is an old woodland indicator species. Smells fishy when wet.

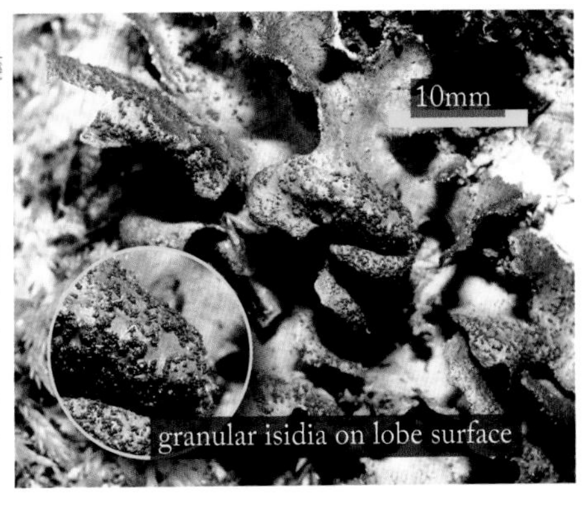

granular isidia on lobe surface

Teloschistes chrysophthalmus

TELOSCHISTES – 2 species recorded in Ireland.

Teloschistes chrysophthalmus – fruticose

Description: This is an unmistakable lichen, with its dazzling colour and bouquet-like display of gold coloured apothecia. The apothecia are large (1–4mm) and fringed with cilia in an eyelash fashion, giving the gold coloured apothecia a larger than life appearance. The thallus radiates from a holdfast and is richly branched. Branches (0.5–mm wide) are ridged, green-white below and orange above. Rhizines are absent. Soralia are rarely present, pycnidia are common, isidia are absent.
Spot Tests: K+ purple.
Nature Notes: Ireland is the northern limit of this Mediterranean to Tropical lichen. It likes well lit, nutrient enriched hawthorn branches. It also occurs on young beech.

TEPHROMELA – 2 species recorded in Ireland.

Tephromela atra – crustose

Description: Thallus is white to light grey in colour, thick, lumpy (but may be smooth) and often warty. The prothallus is thin and darkly coloured. Soredia are absent and apothecia are usually abundant. Discs are inky black, with rims the same colour as the thallus.
Spot Tests: K+ yellow. UV+ ice blue.
Nature Notes: Rare on trees but common on well lit siliceous rocks and walls.
Confusion: With *Lecanora gangaleoides*.
Inset: *Tephromela atra* var. *torulosa*. Smaller thallus with a green tint and smaller apothecia. Very rare. Occurs on trees.

THELOTREMA – 4 species recorded in Ireland.

Thelotrema lepadinum – squamulose

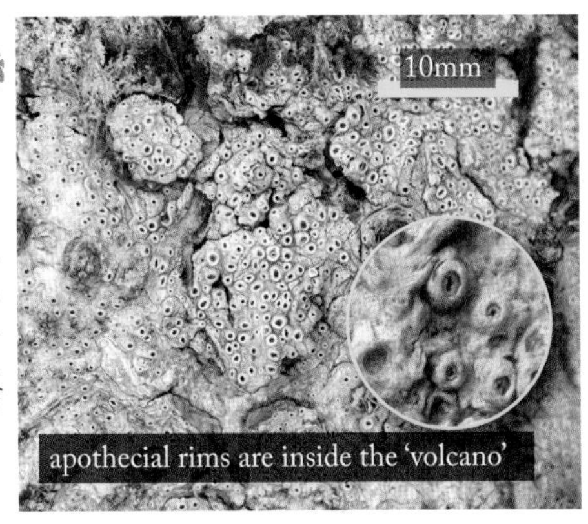

Description: Thallus is smooth to rough and varies from grey to white in colour. Apothecia have volcano-like thalline rims. Inside these are smaller proper rim margins around the disc. Discs are black and may be pruinose. Spot Tests: None.
Nature Notes: Referred to as bark barnacles, it occurs in areas that are shaded (canopy cover). Also found on silica-rich rocks, but this is rare. Sensitive to air pollution and is an indicator of ancient woodlands.
Confusion: With *Thelotrema macrosporum*.

Toninia – 9 species recorded in Ireland.

Toninia aromatica – squamulose

Description: Thallus is made up of dark grey lumpy squamules, sometimes with a hint of green and at times pruinose. Lower cortex is not well developed. Apothecia are black with a diam. of 1.5mm; they may be pruinose. It tends to grow along crevices in rock. Spores, 12–23 × 3–6μm. Spot Tests: None.

Nature Notes: Occurs on shale, slate and limestone. Also found on mortar on old walls, in fissures and other drainage tracks. It is a maritime indicator species. Rarely found on trees.

Trapeliopsis – 6 species recorded in Ireland. Very similar to genus Trapelia.

Trapeliopsis flexuosa – squamulose, granulose

Description: Thallus composed of dark grey to green-black crowded granular areoles that become less so towards the thalline margin. Soredia are farinose to finely granular and green-grey to navy blue. Apothecia, ≤1mm diam., range from pink (in deep shade) to dark grey to black. Discs are flat to convex. Spores, 7–9.5 x 2.5–4μm.

Spot Tests: C+ red, K–, KC+ red. UV+ white.

Nature Notes: Has a preference for lignin (wood posts), but can occur on acid bark and siliceous rocks. Check for C+ red.

Trapeliopsis pseudogranulosa – squamulose, granulose

Description: Catches the eye because of the striking orange colouring on parts of the thallus and soralia. Thallus may cover large areas (<20cm) and has grey to greeny white granular areoles. Apothecia are unknown in Irish specimens. Soralia (<1.6mm) are green and often partially orange. Spores, 10–12 x 3.5–6μm.

Spot Tests: C+ red, Pd–. UV–. Soralia and orange parts: K+ purple. UV deep red.

Nature Notes: Occurs in damp uplands on siliceous rocks and decaying logs and plants.

Tremolecia – 1 species recorded in Ireland.

Tremolecia atrata – crustose

Description: Rust coloured thallus. May occasionally be dark grey to black in shaded areas. Highly areolate with numerous small apothecia that sit between the areoles. Non-thalline margins are raised above the disc. Pycnidia are immersed and difficult to see. The prothallus is dark grey to black. Spores, 10–15 x 6–9μm.

Spot Tests: C–, K–, KC–, Pd–. UV–.

Nature Notes: Occurs on exposed siliceous rocks with a high metal content.

Confusion: With *Rhizocarpon oederi*.

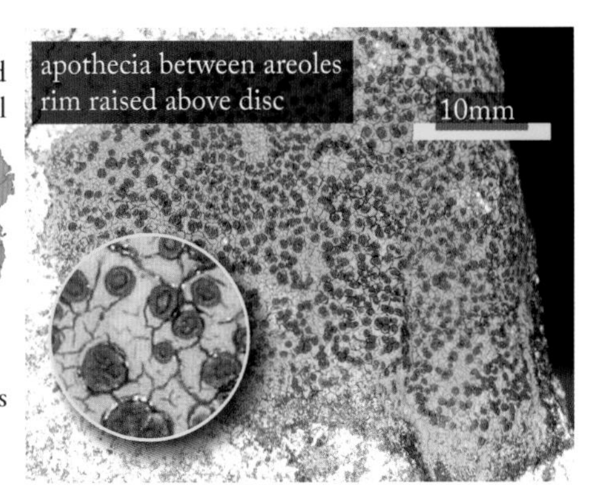

Tuckermanopsis – 1 species recorded in Ireland.

Tuckermanopsis chlorophylla – foliose

Description: A light brown to olive green (when wet) loose, tufted lobed lichen. Lobes may be a little channelled with turned up margins, wavy and often notched or incised. Pale coloured soredia are abundant and run along the lobe margins. Apothecia are very rare. Rhizines are often absent, but when present are pale coloured.

Spot Test: C–, K–, KC–, Pd–. UV–.

Nature Notes: Occurs on branches and twigs of wayside trees, on fences and in woodlands.

Confusion: With *Platismatia glauca*.

Umbilicaria – 6 species recorded in Ireland.

Umbilicaria cylindrica – foliose

Description: Single to multilobed, with rounded wavy lobes and plentiful long black marginal cilia. Upper surface pale grey to brown and ridged or folded upwards. Lower surface smooth and light coloured. Apothecia abundant and distinctly gyrose. Spores, 9–15 x 3–9μm.

Spot Tests: Medulla: C–, K± yellow → red.

Nature Notes: Occurs on siliceous rocks.

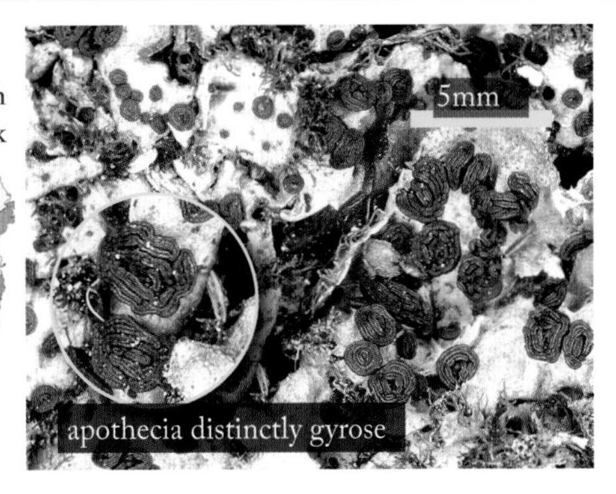

Umbilicaria polyphylla – foliose

Description: Thallus is dark brown to red-brown. It is smooth and shiny with several undulating lobes attached to the substrate by a single stalk or umbilicus. Margins are upturned and wavy. Central area is raised and smaller lobes may be present. Underneath is matt, black and smooth and lacks rhizines. Apothecia are rare. Discs are gyrose. Spores, 12–19 × 4–8μm.

Spot Tests: Medulla: C+ red, K–, KC+ red, Pd–.

Nature Notes: Occurs in well lit exposed upland regions, especially on the tops of quick drying siliceous boulders.

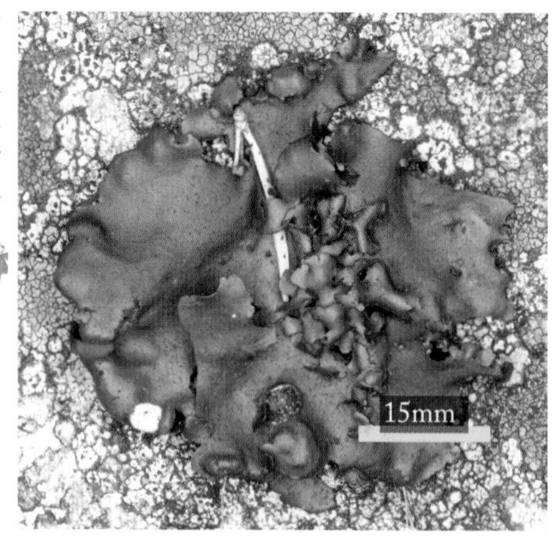

Usnea – 15 species recorded in Ireland. Difficult to id. Use spot tests to help.

Usnea articulata – fruticose

Description: A giant among lichens. The thallus can reach up to 1m in length of inflated sausage-like segments (3mm diam.), joined by axils of cartilaginous connective tissue. Surface is smooth, pale grey to grey-green, sometimes marked with pseudocyphellae and tiny papillae. Apothecia unknown in Ireland. Lacks soredia.

Spot Tests: Medulla: C–, K–, KC–, Pd+ red.

Nature Notes: Occurs on well lit tree tops or high branches. Sensitive to pollutants.

Confusion: When young it may resemble *Usnea flammea* which is K+ orange.

Usnea esperantiana – fruticose

Description: Thallus is erect, rough and hooked at the tips. Side branches twist and are narrower than the main stem. The base of the holdfast is not black (unlike some *Usnea*). Branches are covered in soralia. Spot Tests: C–, K+ yellow → red (characteristic), Pd+ orange → red.

Nature Notes: Occurs on small twigs, shrubs and trees, often in gardens.

Usnea florida – fruticose

Description: Thallus is green-grey, large, bushy and densely branched, reaching 5–10cm. The base is blackened, with horizontal cracking. Apothecia form at the tips of branches and are usually abundant and conspicuous. Discs are smooth textured, flat to concave and fringed with long eyelash-like cilia. Isidia and soralia are absent. Spines and pimples grow on the main stem.

Spot Tests: K+ deep yellow on the medulla, Pd+ orange.

Nature Notes: Very sensitive to pollutants. Occurs in well lit situations, typically in the canopy of broadleaved trees. Sometimes found on fence posts.

Usnea subfloridana – fruticose

Description: Bushy pendulous thallus, grey-green to yellow-green, with a distinctive blackened base and annular rings or cracks. Branches are cylindrical and tapered. Side branches are not narrowed where they attach to the trunk (they are in some species). Trunk and branches are covered in patches of soredia or isidia. Apothecia are rare but when present there are very few.

Spot Tests: K+ yellow. Medulla: Pd+ orange.

Nature Notes: Occurs on well lit trees and fences. Common in Ireland, the most pollution resistant of the genus *Usnea*.

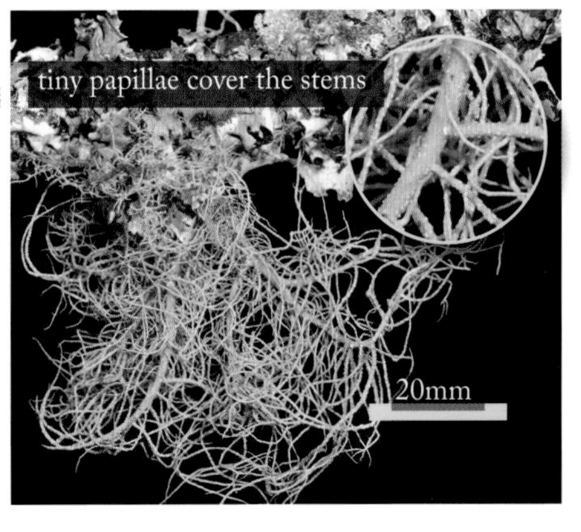

Verrucaria – 43 species recorded in Ireland.

Verrucaria baldensis – crustose

Description: Thallus is white or very pale grey, thin and often immersed. Numerous perithecia with fine cracks at the top, giving the appearance of a hot cross bun. Perithecia leave empty holes when they fall out. Spores, 15–21 x 7–10μm.

Spot Tests: None.

Nature Notes: Common on hard limestone. Empty perithecial pits may become infected with a reddish parasite *Opegrapha rupestris*.

Verrucaria macrostoma – crustose

DESCRIPTION: Thallus light to dark brown, consisting of slightly convex, rounded areoles. Black perithecia are not immersed in the thallus but sit conical to hemispherical on the areoles.
Spores, 25–31 x 11.5–14.5μm.
SPOT TESTS: None.
NATURE NOTES: Occurs on limestone, mortar and calcareous sandstones, often in areas with nutrient enrichment. Expect to see it in graveyards and on church monuments.
CONFUSION: With *Acarospora impressula, Acarospora fuscata* or *Verrucaria nigrescens.*

Verrucaria maura – crustose

DESCRIPTION: Looks like tar. Needs to be checked with a hand lens to reveal the regular, almost rectangular, areolate pattern. Surface texture is matt with many black dots, and cone shaped perithecia. Distinct ostioles are present at the tips of the perithecia.
SPOT TESTS: None.
NATURE NOTES: Forms the black colour in the rocky seashore black zone (littoral). Occurs on many types of seashore rock. Common around all the coastline of Ireland.

Verrucaria mucosa – crustose

DESCRIPTION: Thallus is a dark olive green, very smooth and oily looking, with irregular cracking. A white prothallus may be present around edges of some of the cracks. Perithecia are black and look more prominent when specimens are dry.
SPOT TESTS: None.
NATURE NOTES: Common on rocky seashores from mid-shore to low tide mark. Prefers exposed shores. Sometimes harbours the parasite *Stigmidium marinum.*

Xanthoria aureola – foliose

DESCRIPTION: Thallus is bright yellow to orange, with strap-like lobes that are crenulate and indented towards the tips. Lobe ends are round and may lie across each other. Small side branches (hapterons) attach the lobe tips to the substrate. Apothecia are rare. Discs convex, becoming flat.
SPOT TESTS: K+ crimson.
NATURE NOTES: A coastal lichen of the orange zone, but may occur to a lesser extent in the grey zone. Also found on vertical surfaces of exposed buildings near the coast. Rarely occurs on calcareous substrates, preferring siliceous rocks.

Xanthoria parietina – foliose

DESCRIPTION: Typically bright orange lobes but turning grey or greeny grey when it is in the shade. Broad marginal lobes. Forms neat circles when it has the space. The centre may die off in mature specimens. Individual lobes are long, especially in seashore specimens, and turned up a little at the tips. Underside is white with rhizines. Apothecia are abundant and have orange discs with paler rims. SPOT TESTS: K+ crimson.
NATURE NOTES: Enjoys nitrogen-rich areas and is common in towns, cities and around farms. Occurs on walls, trees, twigs and almost any substrate, including glass.

Xanthoria polycarpa – foliose

DESCRIPTION: Thallus is bright yellow, small in size and rosette shaped, usually with abundant apothecia. Lobes are convex and sometimes pale greenish at the margins, branched, narrow and often crenulate, widening towards the apex (coral-like). Soredia and isidia are absent. Underneath is white. Spores, 11–15 x 5–8μm.
SPOT TESTS: K+ purple.
NATURE NOTES: Occurs on dead and living twigs. Fond of poplar, larch and Salix species.

References

- Aspen, P. Pedley, I. Sanderson, N. Ward, S. *BLS Field Meeting in the Burren, Ireland, 18-25 April 2009.* British Lichen Society Bulletin, No. 105: Winter 2009
- Blom, H.H. and Lindblom, L. *Degelia cyanoloma*, a distinct species from Western Europe *Lichenologist*, Vol. 42 (1):23-27 (2010)
- Brodo, I.M. Sharnoff, S.D. & Sharnoff, S. (2001) *Lichens of North America.* Yale University Press, New Haven
- Charlesworth, J.K. *The Geology of Ireland, an introduction.* Publ: Oliver and Boyd. 1953
- Coppins, A.M. & Coppins, B.J. (2010). *Atlantic hazel.* Scottish Natural Heritage
- Dalby, C. (2009). *Lichens on Rocky Seashores.* BLS Wallchart
- Dalby, C. (2009). *Lichens on Trees.* BLS Wallchart
- Dalby, K. & Dalby, C. (2005). *Shetland Lichens.* Shetland Amenity Trust
- Dobson, F. (2005). *Lichens, An Illustrated guide to the British and Irish species.* Richmond
- Douglass, J. & Whelan, P. (2009). *Lichen Survey of Skellig Michael*
- Fletcher, A. (1973a). The ecology of marine (littoral) lichens on some rocky shores of Anglesey. *Lichenologist,* 5: 368-400
- Fletcher, Anthony, editor. *Lichen Habitat Management,* . The British Lichen Society
- Gilbert, O.L. (2004b). *The Lichen Hunters.* The Book Guild
- Gilbert, O. *Lichens,* 1st edition, The New Naturalist Library, 2000. HarperCollins*Publishers*
- Guest, Bernadette. *Guidance for the Care, Conservation and Recording of Historic Graveyards,* 2nd edition, September 2011. The Heritage Council of Ireland
- Joint Nature Conservation Committee *Red Data Books of Britain and Ireland: Lichens. Volume 1: Britain.* Joint Nature Conservation Committee, Peterborough
- Knowles, M.C. (1913). *The Maritime and Marine lichens of Howth,* Scientific Proceedings of the Royal Dublin Society, Vol. XIV, 14: 79-143
- Knowles, M.C. (1929). *The Lichens of Ireland.* P. Royal Irish Academy, 38B: 179-434
- Malcolm, W.M. and Galloway, D.J. *New Zealand Lichens, Checklist, Key and Glossary*
- Nash III, Thomas H. *Lichen Biology,* 2nd edition. Cambridge University Press, 2008
- Nevill, W.E. *Geology and Ireland.* Allen & Figgis, Dublin, 1974
- Orange, Alan. James, P.W., White, F.J. *Microchemical Methods for the Identification of Lichens.* The British Lichen Society
- Pettersson, R.B., Ball, J.P, Renhorn, K.E., Esseen, P.A. & Sjoberg, K. 1995. Invertebrate communities in boreal forest canopies as influenced by forestry and lichens with implications for passerine birds. *Biological Conservation* **74**:57-63.
- Plantlife leaflet: *Lichens and bryophytes of Atlantic woodland in Scotland.* Plantlife publication
- Plantlife leaflet: *Lichens of Atlantic Woodlands, Guide 1 and 2.* Plantlife publication
- Richardson, D.H.S. *The Vanishing Lichens, Their History, Biology and Importance.* Publ. David & Charles. 1975
- Seaward, M.R.D. *Census Catalogue of Irish Lichens.* 3rd edition, 2010. National Museums of Northern Ireland
- Simms, Mike. *Exploring the Limestone Landscapes of the Burren and Gort Lowlands*
- Smith, Aptroot, Coppins, Fletcher, Gilbert, James, Wolseley. *The Lichens of Great Britain and Ireland* (2009). The British Lichen Society
- Thompson, Robert. *Close-up and Macro: A Photographer's Guide,* (2007 edition)
- Webb, D.A. *Vice-county maps.* Proceedings of the Royal Irish Academy, Vol. 80B, 179-196 (1980)
- Whelan, P. (2008). *Data Collection Survey of Lichens on selected Rocky Shores on the South Coast of Ireland.* Heritage Council of Ireland

Internet Resources

The Internet is a wonderful resource for lichenologists, giving access to photographs, descriptions, maps and scientific papers. However it changes regularly and the web sites listed below may or may not exist by the time you get to them, but you can always use a search engine.
I can recommend the web sites below as good starting points.

- Ireland's lichens with photographs, descriptions, vice-county maps, and Matilda Knowles' paper on the History of Irish Lichens (1939) – www.lichens.ie
- Jenny Seawright's photographic library of Irish lichens. This is an excellent site, offering several photographs per species. See www.irishlichens.ie.
- To download a pdf file guide to Ireland's lichens for primary school children (and their teachers) see www.ispynature.com. Pupils can place their local wildlife on a map.
- The Botanic Gardens, Glasnevin, Dublin is home to Ireland's lichen herbarium. This web site makes available several interesting papers on lichens. See www.botanicgardens.ie
- The Biological Vice-Counties of Ireland: http://www.botanicgardens.ie/herb/census/webbvcs.htm
- The British Lichen Society: www.thebls.org.uk
- Plantlife is part of Plantlife International. Their website incudes downloadable leaflets on lichens. Well worth a visit. See www.plantlife.org.uk
- LichenIreland website with simplified but accurate descriptions of Ireland's lichens. See www.habitas.org.uk/lichenireland/
- Skellig Michael web site has a downloadable photographic guide to some of the island's lichens. See http://www.worldheritageireland.ie/skellig-michael/natural-heritage/lichens/
- Alan Silverside's Lichen Pages. An excellent and reliable set of photographs of lichens run by Alan. See www.lichens.lastdragon.org
- Scottish Natural Heritage on lichens at www.snh.gov.uk/about-scotlands-nature/species/lichens/
- Stephen Sharnoff's lichen photographs identified to both genus and species level. See www.sharnoffphotos.com/lichens/lichens_home_index.html
- Field Studies Council: keep an eye on the site for UK based lichen courses. They also produce leaflets on lichens in various habitats. See www.field-studies-council.org
- The Lichenologist, free to members of the British Lichen Society. See http://journals.cambridge.org/action/displayJournal?jid=LIC
- Ireland's National Biodiversity Data Centre: www.biodiversityireland.ie
- Royal Botanic Garden, Edinburgh, the centre of Scottish lichenology. See http://rbg-web2.rbge.org.uk/lichen/index.html
- Lichens of Wales: http://www.wales-lichens.org.uk/
- Coastal Lichens and Hazelwoods: http://www.treesforlife.org.uk/tfl.hazel_coastal.html
- Lichenology of Iran: http://www.myco-lich.com/
- Natural History Museum Oslo: http://nhm2.uio.no/lav/web/index.html
- Alan Strivall - Lichens of Sweden: http://www.stridvall.se/la/galleries.php#lichens
- Pictures of Tropical Lichens: http://www.tropicallichens.net/
- Lichens of Tibet: http://uni-graz.at/~oberma/tibet-lichens-images/tibet-lichens-images.html
- New Zealand: http://www.hiddenforest.co.nz/index.htm
- The New York Botanical Gardens 'An Introduction to Lichens by Salvatore De Santis': http://www.nybg.org/bsci/lichens/lichen.html

Glossary

- Downloadable Glossary for *Lichens of Ireland* (this book) is available at www.lichens.ie